REAL VIETNAMESE COOKING

by TRACEY LISTER & ANDREAS POHL

For our daughter, Franka

REAL VIETNAMESE COOKING

by TRACEY LISTER & ANDREAS POHL

Photography by Michael Fountoulakis

hardie grant books

MELBOURNE · LONDON

CONTENTS

BALANCE & HARMONY

A SHORT INTRODUCTION TO VIETNAMESE CUISINE

Tracey and I are often asked to describe Vietnamese food and it is a question we always find difficult to answer. How is it even possible to define a national cuisine with the breadth and depth of Vietnamese food? A cuisine that encompasses food from both the mountains close to the Chinese and Lao borders and from a 3400 kilometre-long coastline. A cuisine that is marked by both the four seasons of the Red River Delta in the north and the tropical wet and dry seasons of the Mekong Delta in the south. A cuisine that has assimilated an array of culinary influences ranging from French and Chinese cooking to Khmer and Cham food traditions.

We feel that the most fitting phrase to describe the common characteristics within all that diversity is "understated elegance", because as a national cuisine,

Vietnamese dishes combine simplicity with sophistication and display a light touch even in the more rustic dishes. It is a food culture that has been shaped by a subtropical climate, a long history of wet rice cultivation and the ability to readily absorb foreign influences.

Rice, fish and herbs are the cornerstones of Vietnamese cuisine. Wet rice cultivation requires a lot of terrain and there is very little tradition of animal husbandry given the scarcity of land not earmarked for growing the nation's staple. Meat is used sparingly, mainly for an additional layer of taste and texture and, in the past, it was mainly reserved for guests, pregnant women, children and the ill.

Only since the French colonised the country and the Vietnam War has there been more emphasis on eating meat. Western eating habits have been responsible for new, phonetic word creations in the Vietnamese language such as "bit tet" for beef steak or "xuc xich" for sausage, illustrating how the consumption of beef and pork has assumed greater importance.

In a country dotted with ponds and paddies, crisscrossed by rivers and canals and bordered on the east by a 3400 kilometre long coastline, however, it is no surprise that fish and crustaceans are the main source of protein. And that includes the ever-present fish sauce, nuoc mam: the slightly pungent mainstay of Vietnamese cuisine and an ingredient in virtually every recipe.

Yet what really sets Vietnamese cuisine apart from the food of other countries in the region is its judicious use of aromatics. Visit any market and you will find stalls laden with bunches of fresh herbs in vibrant shades of green. It is herbs

REAL VIETNAMESE COOKING

such as coriander (cilantro), fragrant knotweed and mint that give Vietnamese dishes that certain finesse, often arising from the surprising interplay between strong tastes such as nuoc mam and the delicate flavours and aromas of these leaves.

Acculturation is the final building block of the country's cuisine, with the locals adopting foreign influences and twisting them to meet their tastes. Even Vietnam's most famous dish, pho, is a product of acculturation, marrying Chinese and French influences to create something uniquely Vietnamese.

The Chinese occupied the country for more than 1000 years and had a strong influence on Vietnamese cooking, but their influence also serves as a good example of how very selective the Vietnamese are in what they choose to adopt. While happy to embrace new cooking techniques and utensils such as the steamer and the wok, the Vietnamese stopped short of taking on board other culinary customs.

Traditionally, Chinese food is characterised by its intricate, complicated cooking methods and rare and expensive ingredients, from which it derives much of its prestige. The Vietnamese, in contrast, insist that they have retained a people's cuisine based on the delicate combination of simple and accessible ingredients. Interestingly, notwithstanding Vietnam's rapid economic growth, peasant food, such as Cabbage with Nuoc Mam and Boiled Duck Eggs, is starting to appear on the menus of fashionable city restaurants. "Maybe rich people are looking for a more authentic experience nowadays," muses Hanoi veteran publicist Huu Ngoc about this recent phenomenon which sits well with the nostalgic idealisation of the country-side and village life in Vietnam.

While the Vietnamese rejected the Chinese traditions of manipulating exotic ingredients, they readily integrated Chinese spiritual traditions into their food philosophy: the impact of Taoism and particularly Confucianism can be clearly seen in Vietnamese cooking.

One key concept of Taoism is the notion of complementary opposites, best illustrated in the famous Yin and Yang emblem. This idea extends to eating, with food being categorised as either "cold" or "hot". In keeping with the Taoist philosophy of uniting opposites, a healthy diet should include both. Pineapple, for example, is considered "cold" and is therefore served with a "hot" chilli and salt dip. For the same reasons, "cold" snails are often paired with "hot" ginger.

The influence of Confucianism is even more pronounced and the figure of 5 plays a central role. In Confucian philosophy the natural world is made up of five elements — wood, fire, earth, metal and water — and everything follows on from there. A balanced meal should contain five nutrients (carbohydrates, fat, protein, minerals and water) and should appeal to all five senses, including sound, smell and sight. This might explain the fact that eating noisily is not necessarily frowned upon and that the fashion of intricate vegetable carving discarded in the West is popular in Vietnam.

Most importantly, however, a complete meal must include all five tastes — sour, bitter, sweet, spicy and salty. Hence the great importance of the dipping sauces which make up any tastes missing from the main dishes. For only with the harmony of all five flavours can one achieve the perfection of a Vietnamese meal.

ABOUT THIS BOOK

REAL VIETNAMESE COOKING IS ABOUT THE DISHES
WE LOVE AND THE RECIPES WE HAVE COLLECTED
OVER THE MANY YEARS WE HAVE BEEN LIVING AND
TRAVELLING IN THIS DIVERSE AND VIBRANT COUNTRY.

It is about the memorable meals we have had at street stalls, countryside eateries, *bia hois* and family gatherings which piqued our culinary interests. It also covers the three main culinary regions of the country: the hearty food of the cooler North, dishes from the Centre with its tradition of the imperial cuisine from Hue, and the sweeter and spicier food from the tropical South. The recipes range from classic Vietnamese fare such as Beef Noodle Soup (Pho Bo), Spring Rolls (Nem) and Banana Flower Salad as well as lesser known recipes like Eel in Caul Fat and Boiled Jackfruit Seeds.

While we have retained the traditional chapter headings such as Pork, Beef and Goat, and Fish and Crustaceans, they are more of a guide rather than a definitive description. The recipes are grouped according to their dominant ingredient. In this way, Prawn and Pork Broth with Rice Noodles (Hu Tieu) is listed under Fish and Crustaceans, because the broth is flavoured with dried squid. My Quang Noodles with Prawn and Pork, in contrast, can be found in the Pork, Beef and Goat chapter, because of its straightforward pork broth.

Curiously for a country with a Buddhist tradition, there are very few strictly vegetarian dishes, apart from the quite specialised vegan pagoda cooking. The reason for this is probably that vegetarianism is practised mainly on significant days of the lunar calendar as an exercise of abstinence rather than as a lifestyle. Even vegetable dishes that contain no meat or seafood will quite likely have been prepared with fish sauce. Therefore, we have called this chapter more broadly Vegetables and Salads and it also includes tofu dishes. However, many of the recipes can be adapted to meet a strict vegetarian diet.

The fact that rice is so central to the Vietnamese cuisine warranted a discrete chapter and the all-important dipping sauces, without which no Vietnamese dish would be complete, are also listed separately and are cross-referenced as part of the main dishes with which they are paired.

Traditionally, a Vietnamese meal finishes with platters of freshly cut fruit. The recipes in the Sweets chapter are normally eaten as snacks throughout the day, yet each of them would also be a perfectly suitable way to conclude a meal.

When Vietnamese sit down to eat, it is a communal affair, where family and friends share the food placed in the centre of the table, taking small morsels from the serving platters and bowls, one at a time. There is no hierarchical order of entrée and mains in Vietnamese cuisine. Dishes come out at the same time or whenever they are ready. The only exception is steamed rice which is served at the end of the meal together with a broth (canh).

In keeping with the communal theme, the recipes in the book will serve six unless otherwise stated. Noodle or bowl dishes like Pho Bo, Bun Cha and My Quang are generally not served as part of a banquet, but are eaten individually.

To put together a banquet, select four or five dishes covering different cooking techniques and ingredients. A typical selection would be spring rolls, a fried or grilled meat or fish dish, a braised or stir-fried dish such as tofu with pork and a salad or vegetable dish. This selection should be accompanied by rice and, if you like, a canh. Alternatively, for a quicker and more casual meal, you could select one or two dishes and serve them with rice.

VIVE LA FRANCE!

IN OUR EARLY YEARS IN VIETNAM WE
LOVED TO GO TO A HIDDEN RESTAURANT
CALLED LA BIBLIOTHEQUE WHENEVER
WE FOUND OURSELVES IN HO CHI MINH
CITY. IT WAS CENTRALLY LOCATED IN A
FRENCH VILLA CLOSE TO THE CATHEDRAL,
BUT STILL HARD TO FIND WITHOUT
ANY SIGNAGE.

The place was run by Madame Dai, a lawyer and politician in South Vietnam from a prominent, French educated family. Forbidden from practising law after the communist victory in 1975, she turned the library of the family home into a clandestine restaurant to make ends meet, serving simple bistro classics such as casseroles and coq-au-vin. An evening at La Bibliotheque was like stepping back in time, sitting at one of only six tables surrounded by dusty legal tomes in glassed-in bookcases. A slight woman with a patrician air, dressed in a traditional Ao Dai, Madame Dai would personally host the small number of patrons fluently conversing in French. The restaurant closed in 2000 and Madame Dai passed away not long after, in a small way symbolising the end of the colonial century in Vietnam.

French merchants and missionaries sought economic and political inroads in Vietnam as early as the 17th century. In fact, a French Catholic priest, Alexandre de Rhode, is credited with inventing the romanised script which replaced the Chinese-style Nom ideograms.

France's colonial adventure started in earnest with the attack on the port city of Danang in 1858 and finished with

the inglorious defeat of French paratroopers near Dien Bien Phu in the northern highlands. Colonisation initially focused on the south, driven by the impossible dream of using the Mekong River as a trade route to China. Realising the Mekong River was too treacherous, the French turned their attention to the north, pushing to open the Red River to international trade instead. After three decades of gunboat diplomacy and many treaties, they finally brought the entire country under French control in 1895, renaming the south Cochin China, the centre Annam and the north Tonkin.

As colonial masters the French were not very interested in establishing industry, but keen to export rice, rubber and other agricultural products back to Europe. They were also keen to remodel Saigon and Hanoi in their own image. French villas still give the capital much of its old-world charm, as do the scaled-down replicas of the Cathedral of Notre Dame and the Paris Opera House. For entertainment, the French even built a velodrome and racetrack. The residence of the French Governor-General turned out to be so palatial that when Ho Chi Minh became president of Vietnam in 1954, he famously refused to live in such colonial splendour, preferring a simple, traditional stilt house.

To pay for these ambitious buildings, the French imposed high taxes on the local population and turned salt and alcohol production into state monopolies.

Salt producers had to sell their products to a state company at a fixed price. This had far-reaching consequences for a country which at the time consumed more than double the amount of salt per person than the average European. The two main sources of protein in Vietnamese cuisine, fish sauce and preserved fish, required copious amounts of salt and suddenly became almost unaffordable for locals. The colonial administration also banned traditional rice wine distilling in the villages in an attempt to force the Vietnamese to buy the much stronger, industrially produced liquor from a licensed French company.

Not only did these policies turn scores of villagers into salt smugglers and bootleggers, they also ensured there wasn't much love lost between the locals and the French – which fortunately did not prevent the Vietnamese from borrowing from their cuisine. While the French mostly stayed away from the local fare, preferring a diet based on imported tinned goods, the Vietnamese freely experimented with the new, European foods: kohlrabi with tofu, baguette made with rice flour, pâté with fish sauce and coriander (cilantro), spring rolls with mayonnaise or cha ca with dill.

French influences on Vietnamese cuisine are manifold, ranging from a love of crème caramel and coffee to cooking with wine and beer. France's most enduring culinary legacy, however, might well be the humble tin of sweetened, condensed milk. It all started with an advertising campaign by French brand La Petite Fermiere in 1915 which initially marketed it as a health drink for children. Condensed milk certainly hit the sweet tooth of young and old Vietnamese alike. It is still used in sweets, desserts and particularly with coffee, and has maintained its incredible popularity long past the demise of colonial Indochine.

RICE AND BREAD

BOILED RICE

Cơm trắng

Boiled rice is the backbone of Vietnamese cuisine, and the most common way of enjoying rice as part of a Vietnamese meal.

600 G (1 LB 5 OZ/3 CUPS)
LONG-GRAIN WHITE RICE

SERVES 6

Put the rice in a large colander or sieve and rinse under cold running water. Place your hand in the centre of the rice and move it in a circular motion to make sure the water runs freely over all the rice. When the water runs clear, allow the rice to drain.

Transfer the rice to an electric rice cooker and cover with water. The water should come up to the first knuckle when the tip of your index finger is resting on top of the rice. Cook according to the rice cooker's instructions.

Alternatively, place the rice and 1.125 litres (38 fl oz/4½ cups) water in a saucepan and bring to the boil. Cover immediately and reduce the heat. Simmer for 20 minutes, then allow the rice to rest for a further 10 minutes before serving.

BROKEN RICE

Cơm tấm

Traditionally, it was very difficult for farmers to sell rice that had been broken during the harvest, so they mostly ate it themselves. Later it became part of a cheap worker's lunch, and over time city dwellers developed a taste for it, in part as a nostalgic reminder of a simpler country life.

You normally buy the rice already broken — but if you aren't able to obtain any, you can simply break some white rice yourself using a mortar and pestle.

400 G (14 OZ/2 CUPS) BROKEN LONG-GRAIN WHITE RICE

SERVES 6

Put the rice in a fine colander or sieve and rinse under cold running water. Run your fingers through the rice to ensure the water runs over all the grains, to wash away the starch. When the water runs clear, drain the rice for a few moments.

Transfer the rice to an electric rice cooker and pour in 625 ml (21 fl oz/2½ cups) water. Cook according to the rice cooker's instructions.

Alternatively, place the rice and 625 ml (21 fl oz/2½ cups) water in a saucepan and bring to the boil. Cover immediately and reduce the heat. Simmer for 20 minutes, then allow the rice to rest for a further 10 minutes before serving.

CRISPY RICE FROM THE POT

Cơm cháy

We like this rice with braised meats, or to scoop up one of the salads from this book.

It takes a bit of practice to lift the rice out of the pot in one piece. Don't worry if it doesn't work the first time: it still tastes the same, even if it breaks up!

600 G (1 LB 5 OZ/3 CUPS) LONG-GRAIN WHITE RICE
⅓ TEASPOON SALT

60 ML (2 FL OZ/¼ CUP) VEGETABLE OIL

SERVES 6

Put the rice in a large colander or sieve and rinse under cold running water. Place your hand in the centre of the rice and move it in a circular motion to make sure the water runs freely over all the rice. When the water runs clear, allow the rice to drain.

Transfer the rice to a saucepan and cover with 1.125 litres (38 fl oz/4½ cups) water. Bring to the boil, then cover immediately with a tight-fitting lid and reduce the heat to a simmer.

Cook for 18 minutes, then turn the heat up and cook for a final 2 minutes. Remove from the heat and let the rice rest for 10 minutes before serving.

Scoop the rice from the pan, except for the rice that has stuck to the base and side.

Return the pan to the heat. Season the rice in the pan with the salt and a pinch of freshly ground black pepper. Run the oil down the side and onto the base of the pan.

Cook until the rice lifts away from the pan and has a golden brown colour and crisp texture.

FRIED STICKY RICE

Cơm nếp chiên

Usually served with grilled meats, sticky rice also makes a healthy snack. When it is fried, you should end up with delicious pillows of creamy rice within a crisp, golden crust. In Vietnam, this dish is often accompanied by a cold beer or two.

500 G (1 LB 2 OZ/2½ CUPS) GLUTINOUS RICE
½ TEASPOON SALT
50 G (1¾ OZ/⅓ CUP) SPLIT, PEELED YELLOW MUNG BEANS
1 TEASPOON BAKING POWDER

VEGETABLE OIL, FOR DEEP-FRYING
SOY CHILLI DIPPING SAUCE (SEE PAGE 340), TO SERVE

SERVES 6

Wash the rice under cold running water until the water runs clear. Place in a saucepan or electric rice cooker, then add 750 ml (25½ fl oz/3 cups) water and the salt. Cook for 30 minutes, then drain well and place in a large sturdy bowl.

Meanwhile, put the mung beans in a saucepan and cover with cold water. Bring to the boil, then reduce the heat and simmer for about 15 minutes, until the beans are soft. Drain and add to the rice, along with the baking powder.

Using a pestle, work the rice mixture until all the grains are broken and the ingredients combined.

Transfer the mixture to a tray measuring 30 cm x 24 cm (12 inches x 9½ inches), and at least 4 cm (1½ inches) deep.

Smooth out with dampened hands. Chill in the refrigerator for about 4 hours, or until set.

When the rice has set, heat about 10 cm (4 inches) of oil in a wok or large saucepan over high heat.

Cut the rice into 5 cm (2 inch) batons, or use a spoon to scoop out the rice into ball shapes.

Immediately add the rice portions to the hot oil and cook in batches until lightly coloured. Remove from the oil and drain on paper towel.

Arrange the fried sticky rice on a platter and encourage diners to dip their portions in the dipping sauce.

GRAINS OF LIFE

LEGENDARY HANOIAN PUBLICIST
HUU NGOC RECALLS THAT AS A CHILD
HE ONCE ACCIDENTALLY DROPPED SOME
GRAINS OF RICE ON THE FLOOR. HIS
MOTHER CLIPPED HIM AROUND THE EARS
AND SCOLDED HIM WITH THE WORDS:
'EVERY GRAIN OF RICE IS LIKE A PEARL!'

This anecdote illustrates the high regard in which this everyday food staple is held, in a country whose culture has been defined by millennia of wet rice cultivation.

Rice does, quite simply, belong to the very fabric of Vietnamese life. No meal is complete without rice. No wedding, no funeral, no New Year's Eve celebration can be held without a rice dish carrying a special meaning. Rice is turned into flour, paper, noodles and even into alcohol. Almost half the population is connected with rice production in one way or another. Rice is everywhere. In the countryside, every available plot of land seems to be turned into a rice paddy, to the point where currently more than 1.2 million hectares of farmland are devoted to growing this grain.

Rice is considered a gift from the gods, and many myths and rituals illustrate its importance. One of the most endearing and poignant traditions is that the King himself had to be the first person to plough a rice paddy at the beginning of the lunar year.

Glutinous rice was the first variety under cultivation, with hard rice being introduced much later. Despite that late arrival, hard rice quickly overtook the sticky varieties in importance as it was easier to grow and had a much higher yield. Sticky rice was soon used mainly for special occasions such as ancestor worship and other rites and celebrations. By the late 18th century, some 70 different rice strains were under cultivation, and a cookbook written by the scholar Le Huu Trac in 1760 contained no less than 16 different recipes for cooking glutinous rice.

Historians have long assumed that the Chinese, who had been practising irrigation agriculture in the Yellow River Valley before invading Vietnam in the first century AD, introduced rice to the Red River Delta. More recent archaeological finds, however, show evidence of domestication of wild rice on the slopes north of the Red River as early as 4000 BC. Dykes, initially built as protection against flooding, were later used to regulate irrigation.

The influences of rice cultivation on Vietnam's culture might even run deeper than myths, history and traditions. Huu Ngoc maintains that growing rice and the village culture associated with it have formed the national character itself. Centuries of toiling in the paddies have ingrained the ethics of hard work and of valuing collective needs over individual ones, as well as a belief in the necessity of cooperation.

Being a foodstuff and a national symbol has also turned this humble staple into a political subject matter. Preoccupied with nation building, 19th century emperor Minh Mang promoted a unified national cuisine based on wet rice, fish sauce and the use of chopsticks. Ever since, the foundations of political power in Vietnam have firmly sat in the nation's rice paddies.

The political travails of his successor, emperor Gia Long, provides a case in point. Faced with the dilemma of whether to ship the surplus rice from the fertile Mekong region up north to shore up his political rule or to sell it off to other countries for hard cash, his solution was to officially ban exports, but turn a blind eye to members of his dynasty selling the grains on the sly.

The seesaw of abundance and scarcity has preoccupied the country's rulers and citizens ever since rice became a major trading commodity in the 19th century, and famines and shortages are still etched in the country's collective memory.

Most recently, the fact that after the Vietnam War, a country full of rice paddies had to import this staple triggered the Doi Moi policies of economic reforms in 1986, and set Vietnam on the path to becoming the second largest rice exporter globally that it is today.

STICKY RICE

Xôi

Sticky rice is ideal for soaking up the juices of your favourite dishes at the end of a meal.

600 G (1 LB 5 OZ/3 CUPS) GLUTINOUS RICE
1 TEASPOON SALT

PEANUT AND SESAME MIX (SEE PAGE 334), TO SERVE

SERVES 6

Soak the rice in cold water for a minimum of 4 hours, or overnight if more convenient.

Drain the rice and rinse under cold water until the water runs clear.

Sprinkle the rice with the salt and place in a bamboo steamer lined with muslin (cheesecloth). Cover and steam for 30 minutes. Remove the lid from the steamer and check that the rice is cooked — it should be tender all the way through.

Serve immediately, or cover with a damp cloth to prevent the rice drying out and hardening.

Eat the rice with your fingers, dipping it into the peanut and sesame mix.

STICKY RICE LOGS

Xôi chiên

This is a snack from the countryside, easily transportable for workers to take to the rice paddies. It is great on its own, but can also be served as a side dish for grilled and fried meat or fish.

555 G (1 LB 4 OZ/3 CUPS) COOKED STICKY RICE (SEE OPPOSITE PAGE)

125 ML (4 FL OZ/½ CUP) RENDERED CHICKEN FAT (SEE PAGE 337)

SERVES 6

Take a small handful of the cooked sticky rice and form into an oblong shape with damp fingers, applying a small amount of pressure so the grains stick together.

Heat the chicken fat in a frying pan and fry the rice logs in batches over high heat for about 3 minutes on each side, until slightly crunchy on the outside.

Serve warm or cold.

RICE CRACKERS

Bánh đa vừng

Buy some rice crackers from an Asian supermarket. Usually, two rice crackers for every three people is sufficient.

Cook the rice crackers for about 3 minutes, or until crisp and golden — either in a preheated 180°C (350°F) oven, or on a hot grill.

VIETNAMESE BAGUETTE

Bánh mỳ

The French claim that the term 'banh my' is derived from 'pain de mie', both being sandwich loaves with soft centres. However, the rice flour gives the Vietnamese version of the French baguette its distinct thin, flaky crust.

375 G (13 OZ/2½ CUPS) PLAIN (ALL-PURPOSE) FLOUR
60 G (2 OZ/⅓ CUP) RICE FLOUR
2 TEASPOONS SUGAR
2 TEASPOONS SALT

340 ML (11½ FL OZ/1⅓ CUPS) LUKEWARM WATER
2 TEASPOONS (7 G) DRIED YEAST
MAKES 6 ROLLS

Sift the flours, sugar and salt into a bowl and make a well in the centre. Whisk together the water and yeast, then pour the mixture into the well. Start in the centre of the well and incorporate the wet and dry ingredients with your hand. Move your hand in increasingly larger circles, slowly bringing the ingredients together.

Place the dough on a lightly floured work surface. Knead by stretching the dough away from you, then winding it back, rotating the dough as you go. Continue with this motion for about 8–10 minutes. You should end up with a smooth, elastic dough.

Place the dough in a bowl, cover with a damp cloth and leave in a warm, draught-free spot for about 1 hour, or until doubled in size.

Divide the dough into six equal portions. Roll each piece into a log shape and place on a sheet of baking paper. Leave in a warm spot to prove a second time, for 30–40 minutes.

Meanwhile, heat the oven to 220°C (430°F) and preheat a baking tray in the oven.

Test to see if the rolls are ready by lightly pressing the sides to form a dimple. If the dimple slowly fills out, the dough is ready. Using a sharp knife, score the bread from end to end, in one long line, but not too deep.

Slide the rolls, still on the baking paper, onto the preheated tray and into the oven. Have a small bowl of water at the ready and flick water into the oven before shutting the door. Bake the bread for 20 minutes, flicking water into the oven three more times for a crispy crust.

Slide the rolls off the tray and finish by baking them directly on the oven racks for an additional 5 minutes.

To test if they are cooked, tap the base of the rolls — you should hear a hollow sound.

Remove from the oven and cool on a wire rack.

These baguettes are best enjoyed soon after making.

VEGETABLES AND SALADS

BANANA FLOWER SALAD

Nộm hoa chuối

The large purple petals of the banana flower are often used in Vietnamese cooking. The outer layers are too tough and bitter to eat, but are kept for decoration, for an added splash of colour. The inner petals, which are almost white at the stem and turn a light purple towards the tip, add a delicately bitter taste to salads and curries.

Originally a local Hanoi dish, this salad is now widely available throughout Vietnam. It works equally well with duck or chicken.

JUICE OF 2 LIMES

1 BANANA FLOWER

1 x 180 G (6½ OZ) PORK FILLET

VEGETABLE OIL, FOR PAN-FRYING

12 COOKED TIGER PRAWNS (SHRIMP), PEELED AND DEVEINED

3 RED ASIAN SHALLOTS, THINLY SLICED

1 HANDFUL BEAN SPROUTS

1 HANDFUL CORIANDER (CILANTRO), ROUGHLY CHOPPED

2 TABLESPOONS ROASTED PEANUTS, CHOPPED, PLUS EXTRA TO GARNISH

DRESSING

90 G (3 OZ/HEAPED ⅓ CUP) SUGAR

100 ML (3½ FL OZ) LIME JUICE

60 ML (2 FL OZ/¼ CUP) FISH SAUCE

1 LONG RED CHILLI, SEEDED AND FINELY CHOPPED

2 GARLIC CLOVES, FINELY CHOPPED

SERVES 6

Add the lime juice to a bowl of water. Pull any bruised outer petals from the banana flower (1). Gently remove six tender petals and set aside for presentation.

Slice the remaining flower very thinly, discarding any banana shoots between the petals (2). Soak the flower slices in the lime juice water, to soften them slightly without discolouring.

Meanwhile, season the pork and fry in a lightly oiled non-stick frying pan over medium heat for 3–4 minutes on each side, or until cooked through. Remove the pork to a board. Leave to rest for 5 minutes, then thinly slice and set aside.

Cut the prawns in half lengthways and set aside.

To assemble the salad, drain the sliced banana flower and pat dry with paper towel. Place in a large bowl with the pork, prawns, shallot, bean sprouts, coriander and peanuts.

Combine the dressing ingredients and whisk until the sugar has dissolved (3). Gently toss the dressing through the salad, evenly distributing the ingredients and dressing.

Divide the salad among the six reserved banana flower petals. Sprinkle with extra chopped peanuts and serve.

BITTER GOURD WITH DUCK EGGS

Mướp đắng xào trứng vịt

Bitter gourd, also known as bitter melon, originated in India and made its way to Vietnam via China. It is a knobbly fruit, reminiscent of cucumber, and grows on vines. It is commonly used in soups.

Duck eggs add richness to this dish, but chicken eggs can also be used. The egg balances out the bitterness of the gourd.

1 BITTER GOURD

2 DUCK EGGS

VEGETABLE OIL, FOR PAN-FRYING

½ TEASPOON FISH SAUCE

LIME AND CHILLI DIPPING SALT (SEE PAGE 328), TO SERVE

SERVES 6

Cut the bitter gourd lengthways, discard the seeds, then thinly slice the flesh.

Break the eggs into a small bowl and lightly whisk with a fork. Season with a pinch of salt and freshly ground black pepper.

Heat about 1 tablespoon of oil in a wok or frying pan. When hot, stir-fry the gourd for 2 minutes.

Pour in the eggs and keep stirring to scramble the eggs. When the eggs are nearly set, sprinkle with the fish sauce and continue stirring.

Remove from the wok and serve with the dipping salt on the side.

BOILED JACKFRUIT SEEDS

Hạt mít luộc

Here's a great example of the Vietnamese not wasting anything. When using jackfruit in other dishes, make sure you keep the seeds for this recipe. The boiled seeds taste a little like chestnuts and make a healthy, nutritious snack.

150 G (5½ OZ/1 CUP) JACKFRUIT SEEDS   **MAKES 1 CUP**

Place the seeds in a saucepan, cover with cold water and bring to the boil. Reduce the heat and simmer for 15–20 minutes, or until a bamboo skewer easily passes through the seeds.

Drain the seeds and allow to cool before eating.

The seeds are best eaten the day they are made, dipped into a little sea salt if desired.

CABBAGE AND CHICKEN SALAD WITH VIETNAMESE MINT

Nộm gà với bắp cải

This salad is very common in the homes of Hanoi, where every family prepares their own version.

2 BONELESS, SKINLESS CHICKEN BREASTS

½ CABBAGE, THINLY SLICED

2 CARROTS, CUT INTO LONG THIN STRIPS

3 RED ASIAN SHALLOTS, THINLY SLICED

1 HANDFUL VIETNAMESE MINT

1 LONG RED CHILLI, CUT INTO RINGS

2 TABLESPOONS ROASTED UNSALTED PEANUTS, ROUGHLY CHOPPED, PLUS 1 TEASPOON EXTRA, TO SERVE

DRESSING

120 G (4½ OZ) SUGAR

100 ML (3½ FL OZ) LIME JUICE

60 ML (2 FL OZ/¼ CUP) FISH SAUCE

2 GARLIC CLOVES, CHOPPED

SERVES 6

Bring a small saucepan of salted water to the boil. Add the chicken, reduce the heat and simmer for 8–10 minutes, or until just cooked through. Transfer the chicken to a chopping board, leave to cool, then cut or shred the chicken into thin strips. Place in a large bowl.

To make the dressing, whisk together the sugar and lime juice until the sugar has completely dissolved. Stir in the fish sauce and garlic.

Add the vegetables, mint, chilli and peanuts to the chicken. Pour the dressing over the salad and gently toss to combine.

Serve on a large platter, sprinkled with the remaining peanuts.

CABBAGE WITH EGG AND FISH SAUCE

Bắp cải luộc chấm nước mắm trứng

A basic countryside dish that is making its way into the cities. The richness of the egg with the salty fish sauce makes it a popular staff lunch at the Hanoi Cooking Centre!

1 CM (½ INCH) KNOB FRESH GINGER,
PEELED AND LEFT WHOLE

¼ CABBAGE

2 EGGS

2 TABLESPOONS FISH SAUCE

SERVES 6

Bring a large saucepan of water to the boil. Add the ginger.

Meanwhile, separate the cabbage leaves and cut each leaf into two or three pieces.

When the water has come to the boil, gently slide the whole eggs into the water using a slotted spoon. Cook for 5 minutes, then remove the eggs and leave to cool.

Working in batches, now blanch the cabbage leaves in the same pan of boiling water, for 2 minutes each time. Drain well and place on a platter.

Peel the eggs and place in separate small bowls. Pour half the fish sauce over each egg.

Immediately before eating, roughly chop each egg into several pieces, so the gooey yolk runs into the fish sauce.

Each diner then dips some cabbage into the eggy sauce.

CHICKEN, SESAME AND JICAMA SALAD

Gà xé phay

Jicama is a root vegetable from South and Central America that resembles a turnip. Like choko, it very likely made its way to Vietnam in the 17th and 18th centuries via trading routes from Central America to the Philippines, then onwards to the trading port of Hoi An.

The taste of its firm white flesh has been described as a cross between water chestnut and apple. Jicama works particularly well in salads, as it adds a crisp freshness and doesn't discolour when exposed to air.

300 G (10½ OZ) BONELESS, SKINLESS CHICKEN BREASTS

1 JICAMA, PEELED AND CUT INTO THIN SLICES

2 TABLESPOONS SESAME SEEDS, TOASTED

3 RED ASIAN SHALLOTS, THINLY SLICED

1 CARROT, CUT INTO LONG, THIN STRIPS

1 HANDFUL CORIANDER (CILANTRO)

4 KAFFIR LIME LEAVES, CUT INTO THIN STRIPS

1 LONG RED CHILLI, SEEDED AND CUT INTO THIN STRIPS

1 TABLESPOON FRIED SHALLOTS (SEE PAGE 326)

DRESSING

100 ML (3½ FL OZ) LIME JUICE

120 G (4½ OZ) SUGAR

60 ML (2 FL OZ/¼ CUP) FISH SAUCE

2 GARLIC CLOVES, FINELY CHOPPED

SERVES 6

Bring a small saucepan of salted water to the boil. Add the chicken, reduce the heat and simmer for 8–10 minutes, or until just cooked through. Transfer to a chopping board, leave to cool, then cut or shred the chicken into thin strips. Place in a large bowl.

Add the jicama, sesame seeds, shallot, carrot, coriander, lime leaves and chilli to the chicken.

To make the dressing, whisk together the sugar and lime juice until the sugar has completely dissolved. Stir in the fish sauce and garlic.

Pour the dressing over the salad and gently toss to combine.

Serve on a large platter, sprinkled with the fried shallots.

CHOKO AND BARBECUED PORK SALAD

Nộm su su thịt nướng

Choko, also known as chayote, is a pear-shaped fruit native to Central America and particularly Mexico, which was most likely imported into Vietnam by Portuguese or Spanish traders. It belongs to the same plant family as zucchini (courgette), pumpkin (winter squash) and gourds, and works well when paired with strongly flavoured ingredients, such as the Chinese pork and chilli used here.

2 CHOKOS
1 CARROT, CUT INTO LONG THIN STRIPS
3 RED ASIAN SHALLOTS, THINLY SLICED
1 HANDFUL MINT
2 TABLESPOONS FRIED SHALLOTS (SEE PAGE 326)
2 TABLESPOONS ROASTED PEANUTS, ROUGHLY CHOPPED
1 LONG RED CHILLI, SEEDED AND CUT INTO THIN STRIPS
200 G (7 OZ) CHAR SIU PORK, CUT INTO 2 CM (¾ INCH) PIECES

DRESSING
120 G (4½ OZ) SUGAR
100 ML (3½ FL OZ) LIME JUICE
60 ML (2 FL OZ/¼ CUP) FISH SAUCE
2 GARLIC CLOVES, FINELY CHOPPED
SERVES 6

To make the dressing, whisk together the sugar and lime juice until the sugar has completely dissolved. Stir in the fish sauce and garlic.

Peel the chokos and discard the skin. Cut the choko into very thin strips, using a mandoline or vegetable peeler.

Place the choko strips in a bowl, pour the dressing over and toss to combine. Leave to soak for 3–4 minutes for the choko to soften.

Now add the carrot, shallot, mint, fried shallot, peanuts, chilli and pork to the choko.

Gently toss together, then pile the salad onto a large platter and serve.

CHOKO TENDRIL SALAD WITH CHILLI, SOY AND PEANUTS

Su su xào

In Australia, choko tendrils are considered a weed by many, and often end up on the compost heap. We didn't realise just how tasty they were until we came to Vietnam.

2 BIG HANDFULS CHOKO TENDRILS
80 ML (2½ FL OZ/⅓ CUP) SOY SAUCE
SQUEEZE OF LIME JUICE

1 LONG RED CHILLI, CUT INTO RINGS
2 TABLESPOONS ROASTED PEANUTS, CHOPPED
SERVES 6

Discard any large or bruised leaves from the tendrils. Cut the tendrils into 5 cm (2 inch) lengths so they are easy to pick up with chopsticks.

Bring a large saucepan of water to the boil. Blanch half the tendrils for 30–40 seconds. Remove with tongs or chopsticks and place in a bowl of iced water to stop the cooking process. Repeat with the remaining tendrils, then drain well.

In a small bowl, combine the soy sauce, lime juice, chilli and a pinch of sugar. Whisk until the sugar has completely dissolved.

Place the tendrils in a bowl, pour the soy sauce mixture over and toss well.

Transfer to a platter and serve sprinkled with the peanuts.

CRISPY NOODLE CAKE WITH SAUTÉED PRAWNS AND VEGETABLES

Bún gạo xào tôm, rau

Popular in southern Vietnam, these noodle cakes crisp up nicely on the outside, but stay soft inside. It is possible to turn this recipe into a vegetarian dish by leaving out the prawns (shrimp) and replacing the oyster sauce with soy sauce.

6 DRIED SHIITAKE MUSHROOMS

50 G (1¾ OZ) DRIED RICE VERMICELLI

VEGETABLE OIL, FOR PAN-FRYING

2 RED ASIAN SHALLOTS, DICED

6 PRAWNS (SHRIMP), PEELED, DEVEINED AND CUT IN HALF LENGTHWAYS

15 G (½ OZ/¼ CUP) SLICED GREEN CABBAGE

15 G (½ OZ/¼ CUP) PEELED AND THINLY SLICED JICAMA

12 GREEN BEANS, BLANCHED, THEN CUT IN HALF

12 CHIVES, CUT INTO 3 CM (1¼ INCH) LENGTHS

1 SMALL HANDFUL BEAN SPROUTS

1 TEASPOON SESAME OIL

1 TABLESPOON OYSTER SAUCE

SERVES 6

Soak the mushrooms in warm water for 20 minutes. Drain and squeeze out any excess water. Discard the stems and cut the caps in half.

Soak the vermicelli in boiling water for 4–5 minutes. Gently stir to separate the noodles, then drain and refresh under cold water.

Heat 2 tablespoons of oil in a 26 cm (10¼ inch) non-stick frying pan. When hot, evenly spread the noodles on the bottom of the pan. Cook over medium heat for 4–5 minutes, until golden and crispy underneath — you might need to run some extra oil around the inside of the rim to stop the noodle cake sticking to the pan. Now turn the cake over and cook evenly on the other side.

Meanwhile, in a separate frying pan, heat 1 tablespoon of oil and fry the shallot over medium heat until fragrant. Add the prawns and cook for a further 1–2 minutes. Remove the mixture from the pan and set aside.

Wipe the pan clean and return to the heat. Add another 1 tablespoon of oil to the pan, then cook the cabbage and mushrooms over high heat for 2 minutes, or until the cabbage softens. Add the jicama and beans and cook for a further 1 minute.

Lastly, add the chives, bean sprouts, sesame oil, oyster sauce and a pinch of salt. Return the prawn mixture to the pan with the vegetables and toss to combine.

To serve, transfer the prawns and vegetables to the centre of a warm plate. Remove the noodle cake from its pan and cut into six wedges using sharp kitchen scissors. Serve the warm noodle wedges on top of the prawns and vegetables.

FRIED EGG NOODLE, TOFU AND VEGETABLE SALAD

Thập nhị nhân duyên

The old imperial capital, Hue, is also the centre of Buddhism in Vietnam. This dish is a good example of the local Buddhist vegetarian cuisine.

The salad should be dressed at the table to preserve the crispness of the fried noodles and tofu.

VEGETABLE OIL, FOR FRYING

300 G (10½ OZ) FIRM TOFU

150 G (5½ OZ) FRESH EGG NOODLES

300 G (10½ OZ/1 CUP) PICKLED LOTUS ROOTS

1 CUCUMBER, CUT INTO STRIPS 5 CM (2 INCHES) LONG

¼ RED CABBAGE, CUT INTO LONG THIN STRIPS

1 CARROT, CUT INTO STRIPS

1 SMALL HANDFUL MINT

1 SMALL HANDFUL CORIANDER (CILANTRO)

DRESSING

40 ML (1¼ FL OZ) LIGHT SOY SAUCE

40 ML (1¼ FL OZ) LIME JUICE

1 TABLESPOON SUGAR

1 LONG RED CHILLI, SEEDED AND THINLY SLICED

2 GARLIC CLOVES, CHOPPED

SERVES 6

Heat about 2 cm (¾ inch) of oil in a wok or a large saucepan. Pat the tofu dry with paper towel. When the oil is hot, fry the tofu in batches until it turns lightly golden and floats to the surface. Using a slotted spoon, remove the tofu and drain well on paper towel.

Now fry the noodles in batches until crispy. Remove from the hot oil and also drain on paper towel.

Rinse the lotus roots to remove some of the pickling liquid. Drain well and pat dry. Cut the lotus roots lengthways into four pieces.

For the dressing, combine the soy sauce, lime juice and sugar with 80 ml (2½ fl oz/⅓ cup) water and stir until the sugar has dissolved. Stir in the chilli and garlic.

Arrange all the salad ingredients on a large plate. Serve the dressing on the side.

GREEN BEANS, LAP CHEONG SAUSAGE AND WATER CHESTNUTS

Đỗ xào lạp sườn, mã thầy

Lap cheong is a garlicky, Chinese pork sausage, available from Asian grocers. It freezes well, so if you need to buy a large pack, freeze the rest for next time you make this dish.

500 G (1 LB 2 OZ) GREEN BEANS, TOPPED AND TAILED
2 LAP CHEONG SAUSAGES, THINLY SLICED
40 G (1½ OZ/¼ CUP) WATER CHESTNUTS, THINLY SLICED

1 TABLESPOON SOY SAUCE

SERVES 6

Cook the beans for about 5 minutes in a saucepan of boiling salted water. Drain well.

Heat a wok and add the lap cheong — there's no need to add any oil to the wok as the sausage contains enough fat to prevent it sticking.

Stir-fry over high heat for 1 minute, then add the beans and water chestnuts. Toss to ensure the water chestnuts are evenly distributed.

Lastly, add the soy sauce and give the beans a final toss.

Remove from the wok and serve on a large plate.

GREEN MANGO AND SUN-DRIED SQUID SALAD

Nộm xoài, mực khô

It is best to buy an Asian mango variety such as 'keow savoy' or 'nam doc mai', as the more common unripe 'kensington pride' lacks the necessary tartness required for this recipe.

Asian mango varieties can be recognised by their slightly longer shape, and a small 'hook' at the end.

1 SMALL DRIED SQUID
2 GREEN MANGOES, PEELED AND CUT INTO LONG THIN STRIPS
3 RED ASIAN SHALLOTS, THINLY SLICED
½ LONG RED CHILLI, SEEDED AND CUT INTO THIN STRIPS
1 SMALL HANDFUL CORIANDER (CILANTRO)
1 SMALL HANDFUL MINT
2 TABLESPOONS FRIED SHALLOTS (SEE PAGE 326)

DRESSING
120 G (4½ OZ) SUGAR
100 ML (3½ FL OZ) LIME JUICE
60 ML (2 FL OZ/¼ CUP) FISH SAUCE
2 GARLIC CLOVES, CHOPPED

SERVES 6

Chargrill the squid for about 3 minutes on each side. Transfer the squid to a mortar and lightly pound with a pestle to remove any of the light film on the skin.

Using kitchen scissors or your fingers, shred the squid against the grain into thin strips and place in a large bowl. Add the mango, shallot, chilli, herbs and half the fried shallots.

To make the dressing, whisk together the sugar and lime juice until the sugar has completely dissolved. Stir in the fish sauce and garlic.

Pour the dressing over the salad ingredients and gently toss.

Serve the salad on a large platter, scattered with the remaining fried shallots.

GREENHOUSE EFFECT: GARDENS OF DALAT

'MY FATHER WAS AMONG THE FIRST GROUP OF NORTH VIETNAMESE FARMERS TO COME TO DALAT,' SAYS 62-YEAR-OLD NGO VAN PHONG. HE PROUDLY HOLDS UP A BLACK AND WHITE PHOTOGRAPH FROM THE EARLY 1940S SHOWING VIETNAM'S LAST EMPEROR PINNING A MEDAL ON THE TRADITIONAL TUNIC WORN BY HIS FATHER, NGO VAN BINH, WHO RECEIVED THE AWARD FOR HIS PIONEERING WORK IN ESTABLISHING MARKET GARDENS IN THE CENTRAL HIGHLANDS.

Ngo Van Binh passed away not so long ago at the ripe old age of 94, but his son Phong still lives in the old family home made from pinewood in Ha Dong village on the outskirts of Dalat. The village is named after the district of the same name in Ha Tay province, now part of greater Hanoi, from where the first settlers came, and the story of how Ha Tay residents came to grow vegetables in Dalat is inextricably linked to Vietnam's colonial past.

The famous French immunologist Alexandre Yersin reportedly discovered the location of what was to become Dalat as early as 1893, and recommended it to the colonial administration as an ideal site for a resort to escape the oppressive heat of the lowlands. The French displaced the ethnic minority who lived in the area, and over the next 30 years built a European-style town, replete with chalets,

cathedral, an artificial lake, and even a replica of the Eiffel Tower. Da Lach, 'the river of the Lach people', turned into the French hill station Dalat.

By 1945, the town boasted 3000 villas, the summer palace of the emperor, and a population of about 5000 French, hungry for European food. Over the previous decade, Dalat had grown at such a fast rate that the small Vietnamese population struggled to provide enough food for the French inhabitants. In response, the townspeople decided to establish so-called 'supply villages' in a conscious effort to move away from the imported tinned foods so prevalent in the French diet in Saigon and Hanoi.

They also decided to tap in to an existing skill base and import labour from the northern provinces of what was then called Tonkin. There, farmers were already growing fruit and vegetables for the French living in Hanoi.

'The first people from Ha Dong came here only for a very short time. It was too cold for them,' chuckles Phong. 'But they brought seeds for European cold-climate vegetables, and cleared a lot of the land.' Back in the north, his father, Binh, had temporarily left the family trade of farming and worked as a journalist at the time. He wrote about the migration scheme to the Central Highlands and this piqued his interest in moving there. When the French administration formalised the process of resettlement in 1937, Binh put his name down for a plot of land. One year later, he and his parents were among the first 33 families to move to Dalat.

This time, the French made sure the migrants stayed on and produced a good crop. Not only did they give the new arrivals enough land, they also stipulated what was to be grown on it. There was no direct contact between the colonisers and farmers, however. Instead, Vietnamese officials acted as go-betweens and even dispatched training officers to assist with setting up the market gardens and to advise on irrigation and the use of machinery.

The temperate climate of an area located 1500 metres above sea level, along with the rich volcanic soil, provided excellent conditions for growing Western vegetables and berries, and the success of the first group of migrants lured more and more farmers from the north to Dalat. Ha Dong proved to be the seed that over the years grew into the agricultural powerhouse that Lam Dong province is today. These days, more than 100 different types of vegetables and over 80 varieties of cut flowers are grown on approximately 20,000 hectares, of which about 10 per cent are covered by greenhouses.

Binh and his family started out with the same produce the family had previously cultivated in the north. Over the years, he became more adventurous and experimented with different crops. He even became the first farmer in the province to grow brown onions — which earned him a spread in *National Geographic* magazine in the early 1960s.

Over the past decade, however, agriculture in the Dalat area has undergone big changes, most notably due to the rise in popularity of cut flowers. The market gardens have moved further away from Dalat and many farmers in Ha Dong village have switched to growing flowers, Binh's son included. Phong switched from cultivating cabbage and carrots to growing marigold flowers for the markets in Ho Chi Minh City. 'The price fluctuates, but profit margins are better,' Phong explains. Asked if he misses anything about growing vegetables, he smiles ironically: 'Only the hard work.'

GREEN PAPAYA SPRING ROLLS

Nem cuốn đu đủ

Vietnamese balm, or kinh gioi, is a native herb with bright green serrated leaves and a lemony mint flavour. It is also sometimes called lemon balm.

In Vietnam, sliced pig's ear is often served with green papaya, and it adds a wonderful chewiness to these spring rolls. You can get pig's ears from your butcher, but if they are not to your liking, you can simply omit them.

1 PIG'S EAR (OPTIONAL)

2 CARROTS, 1 CUT IN HALF, 1 CUT INTO LONG THIN STRIPS

4 RED ASIAN SHALLOTS

1 TABLESPOON ROASTED RICE FLOUR (SEE PAGE 337)

½ GREEN PAPAYA, PEELED AND CUT INTO LONG THIN STRIPS

24 RICE PAPER SHEETS, ABOUT 18 CM (7 INCHES) IN SIZE

1 SMALL HANDFUL VIETNAMESE BALM

30 G (1 OZ) DRIED BEEF, SHREDDED

1 TABLESPOON ROASTED PEANUTS, CHOPPED

CLASSIC DIPPING SAUCE (SEE PAGE 323), TO SERVE

SERVES 6

Place the pig's ear, if using, carrot halves and whole shallots in a saucepan and cover with cold water. Bring to boiling point, then reduce the heat and simmer for 6 hours.

Remove the ear from the liquid and discard the liquid and vegetables. Leave to cool, then refrigerate overnight.

To prepare the spring rolls, thinly slice one-third of the pig's ear and mix with the rice flour. Place in a bowl with the carrot and green papaya strips and mix together well.

Soften the rice paper sheets by dipping them one at a time into warm water for 1 second. Do not soak the sheets as they will become too soft and tear when rolled. Place on a flat surface, wait for 20 seconds, then soak up any excess water with a clean cloth.

In a straight line along the bottom third of a sheet, place a small amount of the papaya mixture, the Vietnamese balm and dried beef. Bring the bottom of the wrapper up over the filling, then roll up. Set aside, seam side down, while preparing the remaining spring rolls.

Scatter the peanuts over the spring rolls and serve straight away, with the dipping sauce.

GREEN PAPAYA SALAD

Nộm đu đủ xanh

There is a tradition among itinerant street vendors of using a particular identifying sound to attract customers. Legend has it that in the days before cars and motorbikes, Hanoi was such a quiet city that the most famous green papaya vendor in town could lure customers out of their houses with the sound of snipping metal scissors — his unique signal.

Nowadays, these subtle signals have often been replaced with a piece of recorded music blaring from a portable speaker to drown out all the other street noise.

1 GREEN PAPAYA
1 HANDFUL BEAN SPROUTS
4 RED ASIAN SHALLOTS, THINLY SLICED
1 SMALL HANDFUL VIETNAMESE BALM
40 G (1½ OZ/¼ CUP) ROASTED PEANUTS, CHOPPED
30 G (1 OZ) DRIED BEEF, SHREDDED
2 TABLESPOONS FRIED SHALLOTS (SEE PAGE 326)

DRESSING
120 G (4½ OZ) SUGAR
100 ML (3½ FL OZ) LIME JUICE
60 ML (2 FL OZ/¼ CUP) FISH SAUCE
1 LONG RED CHILLI, SEEDED AND CUT INTO THIN STRIPS
2 GARLIC CLOVES, CHOPPED
SERVES 6

Peel the papaya, then cut the flesh into thin strips 4–6 cm (1½–2½ inches) long. Place in a bowl with the bean sprouts, shallot, Vietnamese balm, peanuts and dried beef.

To make the dressing, combine the sugar and lime juice in a small bowl and stir until the sugar has dissolved. Stir in the fish sauce, chilli and garlic.

Pour the dressing over the salad and gently toss.

Serve in a large bowl, sprinkled with the fried shallots.

LOTUS ROOT SALAD

Nộm ngó sen

The lotus flower is very versatile. The entire lotus plant is used: the seeds in soups and desserts, the root in salads and stir-fries, the leaves for wrapping foods prior to cooking, and the flower for decoration and for making tea.

Although the ingredient in this recipe is commonly referred to as the 'root', it is in fact the tendril that runs off the large rhizome-shaped root.

1 BONELESS, SKINLESS CHICKEN BREAST
250 G (9 OZ) PICKLED LOTUS ROOTS
100 G (3½ OZ) BEAN SPROUTS
1 CARROT, CUT INTO LONG THIN STRIPS
3 RED ASIAN SHALLOTS, THINLY SLICED
3 TABLESPOONS VIETNAMESE MINT
1 TABLESPOON MINT
2 TABLESPOONS TOASTED SESAME SEEDS, PLUS AN EXTRA 2 TEASPOONS, TO SERVE
2 TABLESPOONS FRIED SHALLOTS (SEE PAGE 326), PLUS AN EXTRA 1 TEASPOON, TO SERVE
1 LONG RED CHILLI, SEEDED AND CUT INTO THIN STRIPS

DRESSING
120 G (4½ OZ) SUGAR
100 ML (3½ FL OZ) LIME JUICE
60 ML (2 FL OZ/¼ CUP) FISH SAUCE
2 GARLIC CLOVES, CHOPPED

SERVES 6

Bring a small saucepan of salted water to the boil. Add the chicken, reduce the heat and simmer for 8–10 minutes, or until just cooked through. Transfer the chicken to a board and leave to cool, then thinly slice and place in a large bowl.

To make the dressing, whisk together the sugar and lime juice until the sugar has completely dissolved. Stir in the fish sauce and garlic.

Rinse the lotus roots to remove some of the pickling liquid. Drain well and pat dry with paper towel. Cut the lotus roots lengthways into four pieces and add to the chicken, along with the remaining salad ingredients.

Pour the dressing over the salad and gently toss to combine.

Serve on a large platter, sprinkled with the extra sesame seeds and fried shallots.

PUMPKIN RICE PORRIDGE

Cháo bí ngô

Although pumpkin (winter squash) is indigenous to the Americas, it is now well entrenched in South-East Asian cuisine. It works well with Vietnamese herbs, spices and fish sauce.

300 G (10½ OZ/1½ CUPS) LONG-GRAIN WHITE RICE

1.25 LITRES (42 FL OZ/5 CUPS) VEGETABLE STOCK OR WATER

1 TABLESPOON VEGETABLE OIL

750 G (1 LB 11 OZ) PUMPKIN (WINTER SQUASH), PEELED AND GRATED

1 TEASPOON SUGAR

½ TEASPOON SALT

1 TABLESPOON FISH SAUCE

½ TEASPOON FRESHLY GROUND BLACK PEPPER

2 CM (¾ INCH) KNOB FRESH GINGER, JULIENNED

4 SPRING ONIONS (SCALLIONS), SLICED

4 TABLESPOONS ROUGHLY CHOPPED THAI BASIL

4 SAW-TOOTH CORIANDER (CILANTRO) STEMS, SLICED

SERVES 6

Put the rice in a large colander or sieve and rinse under cold running water. Place your hand in the centre of the rice and move it in a circular motion, to ensure the water runs freely over all the rice. When the water runs clear, drain the rice.

Place the rice in a dry frying pan and toast over high heat for 1 minute, moving the rice continuously so it colours evenly. Place one-quarter of the rice in a mortar and break the grains with the pestle.

Bring 1 litre (34 fl oz/4 cups) of the stock or water to the boil.

In another saucepan, heat the oil. Add the pumpkin and all the rice and fry over medium heat for 1 minute. Pour in the boiling stock and stir in the sugar, salt, fish sauce and pepper.

Reduce the heat and gently simmer for about 20 minutes, stirring regularly.

Stir the ginger through and simmer for a further 5 minutes, or until the rice is cooked.

Remove from the heat and stir the spring onion and herbs through. Serve in six individual bowls, sprinkled with extra black pepper, if desired.

RICE FLOUR PANCAKES WITH QUAIL EGGS

Bánh căn

These pancakes are a very popular afternoon snack on the streets of the ancient city of Hoi An. There are different versions in other coastal towns; for example, the vendors in Nha Trang use squid instead of eggs.

It is best to cook these in an Asian pancake pan, known as a banh khot pan. These pans have a number of small indentations, about 3–4 cm (1¼–1½ inches) in diameter and 2–3 cm (¾–1¼ inches) deep.

VEGETABLE OIL, FOR PAN-FRYING	**PANCAKE BATTER**
6 QUAIL EGGS	130 G (4½ OZ/¾ CUP) RICE FLOUR
1 SMALL HANDFUL PEELED AND THINLY SLICED GREEN PAPAYA	1 TEASPOON GROUND TURMERIC
½ CARROT, CUT INTO LONG THIN STRIPS	⅓ TEASPOON SUGAR
1 SMALL HANDFUL MINT	¼ TEASPOON SALT
1 TABLESPOON ROASTED PEANUTS, CRUSHED	125 ML (4 FL OZ/½ CUP) COCONUT MILK
2 TEASPOONS CHILLI SAUCE (SEE PAGE 322)	1 SPRING ONION (SCALLION), SLICED
CLASSIC DIPPING SAUCE (SEE PAGE 323), TO SERVE	**SERVES 6**

To make the pancake batter, sift the dry ingredients into a bowl, then make a well in the centre. Add the coconut milk and 125 ml (4 fl oz/½ cup) water and whisk to form a smooth batter. Add the spring onion and stir to combine (1).

Heat the banh khot pan and pour a little oil into the dips. Pour 2 tablespoons of the batter into each of the dips and rotate the pan to coat the sides. Crack a quail egg into six of the dips and cook for about 1 minute over medium heat, until the batter is crisp (2).

Remove the pancakes using a spoon and arrange around the rim of a plate (3).

In a bowl, toss together the papaya, carrot and mint, then place in the centre of the plate. Scatter with the peanuts and top with the chilli sauce. Drizzle the salad and pancakes with the dipping sauce.

The best way to enjoy the pancakes is by placing a small amount of the salad onto them while they are still hot.

SMOKY EGGPLANT WITH DRIED SHRIMP

Cà tím với tôm khô

Our favourite way of cooking eggplant is on a coal- or wood-fired barbecue. Its earthy, smoky flavours work wonderfully with the salty shrimp.

18 DRIED SHRIMP

3 LONG EGGPLANTS (AUBERGINES)

1 TEASPOON SUGAR

1 TABLESPOON RICE VINEGAR

2 TABLESPOONS FISH SAUCE

1 TABLESPOON VEGETABLE OIL

4 GARLIC CLOVES, CHOPPED

3 SPRING ONIONS (SCALLIONS), THINLY SLICED

SERVES 6

Cover the dried shrimp with water and set aside.

Chargrill the whole eggplants over a direct flame, either on a barbecue, or over the flame of a gas burner. Cook for 8–10 minutes, until the eggplant is blackened and blistered on all sides and the flesh has softened.

Remove the eggplants from heat and leave to cool. Peel and discard the blackened skin and squeeze the bitter juices from the flesh. Cut three-quarters of the way through the width of the eggplant in three places for easier handling when eating with chopsticks. Arrange the eggplant on a serving platter.

In a bowl, combine the sugar, vinegar and fish sauce. Mix until the sugar has completely dissolved.

Drain the shrimps, reserving the soaking liquid.

Heat the oil in a hot wok and add the shrimp and garlic. Keep the wok moving to avoid burning the garlic. When aromatic, add the spring onion and the reserved shrimp soaking liquid and cook until the spring onion has just wilted.

Remove the wok from the heat and add the vinegar mixture. Toss together well and season to taste with freshly ground black pepper.

Pour the mixture over the warm eggplant and serve.

SPICY EGGPLANT AND YOUNG JACKFRUIT SALAD

Nộm cà tím và mít non

From Hue, the centre of Vietnamese Buddhism, this vegetarian dish uses the very dense, almost meat-like flesh of the jackfruit.

When you prepare jackfruit, be mindful that it releases a very sticky sap when cut. Oil the blade of your knife so it passes through the fruit easily, and try not to get any of the sap on your fingers.

1 SMALL YOUNG JACKFRUIT

3 LONG EGGPLANTS (AUBERGINES)

½ TEASPOON SALT

VEGETABLE OIL, FOR PAN-FRYING

4 GARLIC CLOVES, FINELY CHOPPED

2 CM (¾ INCH) KNOB FRESH GINGER, THINLY SLICED

1 LONG RED CHILLI, SEEDED AND CUT INTO THIN STRIPS

2 TABLESPOONS SOY SAUCE

JUICE OF ½ LIME

½ TEASPOON SUGAR

⅓ TEASPOON FRESHLY GROUND BLACK PEPPER

2 TEASPOONS CHILLI SAUCE (SEE PAGE 322)

½ TEASPOON SESAME OIL

1 TABLESPOON SESAME SEEDS, TOASTED

3 SPRING ONIONS (SCALLIONS), CUT INTO RINGS

RICE CRACKERS (SEE PAGE 27), TO SERVE

SERVES 6

Using a large sharp knife, cut the jackfruit in half lengthways to make it easier to work with (1). Carefully cut away the tough outer rind and discard. Thinly slice the jackfruit flesh, placing the pieces in water as you go, to stop them discolouring (2).

Drain the jackfruit, place in a saucepan and cover with cold water. Weigh the jackfruit down with a small plate to ensure all the fruit is submerged. Slowly bring to the boil, then reduce the heat and simmer for 20 minutes. Drain well. When cool enough to handle, squeeze out any excess liquid.

Meanwhile, cut the eggplant into 4 cm (1½ inch) batons and place in a colander. Sprinkle with the salt and leave to sit for 30 minutes.

Rinse the salt off the eggplant and pat dry with paper towel. Heat about 1 cm (½ inch) of oil in a wok or frying pan and cook the eggplant over medium heat in two batches, for about 5 minutes per batch, until soft and golden brown. Remove from the pan and drain on paper towel.

Drain any excess oil from the wok, wipe the wok clean and return to the heat. Add 1 tablespoon oil of and cook the garlic, ginger and chilli over medium heat for 1 minute, until fragrant.

Now add the eggplant and jackfruit. Toss to combine, then toss the soy sauce, lime juice, sugar, pepper and chilli sauce through (3). Finally, add the sesame oil, sesame seeds and spring onion and toss to combine. Serve with rice crackers.

SQUID AND POMELO SALAD

Nộm mực, bưởi

Pomelo is the largest of all citrus fruits native to South-East Asia. It also works well with other cooked seafood, such as crab. If pomelo is unavailable, use ruby grapefruit instead.

Like many fruits and vegetables, pomelo has multiple uses: the flesh is used for cooking, and oil is extracted from the thick peel as a natural alternative to shampoos and conditioners.

2 SQUID, EACH ABOUT 8 CM (3¼ INCHES) LONG

1 POMELO

1 CARROT, THINLY SLICED

1 HANDFUL DILL

1 HANDFUL MINT

1 HANDFUL CORIANDER (CILANTRO)

3 RED ASIAN SHALLOTS, THINLY SLICED

1 LONG RED CHILLI, SEEDED AND FINELY CHOPPED

2 TABLESPOONS FRIED SHALLOTS (SEE PAGE 326)

1 LEMONGRASS STEM, WHITE PART ONLY, CRUSHED

4 BLACK PEPPERCORNS, LEFT WHOLE

DRESSING

55 G (2 OZ/¼ CUP) SUGAR

60 ML (2 FL OZ/¼ CUP) LIME JUICE

2½ TABLESPOONS FISH SAUCE

SERVES 6

Clean the squid by holding the body with one hand and the head with the other. Gently pull, taking care not to burst the ink sac; the head and tentacles will come away. Remove the clear cartilage, rinse the squid inside and out, then pat dry. Using a sharp knife, cut the head from the tentacles and discard.

Cut the body open and rinse away any membranes from the surface. Lay the squid flat on a board, with the inside facing up. Score the squid by cutting fine lines into the flesh in a crisscross pattern. Cut the tentacles into bite-sized pieces.

For the dressing, whisk the sugar and lime juice together until the sugar has dissolved, then add the fish sauce.

Peel the pomelo with a sharp knife, taking off all the bitter white pith. Segment the pomelo with your fingers, making sure you remove all the membranes. Break the segments into three or four pieces and place in a large bowl. Add the carrot, herbs, shallot, chilli and half the fried shallots.

Bring a small saucepan of water to the boil and add the lemongrass and peppercorns. When the water is boiling, drop in the squid and cook for 2–3 minutes. Drain immediately.

Add the squid and the dressing to the salad and gently toss. Serve on a large platter, sprinkled with the remaining fried shallots.

STICKY RICE STEAMED IN LOTUS LEAF

Xôi gói lá sen

Green rice is an early autumn delicacy, said to have originated half a century ago in Vong village, near Hanoi. One year, due to flooding, the villagers had to harvest their rice early. Being hungry, they nevertheless roasted the grains, pounded them to remove the husks, and found they had stumbled on a delicious treat. Green rice adds a subtle, nutty flavour to dishes such as this one.

300 G (10½ OZ/1½ CUPS) GLUTINOUS RICE
1 TEASPOON SALT
70 G (2½ OZ/⅓ CUP) DRIED LOTUS SEEDS
5 DRIED CHINESE MUSHROOMS
1½ TABLESPOONS RENDERED CHICKEN FAT (SEE PAGE 337) OR VEGETABLE OIL
3 RED ASIAN SHALLOTS, DICED
2 LAP CHEONG SAUSAGES, DICED

½ TEASPOON FRESHLY GROUND BLACK PEPPER
5 TEASPOONS FISH SAUCE
4 PANDAN LEAVES, BROKEN INTO SMALL PIECES
50 G (1¾ OZ/¼ CUP) GREEN RICE
2 TABLESPOONS GRATED COCONUT
60 G (2 OZ/⅔ CUP) FRIED SHALLOTS (SEE PAGE 326)
2 LARGE DRIED LOTUS LEAVES

SERVES 6

Soak the glutinous rice in cold water for 8 hours, or overnight. The next day, drain the rice and rinse it under cold running water until the water runs clear. Sprinkle the rice with ½ teaspoon of the salt and place in a steamer lined with muslin (cheesecloth). Steam for 30 minutes.

Meanwhile, boil the lotus seeds for 20 minutes; soak the dried mushrooms for 20 minutes. Drain the lotus seeds and place in a bowl. Drain the mushrooms, squeeze the water out and discard the stems. Chop the caps and add to the lotus seeds.

Heat the chicken fat in a frying pan over medium heat. Fry the shallot for 1–2 minutes, until soft. Add the sausage and cook for 1 minute. Add the lotus seeds, mushroom, pepper and 2 teaspoons of the fish sauce. Cook for 2 minutes, then transfer to a large bowl. Add the steamed rice.

Pound the pandan leaves using a mortar and pestle. Wearing kitchen gloves, squeeze the leaves over the steamed rice mixture to extract the juice; discard the leaves. Add the remaining ½ teaspoon salt, remaining 3 teaspoons fish sauce, the green rice, coconut and fried shallots. Mix together well.

Soak the lotus leaves in warm water for 3 minutes, or until softened. Lay a lotus leaf, vein side down, in a deep bowl; put half the rice mixture in the centre and lightly press down (1). Fold the leaf sides over the rice and place a saucer on top (2). Turn the bowl, parcel and saucer over, so the parcel sits on the saucer. Remove the bowl (the weight of the rice will keep the leaf in place) (3). Repeat with the remaining lotus leaf and rice.

Steam, covered, for 30 minutes. Remove from the heat and cut the parcels open, being careful to avoid steam burns.

STIR-FRIED CAULIFLOWER AND PRAWNS

Xúp lơ xào tôm

This is such a quick and easy side dish. For a more substantial meal, you could add some broccoli, green beans, corn or carrots to the stir-fry.

1 CAULIFLOWER, CUT INTO FLORETS

1 TABLESPOON VEGETABLE OIL

½ BROWN ONION, CUT INTO 5 MM (¼ INCH) SLICES

3 GARLIC CLOVES, FINELY CHOPPED

200 G (7 OZ) PRAWNS (SHRIMP), PEELED AND DEVEINED, TAILS INTACT

2 TEASPOONS FISH SAUCE

⅓ TEASPOON SALT

8 CHIVES, CUT INTO 3 CM (1¼ INCH) LENGTHS

SERVES 6

Lower the cauliflower into a saucepan of boiling salted water and cook for 6 minutes. Drain well.

Heat the oil in a wok. Add the onion and cook over medium heat for 2 minutes, until it softens. Add the garlic, keeping the wok moving to stop the garlic burning. Cook for a further 1 minute, then add the prawns and toss for 2–3 minutes, until the prawns start turning pink.

Now add the cauliflower, fish sauce, salt and a pinch of freshly ground black pepper and toss to combine.

Toss the chives through and serve immediately.

STIR-FRIED BAMBOO WITH SESAME SEEDS

Măng xào

Pre-prepared bamboo is available in vacuum-sealed packs from Asian grocers. The unopened packs can be kept in the fridge for up to two months, so it's a wonderful ingredient to keep handy for a quick dish such as this. You can also add prawns (shrimp), pork or beef for a more substantial meal.

300 G (10½ OZ) VACUUM-PACKED BAMBOO
1 TABLESPOON VEGETABLE OIL
3 GARLIC CLOVES, FINELY CHOPPED
2 TABLESPOONS SESAME SEEDS, TOASTED
1 TABLESPOON FISH SAUCE

3 SPRING ONIONS (SCALLIONS), THINLY SLICED
5 SAW-TOOTH CORIANDER (CILANTRO) STEMS,
   ROUGHLY CHOPPED
2 RICE CRACKERS (SEE PAGE 27), TO SERVE
SERVES 6

Remove the bamboo from its packet and rinse under cold running water. Put the bamboo in a saucepan and cover with cold water. Gently bring to the boil, then reduce the heat and simmer for 15 minutes.

Drain the bamboo well. Using a knife or your fingers, pull the bamboo apart into smaller pieces that will be easy to pick up with chopsticks.

Heat the oil in a wok. Add the garlic and cook until fragrant. Add the bamboo and cook for 3–4 minutes.

Add the sesame seeds, fish sauce, spring onion and coriander, tossing to mix the seeds and greens evenly through, and to stop the bamboo sticking.

Serve straight away on a platter, with the rice crackers.

SWEET CORN WITH CHILLI AND SPRING ONION

Ngô xào hành ớt

The combination of corn and chilli in this quick and easy side dish echoes South American cooking. In Hanoi, we like to buy corn from the market gardens on the Red River flood plains, sold by street vendors on the iconic Long Bien Bridge.

3 CORN COBS

1 TABLESPOON VEGETABLE OIL

1/2 TEASPOON SALT

1/3 TEASPOON FRESHLY GROUND BLACK PEPPER

3 SPRING ONIONS (SCALLIONS), THINLY SLICED

1 LONG RED CHILLI, CUT INTO THIN STRIPS

1 LIME, CUT INTO 6 WEDGES

SERVES 6

Bring a saucepan of water to the boil. Remove the husks and silks from the corn, then place the cobs in the boiling water. Simmer for 8–10 minutes, then drain.

When the corn is cool enough to handle, remove the kernels by cutting them off as close as possible to the cob.

Heat the oil in a wok or frying pan over high heat. Add the corn, salt and pepper and cook for 1–2 minutes, keeping the corn moving in the wok so it doesn't burn.

Toss the spring onion and chilli through the corn. Serve immediately, with the lime wedges.

SWEET POTATO, TARO AND TURMERIC CROQUETTES

Chả khoai lang

Another example of peasant food making its way back onto city plates. Reminiscent of French potato croquettes, these make a wonderful snack.

1 SMALL WHITE SWEET POTATO
300 G (10½ OZ) TARO
4 POTATOES
2 CM (¾ INCH) KNOB FRESH TURMERIC, ROUGHLY CHOPPED
4 SPRING ONIONS (SCALLIONS), THINLY SLICED
1 HANDFUL CORIANDER (CILANTRO), ROUGHLY CHOPPED
30 G (1 OZ/⅓ CUP) FRIED SHALLOTS (SEE PAGE 326)
⅔ TEASPOON SALT

⅓ TEASPOON FRESHLY GROUND BLACK PEPPER
2 EGGS
80 ML (2½ FL OZ/⅓ CUP) MILK
PLAIN (ALL-PURPOSE) FLOUR, FOR DUSTING
200 G (7 OZ/2 CUPS) DRY BREADCRUMBS
VEGETABLE OIL, FOR PAN-FRYING

MAKES ABOUT 24

Prepare a steamer by bringing a large saucepan of water to the boil.

Meanwhile, peel the sweet potato, taro and potatoes and cut them into chunks of the same size. Place the vegetables on a steaming tray and cook for 10–15 minutes, until a knife easily passes through the flesh. The taro will need to be removed first as it cooks more quickly than the other vegetables.

Working in batches, put the cooked vegetables and the turmeric in a mortar and pound to a smooth, shiny purée with the pestle; alternatively, you can use a food processor. Transfer each batch to a bowl.

Add the spring onion, coriander, fried shallots, salt and pepper and mix until thoroughly combined.

Using damp fingers or a piping (icing) bag, form the mixture into thick croquettes, about 7 cm (2¾ inches) long.

Mix together the eggs and milk. Lightly dust the croquettes with the flour, cover with the egg wash, then coat with the breadcrumbs.

Heat about 2 cm (¾ inch) of oil in a wok or saucepan. Add the croquettes and fry in batches over high heat for 4–5 minutes, until golden brown.

Drain on paper towel and serve hot.

TOFU AND BANANA FLOWER SALAD

Nộm hoa chuối đậu phụ

The father of Chef Y from the Hanoi Cooking Centre used to make this salad for him. Still very popular in the countryside, the salad is now considered slightly old-fashioned in Hanoi, but has nostalgic value for many people there.

½ TEASPOON VINEGAR

2 BANANA FLOWER PETALS

300 G (10½ OZ) FIRM TOFU

1 HANDFUL BEAN SPROUTS

1 HANDFUL CORIANDER (CILANTRO), ROUGHLY CHOPPED

1 LONG RED CHILLI, SEEDED AND SLICED

JUICE OF ½ LIME

1 QUANTITY PEANUT AND SESAME MIX (SEE PAGE 334)

SERVES 6

Add the vinegar to a bowl of cold water. Thinly slice the banana flower crossways, adding it to the vinegar water. Leave to soak for 15 minutes, to soften the banana flower slightly and prevent discolouration.

Drain the banana flower well and place in a large bowl. Crumble the tofu over it and mix well, further breaking up the tofu as you go.

Add the remaining ingredients and toss until evenly combined. Serve on a large platter.

TOFU AND EGG SOUP

Canh đậu hũ cà chua

'Canh' is a soup traditionally served over rice at the end of a meal. This vegetarian option comes together very quickly, and for meat-eaters can also be enriched with minced (ground) pork.

6 TOMATOES

1 TABLESPOON VEGETABLE OIL

4 RED ASIAN SHALLOTS, FINELY DICED

400 G (14 OZ) FIRM TOFU, CUT INTO 2 CM (¾ INCH) CUBES

12 CHIVES, CUT INTO 3 CM (1¼ INCH) LENGTHS

80 ML (2½ FL OZ/⅓ CUP) FISH SAUCE

½ TEASPOON SUGAR

1 TEASPOON SALT

5 EGGS, LIGHTLY WHISKED

SERVES 6

Remove the core from each tomato. Score the bottom with a cross; this will make it easier to remove the skin later. Place the tomatoes into boiling water and count to ten, then remove with a slotted spoon and immerse them in iced water to stop the cooking process. The skin will now come away easily.

Cut each tomato into eight even wedges and set aside.

Heat the oil in a saucepan and fry the shallot until fragrant. Add the tomatoes and continue cooking for a few minutes, until they soften slightly.

Pour in 1.25 litres (42 fl oz/5 cups) water. Add the tofu, chives, half the fish sauce, the sugar, salt and a pinch of freshly ground black pepper. Slowly bring to the boil, then allow the soup to simmer for 2–3 minutes.

Slowly pour in the eggs, continuously stirring, so the egg will form ribbons in the broth. Turn off the heat and stir in the remaining fish sauce.

Adjust the seasoning if desired; we like to serve the soup with a little extra pepper on top.

TOFU AND ROASTED RICE SPRING ROLLS

Nem thính

'Thính', or roasted rice flour, is often used in Pagoda cooking, where no animal products, chilli or garlic can be used. The slightly nutty flavour imparted by roasting makes vegan dishes feel more substantial and adds complexity.

VEGETABLE OIL, FOR PAN-FRYING

100 G (3½ OZ) FIRM TOFU, CUT INTO 1.5 CM (½ INCH) SLICES

60 G (2 OZ) CELLOPHANE NOODLES

140 G (5 OZ) CARROT, CUT INTO THIN STRIPS

140 G (5 OZ) KOHLRABI, CUT INTO THIN STRIPS

PINCH OF SUGAR

⅓ TEASPOON SALT

¼ TEASPOON FRESHLY GROUND BLACK PEPPER

2½ TABLESPOONS ROASTED RICE FLOUR (SEE PAGE 337)

1 SMALL ICEBERG LETTUCE, SHREDDED

1 SMALL HANDFUL HOLY BASIL

1 SMALL HANDFUL CORIANDER (CILANTRO) LEAVES

24 RICE PAPER SHEETS, EACH ABOUT 18 CM (7 INCHES) IN SIZE

VEGAN DIPPING SAUCE (SEE PAGE 343) OR CLASSIC DIPPING SAUCE (SEE PAGE 323), TO SERVE

SERVES 6

Heat about 2 cm (¾ inch) of oil in a wok or saucepan. Add the tofu and cook over high heat until golden brown. Drain well on paper towel. When the tofu is cool enough to handle, cut the slices into 1 cm (½ inch) strips.

Soak the noodles in hot water for 1 minute, then drain and refresh in cold water. Drain again. Using kitchen scissors, cut the noodles into short lengths and set aside.

Heat 1 tablespoon of oil in a frying pan and cook the carrot and kohlrabi until softened. Season with the sugar, salt and pepper. When the vegetables have wilted, add the tofu and remove from the heat.

Toss the noodles and roasted rice flour through the vegetables, then toss the lettuce and herbs through until well combined.

Soften the rice paper sheets by dipping them one at a time into warm water for 1 second. Do not soak the sheets as they will become too soft and tear when rolled. Place on a flat surface, wait for 20 seconds, then soak up any excess water with a clean cloth.

Place a tablespoon of the tofu and noodle mixture on the bottom third of a sheet. Bring the bottom of the wrapper up over the filling, then fold in the sides and roll up. Set aside, seam side down, while preparing the remaining spring rolls.

Serve straight away, with your choice of dipping sauce.

TOFU PILLOWS WITH CRISPY LEMONGRASS

Đậu phụ xả ớt

In Vietnam, a wooden chopstick is used to work out whether a pan of oil is hot enough for frying. Put the chopstick into the oil: when small bubbles rise to the surface, the temperature is just right.

Make sure you drain the tofu and thoroughly pat dry with paper towel before frying it, or the oil will spit when you add the tofu.

5 LEMONGRASS STEMS, WHITE PART ONLY

1 LONG RED CHILLI, SEEDED

4 KAFFIR LIME LEAVES, THINLY SLICED

500 G (1 LB 2 OZ) FIRM TOFU

VEGETABLE OIL, FOR DEEP-FRYING

⅓ TEASPOON SALT

SERVES 6

Using a sharp knife, thinly cut the lemongrass stems, on an angle, into 2 cm (¾ inch) lengths. Do the same with the chilli, then mix together with the kaffir lime and set aside.

Cut the tofu into 4 cm (1½ inch) cubes and pat dry with paper towel.

Heat about 5 cm (2 inches) of oil in a wok or deep frying pan to 180°C (350°F), or until a cube of bread dropped into the oil browns in 15 seconds.

Fry the tofu in batches for 2–4 minutes, until lightly golden and crisp on the outside. Remove the tofu from the oil and drain on paper towel before arranging on a platter.

Pour out two-thirds of the frying oil and return the wok, with the remaining oil, to the heat. Add the lemongrass and chilli mixture, stirring constantly so it colours evenly. Remove with a slotted spoon and drain on paper towel. Sprinkle with the salt.

Scatter the fried lemongrass, kaffir lime and chilli mixture over the tofu and serve immediately.

TURMERIC TOFU IN BETEL LEAF

Đậu phụ lá lốt

A tasty barbecue option for vegetarians. If betel leaves are unavailable, use young grape leaves.

2 TABLESPOONS GREEN RICE

1 CM (½ INCH) KNOB FRESH TURMERIC, PEELED

700 G (1 LB 9 OZ) FIRM TOFU, ROUGHLY CHOPPED

½ TEASPOON SUGAR

½ TEASPOON SALT

18 BETEL LEAVES, WITHOUT ANY TEARS

VEGETABLE OIL, FOR BRUSHING

CLASSIC DIPPING SAUCE (SEE PAGE 323), TO SERVE

SERVES 6

Put the rice in a small bowl and cover with cold water. Leave to soak for 10 minutes, then drain.

Meanwhile, heat a chargrill or barbecue to medium.

Pound the turmeric using a mortar and pestle, or finely chop using a sharp knife. Set aside.

Working in batches, place the tofu in a clean tea towel (dish towel) and squeeze out as much liquid as possible.

Put the tofu in a bowl and add the drained rice, turmeric, sugar, salt and a pinch of freshly ground black pepper. Mix until well combined.

Prepare the betel leaves by removing any tough stems and wiping them with a damp cloth. Place the leaves, smooth side down, on a work surface, with the point of the leaf furthest away. Divide the tofu mixture equally among the leaves, placing it just below the centre of the leaf. Roll up each leaf, taking care to fold in the sides.

Take six skewers and thread three betel leaf rolls onto each. Brush the skewers with oil and chargrill for about 3 minutes on each side.

Serve warm, with the dipping sauce.

WATER SPINACH SALAD

Nộm rau muống

Water spinach, also known as water morning glory or swamp weed, used to be peasant food grown in village ponds. It is now the country's most popular green vegetable, and part of virtually every meal.

This popular dish from central Vietnam is a great example of local ingenuity, making use of the entire water spinach plant, and also finding a delicious way for preparing the stems, which otherwise would be quite tough.

800 G (1 LB 12 OZ) WATER SPINACH (WATER MORNING GLORY)

4 SPRING ONIONS (SCALLIONS), CUT INTO 4 CM (1½ INCH) LENGTHS, THEN SLICED INTO STRIPS

1 HANDFUL VIETNAMESE MINT

1 HANDFUL MINT

1 LONG RED CHILLI, SEEDED AND CUT INTO THIN STRIPS

2 TABLESPOONS FRIED GARLIC (SEE PAGE 326)

1 TABLESPOON FRIED SHALLOTS (SEE PAGE 326)

1 TABLESPOON SESAME SEEDS, TOASTED, PLUS EXTRA TO SERVE

2 TABLESPOONS PEANUTS, UNSALTED AND ROASTED, TO SERVE

DRESSING

100 G (3½ OZ) SUGAR

100 ML (3½ FL OZ) LIME JUICE

60 ML (2 FL OZ/¼ CUP) FISH SAUCE

SERVES 6

Remove the bottom half of the water spinach stems for use in this salad. (Keep the water spinach leaves to use in the Water spinach with garlic recipe on page 104.)

Using a sharp knife, cut the stems into thin strips and place in iced water, to make them curl. Leave to soak for 30 minutes.

For the dressing, whisk together the sugar and lime juice until the sugar has completely dissolved. Stir in the fish sauce.

Drain the water spinach stems. Separate the stems to make for easy serving, then place in a large bowl. Add the spring onion, herbs, chilli, fried garlic, fried shallots, sesame seeds and peanuts.

Pour the dressing over the salad and gently toss to combine.

Serve on a large platter, sprinkled with the extra sesame seeds and peanuts.

WATER SPINACH WITH GARLIC

Rau muống xào tỏi

I usually reserve the bottom half of the water spinach stems to use in the Water spinach salad on page 102. The stems will keep in an airtight container in the refrigerator for two or three days.

800 G (1 LB 12 OZ) WATER SPINACH
1 TABLESPOON VEGETABLE OIL
3–4 GARLIC CLOVES, THINLY SLICED

CLASSIC DIPPING SAUCE (SEE PAGE 323), TO SERVE

SERVES 6

Bring a large saucepan of water to the boil. Thoroughly wash the spinach and discard any bruised leaves. Cut the leaves into easy-to-manage lengths.

Drop the water spinach into the boiling water and blanch for 1 minute, then drain.

Heat the oil in a wok over high heat. Fry half the garlic for 1 minute. Add half the water spinach and stir-fry for 1–2 minutes. Transfer to a bowl and keep warm, and repeat with the remaining garlic and water spinach.

Serve immediately, with the dipping sauce.

FISH AND
CRUSTACEANS

BARBECUED PRAWNS WITH LEMONGRASS

Tôm xiên sả nướng

A Vietnamese twist on the Australian classic pastime of 'throwing another prawn on the barbie' — guaranteed to be a true weekend afternoon crowd-pleaser.

6 RAW LARGE PRAWNS (SHRIMP)	VEGETABLE OIL, FOR BRUSHING
6 LEMONGRASS STEMS	LIME AND CHILLI DIPPING SALT (SEE PAGE 328)
2 TEASPOONS FISH SAUCE	**MAKES 6**

To remove the intestinal vein from the prawns without peeling them, thread a skewer crossways under the shell and flesh, where the prawn bends. Hook the black vein under the skewer and gently ease it out (1).

Trim the lemongrass stems to about 10 cm (4 inches) in length. Using a sharp knife, shave the tips into a point (2). Make a small hole in each prawn shell with the skewer to allow the lemongrass to slide under the shell (3).

Skewer each prawn lengthways onto a lemongrass stem and place in a shallow tray. Sprinkle with the fish sauce and a good pinch of freshly ground black pepper and leave to sit for 15 minutes.

Meanwhile, heat a chargrill or barbecue to medium.

Brush the prawns with oil and grill on each side for 3–4 minutes, until the shells turn an even bright pink.

Serve with the dipping salt.

BARBECUED CRAYFISH WITH SPICY SATAY SAUCE

Tôm hùm nướng sốt satay

In Nha Trang, itinerant food vendors prepare this dish on the footpaths or at the beach, on small hibachi-style barbecues.

Crayfish has such sweet delicate meat that it doesn't need a lot of work to let its flavour shine. For this simple dish, select a live crayfish that has not been in a tank for too long, as the taste diminishes in animals kept in tanks.

1 KG (2 LB 3 OZ) LIVE CRAYFISH
VEGETABLE OIL, FOR BRUSHING

2 TEASPOONS SPICY SATAY SAUCE (SEE PAGE 340)
SERVES 6

Put the crayfish in the freezer for 30 minutes, or until there are no signs of movement.

Meanwhile, heat a chargrill or barbecue to medium.

Holding the crayfish with a cloth to protect your hands from small cuts from the shell, cut it in half lengthways, using a heavy knife or a cleaver. Remove and discard the intestinal tract.

Brush the flesh of the crayfish with 2 teaspoons of oil, and place on the hot barbecue, shell side down. Cook for about 5 minutes, brushing occasionally with a little extra oil. Take

care not to burn the shell, as this imparts a very bitter flavour into the delicate flesh.

Turn the crayfish halves over and cook for 1 minute. Flip them back over, baste with the spicy satay sauce and cook for a further 2 minutes.

Remove from the heat and serve with napkins and a finger bath — eating crayfish can be a messy business!

EEL IN CAUL FAT

Lươn cuốn mỡ chài

Caul is the lacy layer of fat that covers a pig's stomach. Soak the caul fat overnight in salted water to remove any residue or blood. It is then ready to use, or can be frozen for later use.

In this recipe it holds the eel together during frying and creates a crispy exterior — a lovely contrast to the softer flesh of the eel.

3 CM (1¼ INCH) KNOB FRESH TURMERIC, PEELED

JUICE OF 1 LIME

3 EEL, GUTTED, WITH THE BONES, HEAD AND TAIL REMOVED

2 LEMONGRASS STEMS, WHITE PART ONLY, ROUGHLY CHOPPED

4 CM (1½ INCH) KNOB FRESH GALANGAL, ROUGHLY CHOPPED

4 RED ASIAN SHALLOTS, ROUGHLY CHOPPED

4 GARLIC CLOVES, ROUGHLY CHOPPED

200 G (7 OZ) MINCED (GROUND) PORK

1 TABLESPOON FISH SAUCE

⅓ TEASPOON FRESHLY GROUND BLACK PEPPER

½ TEASPOON SUGAR

200 G (7 OZ) CAUL FAT

VEGETABLE OIL, FOR PAN-FRYING

1 HANDFUL PERILLA, ROUGHLY CHOPPED

6 BETEL LEAVES, ROUGHLY CHOPPED

CLASSIC DIPPING SAUCE (SEE PAGE 323), TO SERVE

SERVES 6

Pound the turmeric using a mortar and pestle. Over a bowl, squeeze out all the juice from the pounded turmeric. Mix in the lime juice.

Using a sharp knife, cut each eel into thirds (1). Add to the turmeric mixture and toss to coat; leave to marinate while preparing the filling (2).

Heat a chargrill or barbecue to medium.

In a mortar, pound the lemongrass, galangal, shallot and garlic into a fine paste. Transfer to a small bowl. Add the pork, fish sauce, pepper and sugar and mix until well combined.

Cut the caul fat into pieces large enough to enclose the eel pieces — about 8 cm (3¼ inches) square.

Place a piece of eel on a chopping board, skin side down. Put a spoonful of the pork mixture into the centre and fold over. Place the eel on the caul fat and roll to encase (3). Repeat with the remaining ingredients.

Heat about 1 cm (½ inch) of oil in a frying pan over medium heat. When the oil is hot, fry the eel in batches for about 2 minutes on each side. Remove and drain on paper towel.

Finish the cooking process by charring the eel parcels on the hot chargrill or barbecue for 3–4 minutes on each side.

Serve with the perilla and betel leaves, with the dipping sauce on the side.

EEL COOKED WITH MUNG BEANS

Cháo lươn

This dish, hailing from the Mekong Delta, is reminiscent of the popular porridge from the north, but is spicier and more aromatic.

500 G (1 LB 2 OZ) DRIED GREEN MUNG BEANS

1 TABLESPOON VEGETABLE OIL

3 RED ASIAN SHALLOTS, FINELY DICED

95 G (3¼ OZ/½ CUP) BOILED RICE (SEE PAGE 18)

1 TEASPOON SALT

3 LEMONGRASS STEMS, WHITE PART ONLY, FINELY CHOPPED

1 EEL, HEAD REMOVED, GUTTED, LEFT WHOLE

80 ML (2½ FL OZ/⅓ CUP) FISH SAUCE

1 LONG RED CHILLI, THINLY SLICED (NOT DESEESED)

1 HANDFUL RICE PADDY HERB

6 SAW-TOOTH CORIANDER (CILANTRO) STEMS

100 G (3½ OZ) BEAN SPROUTS

SERVES 6

Rinse the mung beans under cold running water, then place in a bowl, cover with water and soak for 2 hours.

Heat the oil in a saucepan over medium heat and sauté the shallot for 1 minute.

Add the drained mung beans, rice, salt and two-thirds of the chopped lemongrass. Pour in 1 litre (34 fl oz/4 cups) water and bring to a simmer. Cook for 30 minutes, until the mixture reaches a porridge-like consistency.

Meanwhile, preheat the oven to 200°C (400°F).

Place the eel in a clay pot or baking dish, then cover with the mung bean mixture. Transfer to the oven and bake for 7–9 minutes, or until the eel is cooked through.

Combine the fish sauce and chilli in a bowl. Arrange the herbs and bean sprouts on a platter and place on the table.

Remove the eel from the oven and sprinkle the remaining lemongrass on top.

Have your guests serve themselves, adding the herbs, bean sprouts and the fish sauce mixture to their individual bowls to their own liking.

CARAMEL FISH WITH GALANGAL

Cá kho tộ

We came across this dish during our very first journey to Vietnam in 1994, on a trip to the Mekong Delta, where it is prepared from carp at roadside stops. On the coast, it is made with mackerel.

The recipe below, which uses galangal and coconut milk, is typical of the version served in the southern beach town of Nha Trang.

3–4 MACKEREL CUTLETS, EACH 2–3 CM (¾–1¼ INCHES) THICK

3 RED ASIAN SHALLOTS, FINELY DICED

2½ TABLESPOONS FISH SAUCE

1 TEASPOON FRESHLY GROUND BLACK PEPPER

1½ TABLESPOONS SUGAR

1 TABLESPOON VEGETABLE OIL

150 ML (5 FL OZ) COCONUT MILK

3 CM (1¼ INCH) KNOB FRESH GALANGAL, CUT INTO THIN STRIPS

1 LONG RED CHILLI, CUT INTO 5 MM (¼ INCH) RINGS

4 SPRING ONIONS (SCALLIONS), THINLY SLICED

1 SMALL HANDFUL CORIANDER (CILANTRO) SPRIGS

SERVES 6

Coat the mackerel with the shallot, 1 tablespoon of the fish sauce and the pepper. Set aside to marinate for 20 minutes.

Preheat the oven to 180°C (350°F).

Meanwhile, put the sugar and 1½ tablespoons water in a heavy-based saucepan over medium heat and stir until the sugar has dissolved. Bring to the boil, then cook for 3–5 minutes, until the sugar becomes richly golden; do not stir the mixture during the boiling process.

Standing away from the pan, pour in 250 ml (8½ fl oz/1 cup) water. When the spluttering has stopped, stir until the caramel sauce is smooth.

Heat the oil in a frying pan over medium heat. Brown the marinated mackerel on both sides, leaving the shallot sticking to the fish.

Add the caramel sauce, coconut milk, galangal, chilli and remaining fish sauce to the pan. Bring to the boil, then remove from the heat.

Transfer the fish and sauce to a clay pot or casserole dish. Cover and bake for 10 minutes, then remove the lid and bake for a further 4–5 minutes.

Serve the fish in the clay pot or dish, sprinkled with the spring onion, coriander and some extra black pepper.

CLAM AND DILL BROTH

Canh ngao

The clams can be replaced by other seafood — mussels, for example, would also work well. You might need to adjust the seasoning of the finished dish to your own liking, but keep in mind that clams can be quite salty, so resist seasoning the broth until the very end.

2 TEASPOONS VEGETABLE OIL

5 RED ASIAN SHALLOTS, FINELY DICED

3 TOMATOES, PEELED, SEEDED AND ROUGHLY CHOPPED

160 G (5½ OZ/1 CUP) CHOPPED UNRIPE PINEAPPLE FLESH, CUT INTO BITE-SIZED PIECES

½ TEASPOON SALT

3 TEASPOONS SUGAR

1 LITRE (34 FL OZ/4 CUPS) CHICKEN STOCK OR WATER

2 TABLESPOONS TAMARIND WATER (SEE PAGE 341)

1 LONG RED CHILLI, THINLY SLICED

1 HANDFUL DILL FRONDS

500 G (1 LB 2 OZ) CLAMS (VONGOLE), WASHED

1 TABLESPOON FISH SAUCE, APPROXIMATELY

3 SPRING ONIONS (SCALLIONS), THINLY SLICED

½ TEASPOON FRESHLY GROUND BLACK PEPPER

JUICE OF ½ LIME

BOILED RICE (SEE PAGE 18), TO SERVE

SERVES 6

Heat the oil over medium heat in a saucepan and fry the shallot until fragrant. Add the tomatoes, pineapple, salt and sugar and cook for 2 minutes, or until the tomatoes soften.

Pour in the stock and tamarind water. Stir in the chilli and dill and bring to the boil.

When the stock is boiling, add the clams and cover the pan. Shake the pan about to evenly cook the clams — you will start to hear them popping open. After 2–3 minutes, check the clams and discard any that have not opened.

Add the fish sauce, spring onion, pepper and lime juice. Check the seasoning, as you might wish to add more fish sauce.

Serve in a large bowl at the table and enjoy over boiled rice.

COCONUT SEAFOOD CAKES

Bánh dừa hải sản

This tasty snack could also be made in a smaller size and served as finger food with drinks. If you can't get hold of sweet potatoes, just use regular potatoes.

100 G (3½ OZ/⅔ CUP) PLAIN (ALL-PURPOSE) FLOUR

2 TABLESPOONS RICE FLOUR

½ TEASPOON BAKING POWDER

⅓ TEASPOON SALT

PINCH OF SUGAR

1 EGG YOLK

1 TEASPOON RICE VINEGAR

80 ML (2½ FL OZ/⅓ CUP) COCONUT MILK

1 SMALL SQUID

4 RAW PRAWNS (SHRIMP), PEELED, DEVEINED AND CHOPPED INTO 2 CM (¾ INCH) PIECES

50 G (1¾ OZ) CRABMEAT

2 TEASPOONS FISH SAUCE

¼ TEASPOON FRESHLY GROUND BLACK PEPPER

1 PALE-FLESHED SWEET POTATO

VEGETABLE OIL, FOR DEEP-FRYING

VEGETABLE PICKLE (SEE PAGE 343), OR CLASSIC DIPPING SAUCE (SEE PAGE 323) TO SERVE

SERVES 6

Sift the flour and rice flour into a bowl. Add the baking powder, salt and sugar, then make a well in the centre. Add the egg yolk, vinegar, coconut milk and 125 ml (4 fl oz/½ cup) water to the well then mix to form a batter. Cover with a damp cloth and leave to rest for 15 minutes.

Clean the squid by holding the body with one hand and the head with the other. Gently pull, taking care not to burst the ink sac; the head and tentacles will come away. Remove the clear cartilage, rinse the squid inside and out, then pat dry. Using a sharp knife, cut the head from the tentacles and discard the head.

Cut the body open and rinse away any membranes from the surface. Lay the squid flat on a board, with the inside facing up. Cut the body and the tentacles into 2 cm (¾ inch) pieces.

Marinate the squid, prawns and crabmeat in the fish sauce and pepper for 15 minutes.

Peel the sweet potato and cut into thin strips about 4 cm (1½ inches) long.

Mix the sweet potato and seafood into the batter.

Heat about 12 cm (4¾ inches) of oil in a wok or deep saucepan. To test the oil, place the tip of a wooden chopstick into the oil — when bubbles slowly rise to the surface, the oil is hot enough to use.

Gently place a mould or ladle into the hot oil to heat up; this will prevent the cakes sticking to the mould. Remove from the oil and place 2 generous tablespoons of the mixture into the mould. Lower into the hot oil. When the cake floats, turn it over and remove the mould from the oil. Cook for 3–4 minutes, until golden brown.

Remove from the oil and drain on paper towel. Repeat with the remaining batter.

Serve hot, with the pickle or dipping sauce.

CRAB BROTH STEAMBOAT

Lẩu cua

Here's a great spin on the classic steamboat, which we first tasted at a lunch during a bike ride through villages outside Hanoi. It is very popular in the countryside because of the abundance of rice-paddy crabs. The rich broth works particularly well with tofu and beef.

Wombok cabbage originated in China and is milder and sweeter than the regular variety. However, you could also use a savoy cabbage here.

2 BLUE SWIMMER OR SAND CRABS

½ TEASPOON SALT

2 TEASPOONS VEGETABLE OIL

2 RED ASIAN SHALLOTS, FINELY DICED

3 TOMATOES, CORED AND CHOPPED

½ TEASPOON SUGAR

2 TEASPOONS FISH SAUCE

600 G (1 LB 5 OZ) DRIED RICE VERMICELLI

400 G (14 OZ) BEEF FILLET, THINLY SLICED

300 G (10½ OZ) FIRM TOFU, CUT INTO 3 CM (1¼ INCH) CUBES AND FRIED UNTIL GOLDEN

1 HANDFUL PERILLA

1 SMALL HANDFUL SAW-TOOTH CORIANDER (CILANTRO), ROUGHLY CHOPPED

2 BANANA FLOWER PETALS, THINLY SLICED

¼ WOMBOK CABBAGE, LEAVES SEPARATED, THEN CUT INTO 3–4 PIECES EACH

CLASSIC DIPPING SAUCE (SEE PAGE 323)

SERVES 6

Clean the crabs, taking care to wash away any grit lodged in the crevices. Pull off and discard the top shell, then remove any 'mustard' (the crab's digestive system).

Cut the crabs into small pieces along the joints. Working in batches, use a mortar and pestle to pound the crabs, shell and all, as finely as possible. Then transfer to a food processor and break them down even further. Pass the mixture through a fine sieve to remove any larger bits of shell.

Pour 1 litre (34 fl oz/4 cups) water into a saucepan. Add the crushed crab and salt and stir. Slowly bring to the boil, without stirring any further at this stage. As the liquid comes to the boil, the crab will float to the surface and form crab 'cakes'. With a slotted spoon, remove these cakes from the broth, then set the broth and the crab cakes aside.

Heat the oil in a separate saucepan and sauté the shallot over medium heat until fragrant. Add the tomatoes and sugar. Cook for a few minutes, until the tomatoes soften, then add

the crab cakes and fish sauce and cook for a further 2–3 minutes. Now add the crab broth and bring to a simmer.

Meanwhile, soak the vermicelli in boiling water for 4–5 minutes. Gently stir to separate the noodles, then drain and refresh under cold water. Use kitchen scissors to cut the vermicelli into easy-to-manage lengths. Divide among six deep bowls.

Arrange the beef, tofu, herbs, banana leaf petals and cabbage on platters. (You can do this ahead of time and refrigerate until you are ready to eat.)

To serve, place the platters, chopsticks and small individual bowls of dipping sauce on the table.

Pour the crab broth into a steamboat, three-quarters of the way to the top, and again bring to a simmer.

Invite your guests to poach their own beef, tofu, cabbage and herbs and ladle into their bowls, over the noodles.

CRAB FRIED RICE

Cơm chiên cua

Here is Tracey's favourite fried rice — a very stylish and delicious dish that can be served on its own, but equally fits a banquet-style meal. It is best to use rice that has been cooked the day before, as it dries out a little and makes for easier frying.

1 TABLESPOON VEGETABLE OIL

3 EGGS, LIGHTLY BEATEN

2 TABLESPOONS ANNATTO OIL (SEE PAGE 320)

2 GARLIC CLOVES, FINELY CHOPPED

1.11 KG (2 LB 7 OZ/6 CUPS) BOILED RICE (SEE PAGE 318), OR BOIL UP 400 G (14 OZ/2 CUPS) UNCOOKED LONG-GRAIN WHITE RICE

115 G (4 OZ/¾ CUP) PODDED PEAS, BLANCHED, OR UNTHAWED FROZEN PEAS

250 G (9 OZ) CRABMEAT

3 TABLESPOONS FRIED SHALLOTS (SEE PAGE 326)

2 LIMES, CUT INTO WEDGES

SOY CHILLI DIPPING SAUCE (SEE PAGE 340), TO SERVE

SERVES 6

Heat the vegetable oil in a wok over medium heat. Pour the eggs over the base of the wok and cook for 1–2 minutes, rotating the wok to ensure the omelette cooks evenly. Remove from the wok. When cool enough to handle, roll into a cigar shape and thinly slice.

Wipe out the wok, return to the heat and add the annatto oil. When the oil is hot, add the garlic and cook over medium heat until fragrant. Add the rice, tossing it around in the wok to evenly colour the grains.

Add the peas and continue tossing, as the rice will easily stick to the wok. When the rice has heated through, add the crabmeat and half the fried shallots. Toss to mix together, then remove from the heat.

Serve the rice topped with the omelette strips and the remaining fried shallots, with the lime wedges and dipping sauce on the side.

CRAB POACHED IN BEER WITH LEMONGRASS AND CHILLI

Cua hấp bia, xả ớt

We first discovered this dish in the popular coastal town of Nha Trang. The simple combination of seafood, aromatics and beer makes for a wonderfully relaxed meal for a hot day on the beach.

2 BLUE SWIMMER OR SAND CRABS

250 ML (8½ FL OZ/1 CUP) BEER

2 LONG RED CHILLIES, CUT INTO THIN RINGS

2 LEMONGRASS STEMS, WHITE PART ONLY, CHOPPED

4 KAFFIR LIME LEAVES, CUT INTO VERY THIN STRIPS

LIME AND CHILLI DIPPING SALT (SEE PAGE 328), TO SERVE

SERVES 6

Prepare the crabs by removing the top shell, then rinse to remove the gills. Cut each crab into four pieces with a cleaver.

Pour the beer into a large saucepan and add the chilli and lemongrass. Bring to the boil, then reduce the heat and simmer for 10 minutes.

Add the crab and simmer for 4–5 minutes. When the shells are a deep red colour, remove the crab pieces, using a slotted spoon, and place on a platter.

Add the lime leaves to the liquid, then pour this over the crab pieces. Serve with the dipping salt.

VIETNAM AND CHINA

法界蒙薰開佛會日

AMONG THE SILK SHOPS, CAFÉS AND MINI-HOTELS ON BUSY HANG GAI STREET IN HANOI'S OLD QUARTER, THERE IS A MAGNIFICENT, CENTURY-OLD BANYAN TREE IN FRONT OF THE CO VU COMMUNAL HOUSE. REVERED IN BUDDHIST CULTURE, THE TREE HAS SURVIVED THE RAPID URBAN DEVELOPMENT AROUND IT WITH ITS TRUNK AND ROOTS SPILLING ONTO THE FOOTPATH.

In his public lectures, publicist Huu Ngoc likens Vietnamese culture to the banyan tree with its trunk representing the national identity forged in the Red River Delta and its branches symbolising foreign influences. The thickest branch of his symbolic tree would be reserved for China. For all the vestiges of French colonialism, it was the Chinese occupation and the subsequent uneasy relationship between Vietnam and its powerful northern neighbour that has made Vietnam the country it is today.

In the second century BC, a Chinese army invaded the fertile Red River Delta and stayed for an entire millennium. There were numerous revolts — often headed by women. The most famous was led by the Trung sisters, Joan of Arc–like characters who were able to take power for a couple of years before being defeated by ruthless veteran commander, Ma Yuan. Myth has it that, distraught by their loss, the sisters committed suicide by drowning themselves. Today, nearly every city and town has a Hai Ba Trung Street in honour of that early struggle for independence. It would

take another eight centuries before Vietnamese forces, in 939 AD, were finally able to defeat the Chinese army at the famous battle of Bach Dang.

The Chinese brought Buddhism, Taoism and Confucianism, with the latter the most powerful influence. It introduced a new, strict hierarchy into public and private life, demanding respect of subjects for their rulers, children for their parents and wives for their husbands. While this philosophy made significant inroads into Vietnamese culture, it could not entirely displace the tradition of ancestor worship. Village life remained, to a large extent, beyond the grasp of the Chinese occupiers, as expressed in the popular proverb: "The Kings decrees yield to the customs of the village." To this day, Confucian culture and ancestor worship live side-by-side in almost every Vietnamese household.

Chinese influence extended to food and food production through the introduction of modern agricultural practices. The ploughshare, water buffalos and fertiliser changed the landscape of the Red River Delta into a patchwork of rice paddies and wet rice cultivation established the concept that a meal consists of rice with supplementary food. The Chinese also introduced chopsticks which quickly became a symbol of civilisation.

The Vietnamese victory of 939 did not end the influence of Chinese culture on Vietnamese cuisine. In the 17th century, the emperor Le Than Tong accepted 3000 Chinese refugees after the overthrow of the Ming dynasty. They arrived on board fifty junks, sailing up the Mekong River and settling outside what was to become Saigon.

Over the centuries, the trading community became part of the greater Saigon region and the hub of Chinese culture in Vietnam centred on the district of Cholon, which literally means "great market" — Vietnam's very own Chinatown. The trade was mostly divided along ethnic lines. Traders from Hakka controlled the import of Chinese herbs, Hokkien speakers the rice and migrants from Teochow the tea trade. Merchants from those different backgrounds also organised themselves into "Congregations" to deal with the Vietnamese and later French authorities. Many of the colourful Congregation Halls are now main tourist attractions.

The Chinese migrants brought new dishes from their home country such as roast pork buns, stewed pork belly and Cantonese noodle soups which formed the basis of the famous pho. They also introduced a restaurant culture to a country which, up to that point, was unfamiliar with the joys of eating out. At the height of the Vietnam War, Cholon was a vibrant commercial centre with a population of 800,000 ethnic Chinese and countless restaurants and gambling dens.

The great commercial success of the Chinese merchants, however, also attracted hostility. They were excluded from the rice trade in the 1940s, for example. After the communist victory in 1975, the Chinese trading community had to face even greater pressures from a government that was deeply suspicious of private business. As a result, many of the boat people who settled in Australia and other countries were of Chinese heritage and the Vietnamese restaurants in the West commonly serve the southern food they brought with them.

FISH CARPACCIO FROM CENTRAL VIETNAM

Gỏi cá linh

Putting the green bananas into the lemon water in this recipe will remove some of the sticky liquid, which has an unwanted texture. It will also stop the bananas discolouring.

The closer the fish is prepared to serving time, the better. Avoid letting the cut fish sit in the refrigerator any longer than 1 hour.

700 G (1 LB 9 OZ) SNAPPER FILLETS, SKIN AND BONES REMOVED

JUICE OF 1 LIME

2 GREEN BANANAS

1 CARAMBOLA (STAR FRUIT), CUT INTO 5 CM (2 INCH) LENGTHS

1 SMALL CUCUMBER, CUT INTO 5 CM (2 INCH) LENGTHS

1 SMALL HANDFUL VIETNAMESE MINT

1 SMALL HANDFUL THAI BASIL

1 LONG RED CHILLI, CUT INTO RINGS

½ WHITE ONION, THINLY SLICED

5 CM (2 INCH) KNOB FRESH YOUNG GINGER, CUT INTO THIN STRIPS

1 HANDFUL MINT

2 TABLESPOONS ROASTED PEANUTS, CHOPPED

PEANUT SAUCE (SEE PAGE 334), TO SERVE

SERVES 6

Using a sharp knife, cut the fish across the grain into strips about 1 cm (½ inch) wide. Arrange on a plate and drizzle with half the lime juice. Cover with plastic wrap and keep chilled, either over an ice bath or in the fridge, while preparing the remaining ingredients.

Add the remaining lime juice to a bowl of cold water. Using a sharp knife, peel off the outer layer of skin from each banana, leaving on a thin layer of the skin for texture (1). Cut the bananas into strips about 5 cm (2 inches) long and 5 mm (¼ inch) thick, then place in the lime water for 5 minutes.

Arrange the carambola, cucumber, Vietnamese mint, basil and chilli on a platter. Drain the banana and add to the platter.

Uncover the fish and scatter the onion, ginger, mint and peanuts over the top.

Invite your guests to roll the fish up in the herbs with the fruits, cucumber and chilli, then dip their rolls into small individual bowls of peanut sauce.

FISH TOSSED WITH LEEK AND CELERY LEAF

Cá xào cần tỏi

This quick and easy dish can also be prepared with squid or prawns (shrimp) instead of the fish.

Make sure you use Chinese celery leaf here. It is different to the European variety and is available in Asian supermarkets. The Chinese leaf has the typical celery flavour, but is more delicate.

800 G (1 LB 12 OZ) FIRM FISH FILLETS, SKIN AND BONES REMOVED

RICE FLOUR, FOR DUSTING

VEGETABLE OIL, FOR PAN-FRYING

2 GARLIC CLOVES

1 LONG RED CHILLI, THINLY SLICED

2 LEEKS, WHITE PART ONLY, WASHED THOROUGHLY, CUT INTO STRIPS

100 G (3½ OZ) BABY CORN, CUT IN HALF LENGTHWAYS

160 G (5½ OZ/1 CUP) CHOPPED PINEAPPLE, CUT INTO BITE-SIZED PIECES

2 HANDFULS CELERY LEAVES

150 G (5½ OZ) CHERRY TOMATOES, CUT IN HALF

1 HANDFUL DILL FRONDS

2 TABLESPOONS FISH SAUCE

LIME AND CHILLI DIPPING SALT (SEE PAGE 328), TO SERVE

SERVES 6

Cut the fish into pieces about 3 cm (1¼ inches) long, then dust in the rice flour. Shake off any excess flour.

Heat about 2 tablespoons of oil in a wok over high heat. Fry the fish in batches for 1–2 minutes, until lightly golden on all sides then set aside.

Wipe the wok clean and return to a medium heat. Add a little more oil, then fry the garlic and chilli until fragrant.

Add the leek, corn and pineapple and toss for 2 minutes, or until the leek has wilted. Add the celery leaves and tomatoes and keep tossing. If the vegetables are starting to stick, add a few tablespoons of water.

When the celery leaves have wilted and the tomatoes have softened but have not yet lost their shape, add the dill, fish sauce and fish. Toss to combine.

Transfer to a platter and serve with the dipping salt.

FISH CAKES IN YOUNG GREEN RICE

Cá tẩm cốm rang

This is a very versatile dish. As with the Coconut seafood cakes on page 122, you could make these cakes in smaller portions and serve as finger food with drinks. If green rice is unavailable, you can barbecue ordinary white rice for a lighter and slightly smoky flavour. And finally, for a lunchtime twist, try serving the fish cakes in a baguette with the Carrot and daikon pickle on page 321.

600 G (1 LB 5 OZ) SNAPPER FILLETS, SKIN AND BONES REMOVED

2 GARLIC CLOVES, ROUGHLY CHOPPED

1 TABLESPOON FISH SAUCE

1/2 TEASPOON SUGAR

1/3 TEASPOON SALT

1/2 TEASPOON FRESHLY GROUND BLACK PEPPER

3 SPRING ONIONS (SCALLIONS), WHITE PART ONLY, THINLY SLICED

200 G (7 OZ/1 CUP) YOUNG GREEN RICE

VEGETABLE OIL, FOR DEEP-FRYING

CLASSIC DIPPING SAUCE (SEE PAGE 323), TO SERVE

MAKES 6

Cut the fish into chunks. Put them in a food processor along with the garlic and process until the mixture has the consistency of a paste. Add the fish sauce, sugar, salt, pepper and spring onion and further process to incorporate all the ingredients. Place the mixture in a bowl, cover and rest in the refrigerator for 30 minutes.

Using lightly oiled fingers, form the fish mixture into six patties. Now press the patties into the green rice, making sure both sides are well coated.

Heat about 10 cm (4 inches) of oil in a wok. To test the oil, place the tip of a wooden chopstick into the oil — when bubbles slowly rise to the surface, the oil is hot enough to use.

Fry the fish patties for 4–5 minutes, until they are cooked through, and the rice has puffed slightly. Remove and drain well on paper towel.

Serve hot, with the dipping sauce.

FRIED ROCKLING WITH TURMERIC, DILL AND VERMICELLI

Chả cá

The most famous restaurant to eat this dish in Hanoi is Cha Ca La Vong, in the Old Quarter. A specialty of the Doan family, their closely guarded recipe has been handed down through generations, delighting diners huddled around tabletop burners on cold Hanoi evenings, taking in the rich aromas. *Cha ca* literally means 'fried fish'. The special twist with this recipe is that the fish is cooked twice (first grilled, then fried), so you'll need a firm-fleshed fish that does not break apart easily during cooking.

800 G (1 LB 12 OZ) ROCKLING FILLETS, SKIN AND BONES REMOVED, CUT INTO 3 CM (1¼ INCH) CHUNKS

200 G (7 OZ) DRIED RICE VERMICELLI

VEGETABLE OIL, FOR PAN-FRYING

2 LARGE HANDFULS DILL SPRIGS

12 SPRING ONIONS (SCALLIONS), THICKLY SLICED

80 G (2¾ OZ/½ CUP) ROASTED PEANUTS, CHOPPED

1 SMALL HANDFUL THAI BASIL

1 SMALL HANDFUL CORIANDER (CILANTRO) LEAVES

CLASSIC DIPPING SAUCE (SEE PAGE 323), TO SERVE

MARINADE

3 CM (1¼ INCH) KNOB FRESH GALANGAL, ROUGHLY CHOPPED

1 LONG RED CHILLI, SEEDED AND ROUGHLY CHOPPED

2 TABLESPOONS GROUND TURMERIC

1 TABLESPOON SUGAR

60 ML (2 FL OZ/¼ CUP) MAM TOM (FERMENTED SHRIMP PASTE) OR FISH SAUCE

SERVES 6

To make the marinade, pound the galangal, chilli, turmeric and sugar to a paste in a mortar (1). Add the mam tom and 2½ tablespoons water and stir until the sugar dissolves. Smear the marinade over the fish and marinate for about 2 hours (2).

Heat a chargrill or barbecue to medium. Have a hot wok or frying pan ready for the second fish cooking stage.

Meanwhile, soak the vermicelli in boiling water for 5 minutes. Gently stir to separate the noodles, then drain and refresh under cold water. Cut into easy-to-manage lengths.

Thoroughly pat the fish dry with paper towel; excess liquid will make the fish stick to the grill. Chargrill for 2–3 minutes on

each side, until charred areas appear, but remove before the fish is cooked all the way through.

Heat about 2 cm (¾ inch) of oil in the hot wok or frying pan. Test if it is ready by dropping a small piece of bread into the pan: it should quickly turn lightly golden. Add one-third of the fish and cook for 3–4 minutes, turning once. Add one-third of the dill and spring onion and toss until wilted (3).

Divide one-third of the noodles among six deep serving bowls. Top with the fish, then one-third of the peanuts.

Cook the remaining fish and herbs; serve up the remaining ingredients, for diners to help themselves.

FRIED SNAPPER WITH RICE PAPER

Cá chiên bánh tráng

This dish is a fun and easy way to serve spring rolls: have your guests roll their own at the table. It fits in well with the communal spirit in Vietnam, where it is often prepared when entertaining guests at home. This recipe also works well with barbecued snapper.

2 GREEN BANANAS

1 CARAMBOLA (STAR FRUIT), SLICED LENGTHWAYS INTO 5 MM (¼ INCH) STRIPS

1 PINEAPPLE, NOT TOO RIPE, PEELED AND CUT INTO 5 CM (2 INCH) BATONS

50 G (1¾ OZ/⅓ CUP) ROASTED UNSALTED PEANUTS

1 x 600–700 G (1 LB 5 OZ–1 LB 9 OZ) SNAPPER, GUTTED

RICE FLOUR, FOR DUSTING

VEGETABLE OIL, FOR DEEP-FRYING

TO SERVE

1 HANDFUL CORIANDER (CILANTRO)

1 HANDFUL DILL

600 G (1 LB 5 OZ) DRIED RICE VERMICELLI

18 RICE PAPER SHEETS, ABOUT 18 CM (7 INCHES) IN SIZE

CLASSIC DIPPING SAUCE (SEE PAGE 323), TO SERVE

SERVES 6

Using a sharp knife, peel the outer layer of skin from each banana, leaving on a thin layer of the skin for texture (see page 134). Cut the banana into thin strips and arrange on a platter with the carambola, pineapple and peanuts.

Rinse the fish in a bowl filled with salted water. Check for and remove any scales. Using kitchen scissors, cut off the fins and trim the tail. Dry the fish thoroughly with paper towel.

For the fish to cook evenly, make three cuts, about 1 cm (½ inch) deep, on each side. Dust the fish in the rice flour and shake off any excess flour.

Heat about 13 cm (5 inches) of oil in a wok or saucepan. To test the oil, place the tip of a wooden chopstick into the oil — when bubbles slowly rise to the surface, the oil is hot enough to use. Carefully slide the fish in and fry for 8–10 minutes, until the flesh is cooked through and the skin is golden and crisp. Remove and drain well on paper towel. Place the fish on a platter and top with the coriander and dill.

Meanwhile, soak the vermicelli in boiling water for 4–5 minutes. Gently stir to separate the noodles, then drain and refresh under cold water. Use kitchen scissors to cut the vermicelli into easy-to-manage lengths.

Soften the rice paper sheets by dipping them one at a time into warm water for 1 second. Do not soak the sheets as they will become too soft and tear when rolled. Place on a flat surface, wait for 20 seconds, then soak up any excess water with a clean cloth.

Invite your guests to take a sheet of the rice paper and top with the fish, noodles, herbs, fruit and peanuts, before rolling up into a spring roll and enjoying with the dipping sauce.

FRIED SOFT SHELL CRAB

Cua đồng chiên

A 'soft shell' crab is one that has just shed its shell and is in the process of growing a new one. These crabs are full of flavour and easy to eat, as you don't have to pry open a hard shell to get to the meat.

6 SOFT SHELL CRABS
75 G (2¾ OZ/½ CUP) PLAIN (ALL-PURPOSE) FLOUR
45 G (1½ OZ/¼ CUP) RICE FLOUR, PLUS EXTRA FOR DUSTING
¼ TEASPOON SALT
250 ML (8½ FL OZ/1 CUP) COLD SODA WATER

VEGETABLE OIL, FOR DEEP-FRYING
60 G (2 OZ/¼ CUP) MAYONNAISE (SEE PAGE 329)
80 ML (2½ FL OZ/⅓ CUP) CHILLI SAUCE (SEE PAGE 322)

SERVES 6

Carefully pull away the tail of each crab. Remove the gills by folding back the top shell and lifting out the gills with your fingers.

To make the batter, sift the flour, rice flour and salt into a bowl and make a well in the centre. Pour the soda water into the well. Using a whisk, work your way out from the centre until you have a smooth batter.

Heat about 13 cm (5 inches) of oil in a wok. To test the oil, place the tip of a wooden chopstick into the oil — when bubbles slowly rise to the surface, the oil is hot enough to use.

Dry the crabs with paper towel, then dust them in some extra rice flour. Shake to remove any excess flour.

Dip the crabs into the batter, then gently lower them into the oil. Fry for 4–5 minutes, until the crabs are crisp and turning a beautiful golden brown. Remove from the oil and drain well on paper towel.

Serve immediately, with the mayonnaise and chilli sauce.

HOI AN SPRING ROLL

Nem cuốn Hội An

You can pre-prepare the mackerel for this dish; once cooked, the fish will keep in the fridge for up to 1 week. The pickled cabbage also works well alongside grilled and fried meats.

2 x 300 G (10½ OZ) GUTTED WHOLE MACKEREL, OR OTHER OILY FISH

24 RICE PAPER SHEETS, ABOUT 18 CM (7 INCHES) IN SIZE

1 SMALL ICEBERG LETTUCE, OR OTHER CRISP GREEN LETTUCE, THINLY SLICED

¼ QUANTITY PICKLED CABBAGE (SEE PAGE 336)

1 SMALL HANDFUL CORIANDER (CILANTRO) SPRIGS

50 G (1¾ OZ/⅓ CUP) SESAME SEEDS, TOASTED

CLASSIC DIPPING SAUCE (SEE PAGE 323), TO SERVE

MARINADE

190 ML (6½ FL OZ/¾ CUP) SOY SAUCE

1 TABLESPOON SUGAR

1 LEMONGRASS STEM, WHITE PART ONLY, ROUGHLY CHOPPED

3 GARLIC CLOVES, CUT IN HALF LENGTHWAYS

3 RED ASIAN SHALLOTS, ROUGHLY CHOPPED

1 LONG RED CHILLI, CUT IN HALF LENGTHWAYS AND SEEDED

1 TEASPOON FIVE-SPICE

MAKES 24

Combine the marinade ingredients with 125 ml (4 fl oz/ ½ cup) water. Stir until the sugar has dissolved, then marinate the fish in the mixture for 30 minutes.

Transfer the fish and marinade to a frying pan. Slowly bring to the boil, then reduce the heat to a simmer (1). Cover and braise for 15 minutes. Remove from the heat, then leave the fish to cool in the liquid before taking it out of the pan.

Remove all the flesh from the fish and gently flake with your hands. Discard the heads and bones.

Soften the rice paper sheets by dipping them one at a time into warm water for 1 second. Do not soak the sheets as they will become too soft and tear when rolled. Place on a flat surface, wait for 20 seconds, then soak up any excess water with a clean cloth.

Put the lettuce and pickled cabbage in a bowl and mix together (2). Place a small portion of the mixture in a straight line along the bottom third of a sheet; top with some mackerel, coriander and sesame seeds (3). Bring the bottom of the wrapper up over the filling, then fold in the sides and roll up. Set aside, seam side down, while preparing the remaining spring rolls.

Serve with the dipping sauce.

LACY SPRING ROLLS WITH CRAB, PRAWN AND TARO

Chả giò rế

Chef Nguyen Mang Hung from the Hanoi Cooking Centre perfected this lacy spring roll wrapper.

130 G (4½ OZ/¾ CUP) RICE FLOUR

90 G (3 OZ/⅔ CUP) TAPIOCA FLOUR

1 EGG YOLK

VEGETABLE OIL, FOR DEEP-FRYING

CLASSIC DIPPING SAUCE (SEE PAGE 323), TO SERVE

FILLING

6 DRIED BLACK FUNGUS (WOOD EARS)

150 G (5½ OZ) CRABMEAT, CHOPPED

150 G (5½ OZ) PRAWN (SHRIMP) MEAT, CHOPPED

300 G (10½ OZ) MINCED (GROUND) PORK

200 G (7 OZ) TARO, PEELED AND THINLY SLICED

¼ TEASPOON FRESHLY GROUND BLACK PEPPER

1 TEASPOON FISH SAUCE

1 EGG, LIGHTLY WHISKED

SERVES 6; MAKES 24

Sift the flours into a bowl and make a well in the centre. Add the egg yolk and 200 ml (7 fl oz) water. Whisk until you have a smooth, thin batter, then set aside while preparing the filling.

To make the filling, soak the mushrooms in warm water for 20 minutes. Drain the mushrooms and squeeze out any excess water. Discard the stems. Thinly slice the caps, then place in a large bowl. Add the remaining filling ingredients and mix well.

To make the lacy wrappers, heat a 25 cm (10 inch) non-stick frying pan over medium heat. Moisten a piece of paper towel with oil, then rub it over the base of the pan so it leaves a light film of oil. (You will need to repeat this process before cooking each new wrapper.)

Spread your fingers and place them in the batter, then lift your fingers out of the bowl and allow some of the batter to run off. Place your hand, fingers pointing down, over the hot pan and move your hand in a circular motion to form a large lacy pattern in the pan (1). Cook for 10 seconds, just on the one side, then remove from the pan (2). Repeat with the remaining batter.

Place a lacy wrapper on a flat surface. Put a heaped tablespoon of the filling, in an oblong shape, on the bottom third of the wrapper. Lift the side closest to you to encase the filling, then fold in the sides and continue rolling (3). Place on a plate, seam side down, and continue with the remaining wrappers and filling.

Heat about 13 cm (5 inches) of oil in a wok. To test the oil, place the tip of a wooden chopstick into the oil — when bubbles slowly rise to the surface, the oil is hot enough to use. Cook the spring rolls in batches for 2–3 minutes, until crisp, golden and cooked through.

Drain on paper towel and serve immediately, with the dipping sauce.

MOT, HAI, BA — YOH! BEER IN VIETNAM

HALF PAST EIGHT IN THE EVENING AND IT IS CLOSING TIME IN THE LARGE *BIA HOI* BEHIND HO CHI MINH'S MAUSOLEUM, WHICH LOCALS KNOW BY ITS ADDRESS, 19A NGOC HA, RATHER THAN ITS NAME. THE SHOUTS OF 'MOT, HAI, BA — YOH!' ('ONE, TWO, THREE — BOTTOMS UP!') ARE GETTING FEWER AND FURTHER BETWEEN. AN HOUR LATER, THE LAST RED-FACED PATRONS STAGGER OUT, AND THE STAFF SIT DOWN FOR A QUICK MEAL BEFORE THE FINAL CLEAN-UP.

This uniquely Hanoian experience dates back to 1961, when the Hanoi Brewery decided to make bia hoi, literally 'fresh beer': a low-alcohol, unpasteurised brew without any added preservatives — a cheap and refreshing drink for those hot summer months. Since then, the raucous, open-air beer gardens, which the brew's success spawned, have become an integral part of Vietnam's vibrant beer culture.

Bia hoi is collected at sunrise every morning at the factory gates by proprietors who have to accurately forecast the day's consumption, as the beer only lasts one day. It is brewed quickly (hence the alcohol level of only 2–4%), it goes off quickly and is drunk quickly as well. The fact that *bia hoi* continues to ferment during the day makes for slightly different tastes at different vendors, even though the barrels might have been picked up at the same brewery.

These days, two more companies have joined Hanoi Brewery and the fresh beer market is divided up between them. *Bia hoi* is big business: there are hundreds of major outlets in Hanoi alone, not counting the many street stalls that might just buy one or two barrels off the big players to serve on the footpath.

Beer is one more legacy of French colonial times. Initially the French were only interested in importing wine from the motherland to Vietnam, but they switched first to importing beer, and then to brewing it themselves at the end of the 19th century after a devastating case of phylloxera disease wrought havoc on the French vineyards.

In the 19th and early 20th centuries, the Vietnamese were slow to adopt the new drink, preferring their traditional rice wine. In the end, however, they turned to beer for reasons of fashion and policy. Beer made its first appearance outside French colonial society in Chinese gambling houses in an attempt to provide them with a touch of class, and it was subsequently taken up by the middle classes to show off their urban sophistication. The French monopoly on liquor also helped. Instead of switching from rice wine to the harsh, high-alcohol state-produced liquor, many Vietnamese chose beer as a refreshing alternative.

One of the beer pioneers was a decommissioned sergeant who had an interest and some expertise in brewing. He teamed up with a businessman named Monsieur Hommel to establish the 'Breweries and Ice-Houses of Indochina' (BGI), which included the Hanoi Beer company (Habeco for short), and produced a brew made from local rice and imported hops. The French left in 1954 and took with them a lot of beer-brewing know-how. Under j the guise of international solidarity among the newly formed socialist states, Czechoslovakia came to the rescue and in the early days of independence trained a new generation of brewers to make a Czech-style lager, named *Bia Hanoi.*

In the south, the famous '333' beer is another example of how European traditions live on. The French brought the label '33' from Germany in an attempt to introduce some German brewing expertise to France. Production soon shifted to Saigon, where the company continued to brew with German ingredients and technology, right until the North Vietnamese army stormed the city in 1975. After reunification, the new authorities nationalised the company and added another '3' to the name for good luck — which obviously worked, as 'Ba-Ba-Ba' (333) is now one of the highest-selling brands in the country.

MACKEREL GRILLED IN BANANA LEAF

Cá nướng là chuối

Every restaurant in Hoi An has its own version of fish steamed in banana leaf. Grilling fish in banana leaves keeps it moist, while allowing the smoky flavours from the grill to penetrate the sweet flesh.

3 GARLIC CLOVES, ROUGHLY CHOPPED

2 LEMONGRASS STEMS, WHITE PART ONLY, ROUGHLY CHOPPED

2 CM (¾ INCH) KNOB FRESH GINGER, ROUGHLY CHOPPED

80 ML (2½ FL OZ/⅓ CUP) PEANUT OIL

8 SPRING ONIONS (SCALLIONS), SLICED

1 LARGE OR 2 SMALL BANANA LEAVES

1 x 1–1.4 KG (2 LB 3 OZ–3 LB 1 OZ) MACKEREL, GUTTED AND CLEANED

4 TABLESPOONS FRIED SHALLOTS (SEE PAGE 326)

LIME AND CHILLI DIPPING SALT (SEE PAGE 328), TO SERVE

SERVES 6

Heat a chargrill or barbecue to high.

Place the garlic, lemongrass and ginger in a mortar or food processor and pound or process to form a paste.

Put the peanut oil and spring onion in a small saucepan and heat gently over low heat. As soon as the spring onion wilts, remove from the heat.

Cut the banana leaf into seven 30 cm x 20 cm (12 inch x 8 inch) rectangles. Soften the pieces by dropping them into a saucepan of boiling water for 20 seconds. Remove and pat dry with paper towel. They can now be folded easily without tearing.

Place one banana leaf portion, shiny side down, on a work surface. Place a second banana leaf on the top half. Continue with the remaining leaves, working your way around the bottom leaf.

Place the fish on top of the banana leaves. Make a pocket in the fish, by making an incision just below the head, lengthways along the side of the fish. Now carefully cut the fish away from the ribcage. Fold the flesh back to expose the bones. Into this cavity, place the garlic paste, fried shallots, and the spring onions with their oil (1).

To wrap the fish, fold the banana leaves at the head and tail of the fish, then roll up and secure with skewers (2).

Place directly onto the hot grill or use a grilling basket, if desired, for easier handling (3). Cook for 15 minutes, or until the fish is cooked through, turning the fish once.

Remove the fish from the heat. Unwrap the banana leaves, taking care to avoid steam burns.

Serve the fish on the banana leaf, with the dipping salt.

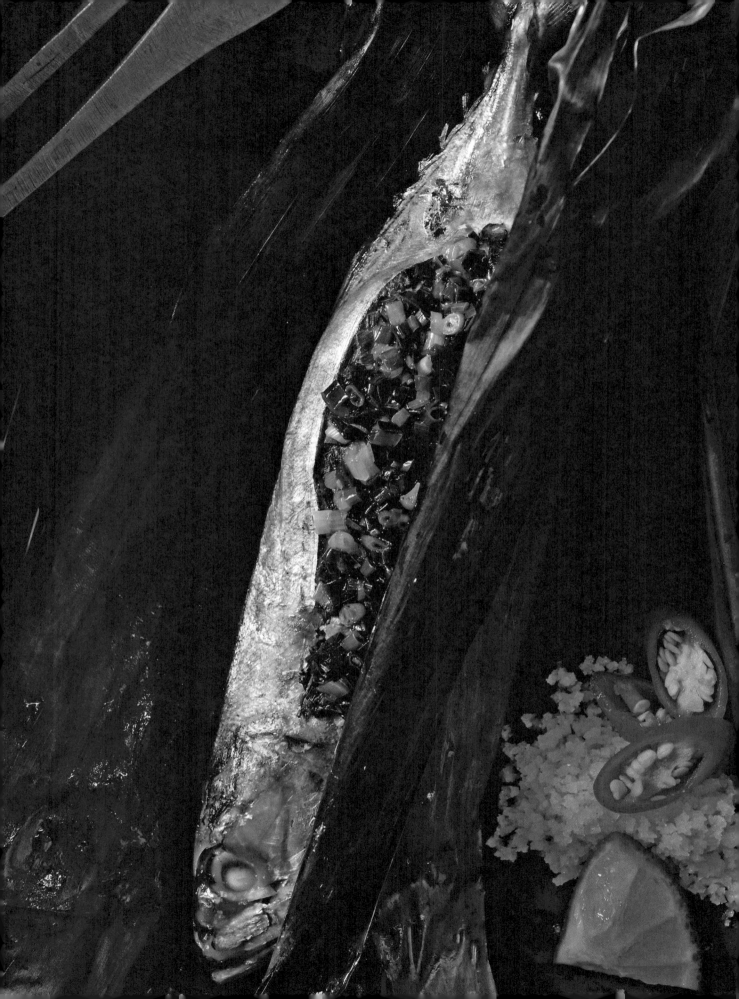

PRAWN AND MUNG BEAN PANCAKES

Bánh khọt

To make these popular Saigon pancakes, you'll need an Asian pancake pan, with indentations roughly 3 cm (1½ inches) in diameter. Called banh khot, these pans are readily available from most Asian kitchen supply stores.

100 g (3½ oz) DRIED GREEN MUNG BEANS

200 g (7 oz) RICE FLOUR

⅓ TEASPOON GROUND TURMERIC

1 TEASPOON SALT

375 ML (12½ FL OZ/1½ CUPS) COCONUT MILK

VEGETABLE OIL, FOR PAN-FRYING

24 SMALL PRAWNS (SHRIMP), PEELED AND DEVEINED

3 SPRING ONIONS (SCALLIONS), BOTH THE WHITE AND GREEN PARTS, CUT INTO THIN RINGS

FISH SAUCE AND COCONUT DIPPING SAUCE (SEE PAGE 323), TO SERVE

MAKES 24

Rinse the mung beans under cold running water, then place in a bowl, cover with water and soak for 2 hours.

Drain the mung beans and place in a saucepan. Cover with cold water and cook for 20–25 minutes, until soft.

Place the flour, turmeric and salt in a bowl. Make a well in the centre and pour in the coconut milk. Whisk until you have a smooth batter; if necessary, you can strain the batter to remove any lumpy bits. Set aside for 10 minutes so the batter doesn't become chewy when cooked.

Heat the banh khot pan over medium heat. When the pan is hot, add about ¼ teaspoon vegetable oil to each hollow.

When the oil is hot, add 1 tablespoon of the batter to each hollow. Sprinkle in some of the mung beans and top each pancake with a prawn. Cover with the lid and cook for 1–2 minutes.

Add some spring onion to each pancake and cook for a further 1 minute, or until the batter has set and the bottom is crisp. Remove from the pan, using a palette knife.

Repeat with any remaining ingredients.

Serve hot, with the dipping sauce.

PRAWN AND PORK BROTH WITH RICE NOODLES

Hủ tiếu

This attractive and utterly delicious noodle soup is to the Saigonese what *pho* is to their northern compatriots. Traditionally served by street vendors as a hearty breakfast, it is now available any time of the day or night. What makes this particular version truly unique is the subtle smoky flavour achieved by adding dried squid to the broth.

250 G (9 OZ) PORK LOIN, FAT AND SINEW REMOVED

18 PRAWNS (SHRIMP), PEELED AND DEVEINED

300 G (10½ OZ) DRIED RICE VERMICELLI

1 SMALL HANDFUL BEAN SPROUTS

4 SPRING ONIONS (SCALLIONS), SLICED

1 SMALL HANDFUL THAI BASIL, CHOPPED

1 SMALL HANDFUL CORIANDER (CILANTRO) LEAVES, CHOPPED

1 RED BIRD'S EYE CHILLI, SLICED

3 LIMES, CUT IN HALF

BROTH

1 DRIED SQUID

5 CHICKEN CARCASSES

1 PIG'S TROTTER, CUT INTO FOUR PIECES

2 ONIONS, QUARTERED

3 CARROTS, EACH CUT INTO THIRDS

3 GARLIC CLOVES, CRUSHED

2 TABLESPOONS FISH SAUCE

½ TEASPOON BLACK PEPPERCORNS

SERVES 6

To prepare the broth, first soak the dried squid in warm water for 30 minutes to remove any excess salt.

While the squid is soaking, place the chicken carcasses and pig's trotter in a large saucepan and cover with cold water. Slowly bring to a simmer, skimming off any froth that rises to the surface.

Drain the squid and add it to the broth, along with the vegetables, garlic, fish sauce and peppercorns. Simmer for 2 hours, skimming regularly to ensure you have a clear broth. Strain the stock and discard the bones, squid, vegetables and peppercorns.

Clean the saucepan and pour the broth back in. Return to a simmer. Gently lower the pork into the broth and poach for 15 minutes. Remove the pork to a board and allow to rest for 5 minutes before slicing.

While the pork is resting, poach the prawns in the broth for 1–2 minutes, until just cooked.

Meanwhile, soak the vermicelli in boiling water for 4–5 minutes. Gently stir to separate the noodles, then drain and refresh under cold water. Use kitchen scissors to cut the vermicelli into easy-to-manage lengths. Divide among six deep bowls.

Top the noodles with the bean sprouts, pork slices, prawns, spring onion, herbs and chilli. Ladle the hot broth into the bowls and serve immediately, with lime wedges on the side, and extra fish sauce, if desired.

PRAWN AND PORK SPRING ROLLS

Nem tôm thịt

Originally from the south of Vietnam, these are the fresh spring rolls most Westerners are familiar with, because south Vietnamese refugees put them on their menus in the United States, Australia and other countries that took them in.

150 G (5½ OZ) DRIED RICE VERMICELLI

24 SPRING ROLL SHEETS, ABOUT 18 CM (7 INCHES) IN SIZE

1 SMALL ICEBERG LETTUCE, OR OTHER CRISP GREEN LETTUCE, THINLY SLICED

200 G (7 OZ) CHAR SIU PORK, CUT INTO 24 PIECES

1 SMALL HANDFUL CORIANDER (CILANTRO) SPRIGS

1 SMALL HANDFUL MINT

24 COOKED PRAWNS (SHRIMP), PEELED, DEVEINED AND CUT IN HALF LENGTHWAYS

24 GARLIC CHIVES, CUT IN HALF

PEANUT SAUCE (SEE PAGE 334), TO SERVE

MAKES 24

Soak the vermicelli in boiling water for 4–5 minutes. Gently stir to separate the noodles, then drain and refresh under cold water. Use kitchen scissors to cut the vermicelli into easy-to-manage lengths.

Soften the rice paper sheets by dipping them one at a time into warm water for 1 second. Do not soak the sheets as they will become too soft and tear when rolled. Place on a flat surface, wait for 20 seconds, then soak up any excess water with a clean cloth.

In a straight line along the bottom third of a sheet, place some lettuce, noodles, pork and herbs. Bring the bottom of the wrapper up over the filling, then fold in the sides. Place two prawn halves and two bits of garlic chive on the wrapper and continue rolling.

Set aside, seam side down, while preparing the remaining spring rolls.

Serve with the peanut sauce.

PRAWN AND CARAMBOLA CLAY POT

Tôm kho khế

Native to Sri Lanka and Indonesia, the carambola (star fruit) tree has been cultivated for centuries in South-East Asia. These trees, with their beautiful foliage and unusually shaped fruit, are a common sight in the south of Vietnam. As well as being visually appealing, the carambola fruit is also a wonderful way of adding tartness to a dish.

12 LARGE PRAWNS (SHRIMP), IN THEIR SHELLS

1 TABLESPOON SUGAR

1 TABLESPOON VEGETABLE OIL

1 TABLESPOON FISH SAUCE

2 TEASPOONS LIGHT SOY SAUCE

1 LONG RED CHILLI, CUT INTO 5 MM (¼ INCH) RINGS

2 SMALL UNRIPE CARAMBOLA (STAR FRUIT), CUT INTO 5 MM (¼ INCH) SLICES

4 SPRING ONIONS (SCALLIONS), SLICED

MARINADE

2 GARLIC CLOVES, FINELY CHOPPED

3 RED ASIAN SHALLOTS, FINELY DICED

1 TABLESPOON FISH SAUCE

¼ TEASPOON FRESHLY GROUND BLACK PEPPER

SERVES 6

Preheat the oven to 180°C (350°F).

Combine the marinade ingredients in a bowl and use it to coat the prawns. Leave to sit for 20 minutes while making the caramel sauce.

Put the sugar and 1½ tablespoons water in a heavy-based saucepan and place over medium heat. Stir until the sugar has completely dissolved. Now boil, without stirring, for about 1 minute, until the sugar becomes richly golden. Standing away from the pan, pour in 250 ml (8½ fl oz/1 cup) water. When the spluttering has stopped, stir until you have a beautiful smooth caramel sauce.

Heat the oil in a frying pan over medium heat and cook the prawns for 1 minute on each side. Add the caramel sauce, fish sauce, soy sauce and chilli. When the liquid comes to the boil, remove the pan from the heat.

Transfer the mixture to a clay pot or casserole dish. Cover with the lid, then place in the oven and bake for 4–5 minutes.

Remove the lid. Add the starfruit, then bake, uncovered, for a further 3 minutes.

Serve in the clay pot or casserole dish, with the spring onion scattered over the top and some freshly ground black pepper.

PRAWN BROTH WITH FISH CAKES AND NOODLES

Bún tôm

Tracey recently discovered this dish at a little stall tucked away near the district post office. The vendor claimed she was preparing the soup in the same way as her mother, who first created this dish.

18 PRAWNS (SHRIMP), PEELED AND DEVEINED (RESERVE THE SHELLS FOR MAKING THE BROTH)

3 DRIED BLACK FUNGUS (WOOD EARS)

600 G (1 LB 5 OZ) DRIED RICE VERMICELLI

VEGETABLE OIL, FOR DEEP-FRYING

4 SPRING ONIONS (SCALLIONS), SLICED

1 SMALL HANDFUL DILL, CHOPPED

BROTH

1 TABLESPOON VEGETABLE OIL

RESERVED PRAWN SHELLS (SEE ABOVE)

2 RED ASIAN SHALLOTS, ROUGHLY CHOPPED

1 LEMONGRASS STEM, WHITE PART ONLY, CRUSHED

FISH CAKES

150 G (5½ OZ) SNAPPER FILLETS, SKIN AND BONES REMOVED, CUT INTO CHUNKS

1 TEASPOON FISH SAUCE

PINCH OF SUGAR

1 TABLESPOON CHOPPED DILL

PORK IN BETEL LEAF

120 G (4½ OZ) MINCED (GROUND) PORK

½ LEMONGRASS STEM, WHITE PART ONLY, FINELY CHOPPED

½ TEASPOON FISH SAUCE

PINCH OF SUGAR

6 BETEL LEAVES, WITHOUT ANY TEARS

SERVES 6

To make the broth, heat the oil in a saucepan over medium heat. Cook the reserved prawn shells, shallot and lemongrass until the shells turn deep red. Add 1.25 litres (42 fl oz/ 5 cups) water and bring to the boil. Reduce the heat and simmer for 15 minutes, skimming off any froth. Turn off the heat and allow the broth to sit for a further 10 minutes before straining. Discard the prawn shells, shallot and lemongrass.

To make the fish cakes, put the fish chunks in a food processor and process to the consistency of a paste. Add the fish sauce, sugar and a pinch of salt and freshly ground black pepper. Process until incorporated, then transfer to a bowl and stir the dill through. Cover and refrigerate for 30 minutes.

Meanwhile, soak the mushrooms in warm water for 20 minutes. Drain the mushrooms and squeeze out any excess water. Discard the stems. Thinly slice the caps and set aside.

Soak the vermicelli in boiling water for 4–5 minutes. Gently stir to separate the noodles, then drain and refresh under cold water. Use kitchen scissors to cut the vermicelli into easy-to-manage lengths.

With lightly oiled fingers, form the fish mixture into six patties. Heat about 10 cm (4 inches) of oil in a wok or saucepan over medium heat. Fry the fish patties for 1 minute, or until cooked through. Remove and drain well on paper towel.

To make the pork in betel leaf, combine the pork, lemongrass, fish sauce and sugar in a small bowl. Add a pinch of salt and black pepper and mix well. Discard any tough stems from the betel leaves and wipe the leaves with a damp cloth. Place the leaves, smooth side down, on a work surface, with the point of the leaf furthest away. Divide the pork mixture among the leaves, placing it just below the centre of each leaf. Roll up the leaves, taking care to fold in the sides. Now take two skewers and thread three betel leaf parcels onto each.

Heat about 2 tablespoons of oil in a frying pan. Cook the betel leaf rolls over medium heat for about 2 minutes on each side.

Reheat the broth and poach the prawns for 2–3 minutes. Divide the noodles and mushrooms among deep bowls and top with the prawns. Add a fish cake, betel leaf roll, some spring onion and dill to each. Ladle the broth over and serve.

PRAWN CAKE

Chả tôm

This classic dish from the imperial cuisine of the old capital, Hue, works equally well at street level, served in a baguette with avocado, or even rolled up in a spring roll sheet.

400 g (14 oz) prawn (shrimp) meat, deveined
2 red Asian shallots, roughly chopped
2 garlic cloves, roughly chopped
3 teaspoons tapioca flour
1 egg, separated
1 long red chilli, seeded and chopped

½ teaspoon salt
⅓ teaspoon freshly ground black pepper
1 banana leaf, cut into a 25 cm (10 inch) square
classic dipping sauce (see page 323), to serve

SERVES 6

Pat the prawns dry with paper towel and place in a food processor. Add the shallot and garlic and process to a smooth, shiny paste.

Mix the tapioca flour with 3 teaspoons water and blend to a thin paste. With the motor running, add the tapioca paste and egg white to the prawn mixture and process to incorporate the ingredients. Transfer the mixture to a bowl and stir the chilli, salt and pepper through.

Put the prawn mixture in the centre of the banana leaf, forming a log shape. Bring up the sides of the leaf, then shake to form a regular shape and to help the mixture stick together. Do this for about 1 minute.

Place the banana leaf in a steamer, but don't fold the leaf over the prawn cake. Set the steamer over a saucepan of boiling water and cook for 10 minutes.

Lightly whisk the egg yolk, brush it over the top of the prawn cake and cook for a further 5 minutes.

Remove the prawn cake from the steamer. When cool enough to handle, cut the cake into wedges and serve with the dipping sauce.

The prawn cake can be served at room temperature, and will keep in an airtight container in the refrigerator for 3–4 days.

PRAWN ON SUGARCANE

Tôm bao mía

※

This popular Vietnamese dish is very easy to make if you let the food processor do the work for you. Make sure you have damp fingers when forming the prawn paste around the sugarcane, as the whole process can become quite messy otherwise.

If you can't obtain sugarcane from your Asian grocer, or for a change, try using lemongrass stems.

The prawns can also be cooked over hot coals — a great addition to your next barbecue.

600 G (1 LB 5 OZ) PRAWNS (SHRIMP), PEELED AND DEVEINED
2 GARLIC CLOVES, ROUGHLY CHOPPED
2 SPRING ONIONS (SCALLIONS), SLICED
100 G (3½ OZ) MINCED (GROUND) PORK FAT
1 TABLESPOON FISH SAUCE
1 TEASPOON SUGAR

⅓ TEASPOON FRESHLY GROUND BLACK PEPPER
3 PIECES OF 12 CM (4¾ INCH) LONG, PEELED SUGARCANE, QUARTERED LENGTHWISE (TO MAKE 12 STICKS) (1)
VEGETABLE OIL, FOR PAN-FRYING
CLASSIC DIPPING SAUCE (SEE PAGE 323), TO SERVE

SERVES 6

Place the prawns, garlic and spring onion in a food processor and blend to a paste. Add the pork fat, fish sauce, sugar and pepper and process again until all the ingredients are combined and you have a sticky paste. Transfer to a bowl, then cover and rest in the refrigerator for 30 minutes.

Divide the prawn mixture into 12 portions. Working with one portion at a time, moisten your fingers in a bowl of tepid water and flatten the portion slightly in the palm of your hand (2). Mould the prawn mixture around the top two-thirds of a sugarcane stick, taking care to seal the edges (3). Place on an oiled tray. Repeat with the remaining portions.

Heat about 1 cm (½ inch) of oil in a frying pan. Fry the prawn skewers over high heat for 5–6 minutes, turning them regularly, until cooked and lightly golden.

Serve hot, with the dipping sauce.

PRAWN TAILS COOKED IN COCONUT MILK

Tôm nấu nước dừa

A popular dish from the Mekong region. Coconut features prominently in South Vietnamese cuisine, and the coconut plant is a true all-rounder. Virtually all parts of it are used: the flesh and milk for cooking, the leaves for roofing and the wood for building.

12 PRAWNS (SHRIMP), PEELED AND DEVEINED, TAILS INTACT

4 GARLIC CLOVES, CHOPPED

1/3 TEASPOON FRESHLY GROUND BLACK PEPPER

1½ TABLESPOONS FISH SAUCE

VEGETABLE OIL, FOR PAN-FRYING

1 LONG RED CHILLI, SEEDED AND CUT INTO THIN STRIPS

190 ML (6½ FL OZ/¾ CUP) COCONUT MILK

4 SPRING ONIONS (SCALLIONS), CUT INTO 4 CM (1½ INCH) STRIPS

SERVES 6

Marinate the prawns in the garlic, pepper and 1 tablespoon of the fish sauce for 15 minutes.

Remove the prawns from the marinade and pat dry with paper towel.

Lightly oil a wok or frying pan and place over medium heat. Cook the prawns for 1–2 minutes, then add the chilli and cook for a further 1 minute, until the prawns start turning pink.

Pour in the coconut milk and bring to a simmer. Cook for 3–4 minutes, or until the prawns are deep pink.

Using a slotted spoon, transfer the prawns to a serving platter or bowl.

Continue cooking the coconut milk mixture for a further 2 minutes to reduce it. Stir in the spring onion and remaining fish sauce, then pour the coconut sauce over the prawns and serve.

PRAWN WONTONS IN A PORK BROTH WITH SESAME OIL

Sủi cảo

This dish comes from Vietnam's Chinatown — Cholon, in Ho Chi Minh City. Wontons were initially introduced to the country by Chinese traders and were quickly adopted into the local cuisine. These wontons can be made up to 12 hours ahead.

3 KG (6 LB 10 OZ) PIG'S TROTTERS, SAWN IN HALF LENGTHWAYS BY YOUR BUTCHER

1 TEASPOON SALT

8 RED ASIAN SHALLOTS, LEFT WHOLE

24 WONTON WRAPPERS

150 G (5½ OZ) CHAR SIU PORK, CUT INTO 24 PIECES, ABOUT THE LENGTH OF THE PRAWNS

12 PRAWNS (SHRIMP), PEELED AND DEVEINED, CUT IN HALF LENGTHWAYS

400 G (14 OZ) BOK CHOY (PAK CHOY), LEAVES SEPARATED

4 SPRING ONIONS (SCALLIONS), WHITE ENDS CUT INTO 4 CM (1½ INCH) LENGTHS, GREEN TOPS THINLY SLICED

1 TEASPOON SESAME OIL

SERVES 6

Wash the trotters under cold running water, then place in a large saucepan and cover with cold water. Add the salt and slowly bring to a simmer, skimming off any froth that rises to the surface.

Chargrill the whole unpeeled shallots on a barbecue or gas burner over medium heat for about 5 minutes, until they are fragrant and the skin is lightly charred. Leave to cool slightly. Using your fingers, flake off the outer thin layer of skin.

Add the shallots to the stock and simmer for 3½ hours. Remove from the heat, strain the stock through a sieve and discard the trotters and shallots.

To make the wontons, place a wonton wrapper on a work surface and brush the edges with water. On one half, place a piece of pork and half a prawn. Fold the other half over and seal the edges with your fingertips, making sure there is no air trapped in the wonton, or it will burst open when cooked.

Place the wonton on a tray and cover with a damp cloth. Repeat with the remaining ingredients, to make 24 wontons.

To serve, bring a saucepan of water to the boil. Briefly blanch the bok choy, then divide among six deep bowls.

In batches, gently lower the wontons into the pan of boiling water and simmer for 2–3 minutes. Remove with a slotted spoon and drain thoroughly.

Place four wontons in each bowl. Ladle the hot broth into the bowls and scatter with the spring onion. Drizzle a little sesame oil into each bowl to serve.

PRAWNS IN YOUNG GREEN RICE

Tôm cốm xanh

What makes this dish special is the wonderful contrast of textures, with the crisp green-rice covering the soft-fleshed prawns. The little orange prawn tails poking through the green on the outside also make the dish look very attractive.

Green rice can be used to crumb other foods, such as chicken or tofu, and is a great alternative to breadcrumbs for people who are gluten intolerant.

400 G (14 OZ) SNAPPER FILLETS, SKIN AND BONES REMOVED, CUT INTO ROUGH CHUNKS

2 GARLIC CLOVES, ROUGHLY CHOPPED

3 TEASPOONS FISH SAUCE

⅓ TEASPOON SUGAR

½ TEASPOON SALT

½ TEASPOON FRESHLY GROUND BLACK PEPPER

12 LARGE PRAWNS (SHRIMP)

RICE FLOUR, FOR DUSTING

200 G (7 OZ) YOUNG GREEN RICE

CLASSIC DIPPING SAUCE (SEE PAGE 323), TO SERVE

SERVES 6

Using a mortar and pestle or food processor, pound or process the fish and garlic until the mixture forms a paste (1). Add the fish sauce, sugar, salt and pepper and further pound or process to incorporate the ingredients. Transfer to a bowl, then cover and rest in the refrigerator for 30 minutes.

Carefully remove the shells from the bodies of the prawns, leaving the head and tail intact. Using a sharp knife, and making sure not to cut too deep, run the blade along the back of each prawn and remove the intestinal tract.

Lightly dust the prawns in the rice flour, shaking off any excess.

Divide the fish paste into 12 portions. Working with one portion at a time, and using lightly oiled fingers, flatten the paste in the palm of your hand. Place a prawn into the centre, then mould the paste around the peeled part of the prawn (2). Press firmly to seal. Lightly press the green rice into the moulded prawns.

Heat about 13 cm (5 inches) of oil in a wok. To test the oil, place the tip of a wooden chopstick into the oil — when bubbles slowly rise to the surface, the oil is hot enough to use.

Fry the prawns for 5–6 minutes, until they are cooked through and the rice has puffed slightly (3). Drain well on paper towel.

Serve hot, with the dipping sauce.

RAW FISH SALAD WITH GALANGAL AND THINH

Gỏi cá cuốn thính

Thinh is roasted rice, which is then ground to a powder. It is used a lot in pagoda food, and adds a depth of flavour. This dish is a specialty from the countryside that the Hanoi Cooking Centre's very own chef, Nguyen Huy Y, grew up in.

250 G (9 OZ) FRESH YOUNG GALANGAL

700 G (1 LB 9 OZ) SNAPPER FILLETS, SKIN AND BONES REMOVED

JUICE OF 1 LIME

100 G (3½ OZ) MUSTARD GREENS, LEAVES SEPARATED

12 BETEL LEAVES OR THAI BASIL LEAVES

150 G (5½ OZ) ROASTED RICE FLOUR (SEE PAGE 337)

GINGER DIPPING SAUCE (SEE PAGE 327)

SERVES 6

Peel the galangal. Cut 100 g (3½ oz) of the galangal into thin strips and set aside. Roughly chop the remaining galangal, place in a mortar or food processor and pound or process to a very fine consistency (1).

Using a sharp knife, cut the fish across the grain into strips about 1 cm (½ inch) wide (2). Place in a bowl or on a tray, add the lime juice and pounded galangal, then gently toss to evenly coat the fish (3). Cover with plastic wrap and leave the fish to sit for 10 minutes to allow the flavours to develop.

Arrange the galangal strips, mustard greens and betel or basil leaves on a serving platter.

When you are ready to serve, sprinkle the rice flour over the marinated fish and toss it through, evenly coating the fish. Place the fish on a platter and serve with the dipping sauce and remaining ingredients.

To serve, put some galangal strips, marinated fish and dipping sauce onto a mustard leaf. Roll up and enjoy.

RICE PORRIDGE WITH DRIED SCALLOPS

Cháo sò điệp

Ladling the hot porridge over the raw eggs in individual serving bowls adds a richness and creamy texture to this dish. However, you can omit the eggs if you wish. We suspect they were added because the porridge is often served for breakfast.

24 DRIED SCALLOPS

300 G (10½ OZ/1½ CUPS) LONG-GRAIN WHITE RICE

1 LITRE (34 FL OZ/4 CUPS) VEGETABLE STOCK OR WATER

1 TABLESPOON VEGETABLE OIL

2 TEASPOONS FISH SAUCE

1 TEASPOON SUGAR

½ TEASPOON SALT

½ TEASPOON FRESHLY GROUND BLACK PEPPER

100 G (3½ OZ) MINCED (GROUND) PORK

6 SPRING ONIONS (SCALLIONS), THINLY SLICED

6 EGGS

½ TEASPOON SESAME OIL

SERVES 6

Soak the scallops in 190 ml (6½ fl oz/¾ cup) water for 2 hours.

Meanwhile, put the rice in a large colander or sieve and rinse under cold running water. Place your hand in the centre of the rice and move it in a circular motion to make sure the water runs freely over all the rice.

When the water runs clear, drain the rice and place in a dry frying pan. Toast over medium heat for 1 minute, moving the rice constantly so it colours evenly. Remove from the pan.

Place one-quarter of the rice in a mortar and break the rice grains with a pestle.

Drain the scallops over a saucepan, to catch the soaking liquid. Slice the scallops 1 cm (½ inch) thick.

Add the vegetable stock to the reserved scallop water and bring to a boil.

In another saucepan, heat the oil over medium heat. Add the scallops, and both the broken and intact rice, and fry for 1 minute. Pour in the boiling stock, then stir in the fish sauce, sugar, salt and pepper.

Reduce the heat and gently simmer for about 20 minutes, stirring regularly.

Stir the pork through and simmer for a further 5 minutes, or until the rice is cooked. Remove from the heat and stir in the spring onion.

Crack an egg into each serving bowl and ladle the rice porridge over the top. Using a chopstick, stir the egg through the rice. Drizzle with the sesame oil and serve with extra pepper and fish sauce, if desired.

SALTED MACKEREL WITH STICKY RICE LOGS

Xôi chiên với cá muối

Traditionally, the fish for this recipe is salted and then dried on bamboo racks in the sun for two days, but we have adapted the recipe to use a slow oven instead. The saltiness makes this dish a popular *bia hoi* snack, which is often served with cucumber sticks to add an element of freshness.

500 G (1 LB 2 OZ) MACKEREL CUTLETS, OR WHOLE GUTTED FISH
2 TEASPOONS COARSE SALT
1 TABLESPOON VEGETABLE OIL

STICKY RICE LOGS (SEE PAGE 27)
2 CUCUMBERS, CUT INTO 4 CM (1½ INCH) BATONS
SPRING ONION OIL (SEE PAGE 341)
SERVES 6

Clean the mackerel, removing all the bones and any blood. Massage the salt onto both sides of the fish. Place on a tray, then cover and refrigerate overnight.

The next day, preheat the oven to 60°C (140°F). Wash the salt off the fish and pat dry with paper towel. Place the fish on a wire rack and dry for 4 hours in the oven.

The mackerel is now ready to be cooked. Alternatively, you can keep it in the fridge for 2–3 days before cooking.

Cut the mackerel into thick batons. Heat the oil in a frying pan over medium heat. When hot, fry the fish for 2–3 minutes on each side, until cooked through.

Serve on a platter with the sticky rice logs and cucumber, and the spring onion oil in dipping bowls on the side.

SALTED FISH FRIED RICE

Cơm chiên cá muối

The salted mackerel, or 'mam ca thu', is available in jars, ready to use, from Asian grocery stores. Save the oil and use it to fry the rice, for a more intense flavour.

1 TABLESPOON VEGETABLE OIL

3 EGGS, LIGHTLY BEATEN

2 SALTED MACKERELS IN SOY BEAN OIL (MAM CA THU), FLAKED, PLUS 1 TABLESPOON OF THE SOY BEAN OIL

4 RED ASIAN SHALLOTS, FINELY CHOPPED

1.11 KG (2 LB 7 OZ/6 CUPS) BOILED RICE (SEE PAGE 18), OR BOIL UP 400 G (14 OZ/2 CUPS) UNCOOKED LONG-GRAIN WHITE RICE

⅓ TEASPOON SALT

2 SPRING ONIONS (SCALLIONS), CUT INTO RINGS

SOY CHILLI DIPPING SAUCE (SEE PAGE 340), TO SERVE

SERVES 6

Heat the vegetable oil in a wok over high heat. Pour the eggs over the base of the wok and cook for 1–2 minutes, rotating the wok to ensure the omelette cooks evenly. Remove from the wok. When cool enough to handle, roll the omelette into a cigar shape and roughly chop.

Wipe the wok clean and place over medium heat. Add the soy bean oil from the salted mackerel, then sauté the shallot until fragrant. Add the salted mackerel and cook for a further 1 minute.

Now add the rice and salt. Keep tossing the rice and fish, as the rice can easily stick to the side of the wok. When the rice has heated through, add the omelette strips. Toss, then remove from the heat.

Serve topped with the spring onion, with the dipping sauce on the side.

SEAWEED AND FISH SOUP

Canh rong biển

Dry seaweed is available from Asian grocers and is a great source of iron. In Vietnam, women often eat it after childbirth. Don't be tempted to use Japanese nori sheets for this soup, as they are too salty.

3 RED ASIAN SHALLOTS, PEELED AND ROUGHLY CHOPPED

1 TABLESPOON VEGETABLE OIL

2 TOMATOES, PEELED AND SEEDED (SEE PAGE 94), EACH CUT INTO 8 WEDGES

½ TEASPOON SUGAR

1 TEASPOON SALT

¼ TEASPOON FRESHLY GROUND BLACK PEPPER

1 TEASPOON FISH SAUCE

2 ROUNDS DRIED SEAWEED, ABOUT 10 CM (4 INCHES) IN SIZE

6 PRAWNS (SHRIMP), PEELED AND DEVEINED, TAILS INTACT

150 G (5½ OZ) FIRM WHITE FISH FILLETS, SKIN AND BONES REMOVED, CUT INTO BITE-SIZED PIECES

4 SPRING ONIONS (SCALLIONS), CUT INTO 3 CM (1¼ INCH) LENGTHS

1 TABLESPOON CHILLI SAUCE (SEE PAGE 322) (OPTIONAL)

SERVES 6

Pound the shallots using a mortar and pestle. Heat the oil in a saucepan over medium heat and sauté the pounded shallot for 1–2 minutes.

Add the tomatoes, sugar, salt and pepper and cook for 1 minute, then pour in 1.25 litres (42 fl oz/5 cups) water and the fish sauce. Tear each seaweed round into four pieces and add to the pan. Bring to the boil, then reduce the heat and simmer for 5 minutes.

Add the prawns and fish and poach for 2 minutes. Lastly, stir in the spring onion and remove from the heat.

For some extra spice, top with the chilli sauce, if desired.

SNAILS WITH RICE NOODLE SOUP

Bún Ốc

Featuring an unusual combination of ingredients, this specialty dish is often served around Hanoi's West Lake, at lakeside tables on weekend afternoons. We particularly like the way the cooked bananas assume a potato-like, starchy consistency, but retain their sweetness.

2 KG (4 LB 6 OZ) PIG'S TROTTERS, SAWN INTO FIVE PIECES EACH BY YOUR BUTCHER

⅓ TEASPOON SALT

8 RED ASIAN SHALLOTS

JUICE OF ½ LEMON

4 GREEN BANANAS

VEGETABLE OIL, FOR PAN-FRYING

400 G (14 OZ) FIRM TOFU, CUT INTO 2 CM (¾ INCH) CUBES

3 CM (1¼ INCH) KNOB FRESH TURMERIC, PEELED

5 TOMATOES, PEELED, SEEDED (SEE PAGE 94) AND ROUGHLY CHOPPED

1 TEASPOON SUGAR

2 TABLESPOONS FISH SAUCE

400 G (14 OZ) DRIED RICE VERMICELLI

1 TABLESPOON TAMARIND WATER (SEE PAGE 341)

18 SNAILS, SHUCKED

6 BETEL LEAVES, THINLY SLICED

1 HANDFUL PERILLA, THINLY SLICED

SERVES 6

Wash the trotters under cold running water, then place in a large saucepan and cover with 2 litres (68 fl oz/8 cups) cold water. Add the salt and slowly bring to a simmer, skimming off any froth that rises to the surface.

Chargrill the whole unpeeled shallots on a barbecue or gas burner over medium heat for about 5 minutes, until they are fragrant and the skin is lightly charred. Leave to cool slightly. Using your fingers, flake off the outer thin layer of skin.

Add the shallots to the stock and simmer for 3½ hours — be careful not to let the stock boil, or it will become very cloudy. Strain the broth through a sieve and discard the trotters and shallots.

Meanwhile, add the lemon juice to a bowl of cold water. Using a sharp knife, peel off the outer layer of skin from each banana, leaving on a thin layer of the skin for texture. Cut the banana into batons and place in the lemon water. This will remove some of the sticky liquid from the bananas.

Heat about 2 cm (¾ inch) of oil in a wok over medium–high heat. Add the tofu and fry for 1–2 minutes on each side, until crisp. Remove with a slotted spoon and drain on paper towel.

Pound the turmeric to a fine paste using a mortar and pestle. Drain the banana and marinate for 15 minutes with the turmeric and 2 tablespoons of oil.

Heat 1 tablespoon of oil in a saucepan and sauté the banana over medium heat. When coloured, add all the pork stock, along with the tomatoes, sugar and 1 tablespoon of the fish sauce. Simmer for 10 minutes.

Meanwhile, soak the vermicelli in boiling water for 4–5 minutes. Gently stir to separate the noodles, then drain and refresh under cold water. Use kitchen scissors to cut the vermicelli into easy-to-manage lengths, then divide among six deep bowls.

Add the tamarind water to the banana mixture and cook for a further 2 minutes. Lastly, add the remaining fish sauce, the snails, tofu, betel leaves and perilla.

Gently stir together, then ladle the soup over the noodles.

SQUID FILLED WITH PORK AND NOODLES

Mực nhồi thịt

One of Andreas' favourites, this dish is popular in the restaurants along the river bank in the old trading port of Hoi An. If you like, you can quickly chargrill the filled squid over hot coals after cooking it in the pan, to impart a smoky flavour.

4 dried Chinese mushrooms

25 g (1 oz) cellophane noodles

8 small squid, about 1.5 kg (3 lb 5 oz) in total

300 g (10½ oz) minced (ground) pork shoulder

2 red Asian shallots, finely diced

2 garlic cloves, finely chopped

1 handful coriander (cilantro) leaves

2 tablespoons fish sauce

½ teaspoon caster (superfine) sugar

⅓ teaspoon freshly ground black pepper

2 tablespoons vegetable oil

Classic dipping sauce (see page 323), to serve

SERVES 6

Soak the mushrooms in boiling water for 20 minutes. Drain the mushrooms and squeeze out any excess water. Discard the stems. Thinly slice the caps, then place in a bowl.

Soak the noodles in hot water for 1 minute, then drain and refresh under cold running water. Drain the noodles, then cut into 2 cm (¾ inch) lengths using kitchen scissors. Add to the mushrooms.

Clean the squid by holding the body with one hand and the head with the other. Gently pull, taking care not to burst the ink sac; the head and tentacles will come away. Remove the clear cartilage, rinse the squid inside and out, then pat dry. Using a sharp knife, cut the head from the tentacles and discard the head. Finely chop the tentacles, or mince (grind) them using a food processor.

Add the minced tentacles to the minced pork, mushrooms, along with the shallot, garlic, coriander, fish sauce, sugar and pepper. Mix together well.

Firmly pack the squid tubes two-thirds of the way with the pork mixture, ensuring there are no air pockets. Secure the ends with skewers or toothpicks.

Heat the oil in a large frying pan over medium heat. Fry the squid for 5 minutes, turning regularly so they brown evenly.

Now pierce the squid several times to release any trapped liquid — this will cause the oil to spit, so take care. Cook the squid for a further 10 minutes, turning occasionally so they colour evenly.

Take the squid out of the pan and remove the skewers. Slice into 2 cm (¾ inch) rounds and drizzle with the cooking juices.

Serve warm, with the dipping sauce.

STEAMED OMELETTE WITH SEAFOOD AND PORK

Trứng hấp hải sản

Steamed omelettes make a tasty and healthy breakfast. They are often available in the wet markets for early risers. Serve with crusty bread or steamed rice.

5 DRIED BLACK FUNGUS (WOOD EARS)
50 G (1¾ OZ) CELLOPHANE NOODLES
8 EGGS
150 G (5½ OZ) PRAWN (SHRIMP) MEAT, ROUGHLY CHOPPED
150 G (5½ OZ) CRABMEAT
100 G (3½ OZ) MINCED (GROUND) PORK

3 SPRING ONIONS (SCALLIONS), SLICED
1 SMALL HANDFUL CORIANDER (CILANTRO), CHOPPED
½ TEASPOON SALT
⅓ TEASPOON FRESHLY GROUND BLACK PEPPER
SOY CHILLI DIPPING SAUCE (SEE PAGE 340), TO SERVE

SERVES 6

Soak the mushrooms for 20 minutes in warm water. Drain the mushrooms and squeeze out any excess water. Discard the stems, then thinly slice the caps.

Soak the noodles in hot water for 1 minute, then drain and refresh under cold running water. Drain the noodles, then cut into 3 cm (1¼ inch) lengths using kitchen scissors.

Lightly whisk the eggs in a large bowl, then add the mushrooms, noodles, seafood, pork, spring onion, coriander, salt and pepper. Combine well, then pour into an 18 cm (7 inch) heatproof dish.

Place the dish in a steamer set over a saucepan of boiling water. Cook for 20–25 minutes, until the eggs have set.

Serve with crusty bread or steamed rice, with the dipping sauce on the side.

TAMARIND PRAWNS

Tôm sốt me

Deliciously messy to eat, this dish should be served with finger bowls, or the wet hand towels popular in Vietnamese restaurants. Because the tamarind sauce is quite sour, a cold beer complements it much better than wine. It is a common dish in the *bia hoi* eateries in the capital.

6 LARGE PRAWNS (SHRIMP), IN THEIR SHELLS

2 TABLESPOONS VEGETABLE OIL

3 GARLIC CLOVES, ROUGHLY CHOPPED

3 SPRING ONIONS (SCALLIONS), WHITE PART ONLY, CUT INTO 4 CM (1½ INCH) LENGTHS

2 TABLESPOONS TAMARIND WATER (SEE PAGE 341)

2½ TABLESPOONS FISH SAUCE

1 TEASPOON ANNATTO OIL (SEE PAGE 320)

1 TEASPOON SUGAR

½ TEASPOON FRESHLY GROUND BLACK PEPPER

SERVES 6

Prepare the prawns by threading a skewer crossways just between the shell and flesh, where the prawn bends. Hook the black intestinal tract over the skewer, then gently ease it out and discard.

Heat the oil in a wok or frying pan over medium heat and cook the prawns for 2 minutes, or until the shells turn red. Set the prawns aside.

Return the wok to medium heat and add the garlic and spring onion, keeping the wok moving to stop the garlic burning.

When the mixture is aromatic, add 80 ml (2½ fl oz/⅓ cup) water and the tamarind water, fish sauce, annatto oil, sugar and black pepper.

Return the prawns to the wok and toss to coat. Increase the heat to high and cook for a further 1–2 minutes, until the sauce has reduced and coats the prawns.

Arrange the prawns on a platter and serve hot.

SOUR FISH SOUP WITH PORK, PRAWN, SQUID AND RICE NOODLES

Bún mắm

A dish from the small town of Soc Trang in the Mekong Delta, which is home to a large community of ethnic Khmers, who often use fermented fish (*mam ca linh xay*) in their cooking. Fermented fish is available in Asian supermarkets, but can be an acquired taste because of its strong aroma.

300 G (10½ OZ) FERMENTED FISH (MAM CA LINH XAY)

1 SQUID, ABOUT 8 CM (3¼ INCHES) LONG

7 LEMONGRASS STEMS, WHITE PART ONLY

VEGETABLE OIL, FOR PAN-FRYING

2 RED BIRD'S EYE CHILLIES, SEEDED AND FINELY CHOPPED

200 G (7 OZ) PORK BELLY, SLICED 5 MM (¼ INCH) THICK

500 ML (17 FL OZ/2 CUPS) COCONUT JUICE

200 G (7 OZ) FIRM WHITE FISH FILLETS

3 TABLESPOONS PALM SUGAR (JAGGERY)

6 LARGE PRAWNS (SHRIMP), PEELED AND DEVEINED, TAILS INTACT

TO SERVE

600 G (1 LB 5 OZ) DRIED RICE NOODLES

1 HANDFUL BEAN SPROUTS

2 LONG EGGPLANTS (AUBERGINES), CUT INTO 4 CM (1½ INCH) BATONS

100 G (3½ OZ) CHAR SIU PORK, SLICED 5 MM (¼ INCH) THICK

18 GARLIC CHIVES, CUT INTO 4 CM (1½ INCH) LENGTHS

2 LIMES, CUT INTO WEDGES

3 RED BIRD'S EYE CHILLIES, CUT INTO RINGS

SERVES 6

Place the fermented fish in a bowl and mash with a fork. Transfer to a saucepan, cover with 500 ml (17 fl oz/2 cups) water and bring to the boil. Reduce the heat and simmer for 15 minutes. Strain through a fine sieve, reserving the liquid.

Clean the squid by holding the body with one hand and the head with the other. Gently pull, taking care not to burst the ink sac; the head and tentacles will come away. Remove the clear cartilage, rinse the squid inside and out, then pat dry. Using a sharp knife, cut the head from the tentacles and discard the head. Cut the body open and rinse away any membranes from the surface. Lay the squid flat on a board with the inside facing up. Score the squid by cutting fine lines into the flesh in a crisscross pattern. Cut the body into 3 cm (1¼ inch) strips and the tentacles into 3 cm (1¼ inch) lengths.

Finely chop 4 of the lemongrass stems; crush the remaining 3 lemongrass stems and set aside.

Heat 2 tablespoons of oil in a wok or frying pan. Fry the squid and tentacles over high heat for 3–4 minutes, until cooked and deeply golden. Remove and drain on paper towel.

Heat another 1 tablespoon of oil in the wok over medium heat. Add the chopped lemongrass and chilli and stir constantly for 1 minute. Add the pork belly and cook for 2–3 minutes, until the meat is coloured. Pour in the reserved fermented fish liquid, coconut juice and 250 ml (8½ fl oz/1 cup) water, then add the crushed lemongrass, fish and palm sugar.

Bring to the boil, then simmer for 12–15 minutes, or until the fish is cooked, skimming off any froth. Using a slotted spoon, remove the fish and pork belly from the soup. Take the pork meat off the bone, shred it and return to the soup.

Meanwhile, soak the vermicelli in boiling water for 5 minutes. Gently stir to separate the noodles, then drain and refresh under cold water. Use kitchen scissors to cut the vermicelli into easy-to-manage lengths, then divide among six deep bowls. Top with the bean sprouts, eggplant, fish and char siu.

Return the broth to the boil. Add the prawns and squid and poach for 1–2 minutes. Divide the pork belly and seafood among the bowls. Ladle the hot broth over, top with the garlic chives, and serve with the lime wedges and chilli on the side.

POULTRY

BABY CHICKEN CHARGRILLED WITH KAFFIR LIME LEAVES

Gà lá chanh

Variations of this dish appear on *bia hoi* menus across the country, but it is the version from central Vietnam we enjoy most. The galangal, lemongrass and chilli in the marinade give it a wonderful perfume during grilling, and create a complex taste sensation on the palate.

1 SMALL CHICKEN, WEIGHING ABOUT 1 KG (2 LB 3 OZ)
12 KAFFIR LIME LEAVES
2 GARLIC CLOVES
½ LONG RED CHILLI, SEEDED
2 CM (¾ INCH) KNOB FRESH GALANGAL, PEELED
1 LEMONGRASS STEM, WHITE PART ONLY
2 RED ASIAN SHALLOTS, PEELED

¼ TEASPOON FIVE-SPICE
¼ TEASPOON BROWN SUGAR
½ TEASPOON FRESHLY GROUND BLACK PEPPER
1 TABLESPOON FISH SAUCE
1 TABLESPOON VEGETABLE OIL
LIME AND CHILLI DIPPING SALT (SEE PAGE 328), TO SERVE

SERVES 4

To bone the chicken, remove the wing tips using a sharp knife. Then run your knife in a straight line down either side of the backbone. Take the backbone in one hand and hold the breast with the other. Pull the backbone towards you. If you have cut all the way through the skin and tendons, the bones should come away easily. Discard the wing tips and the backbone and lay the chicken on a plastic tray while preparing the marinade.

Roughly chop the lime leaves, garlic, chilli, galangal, lemongrass and shallots. Place in a mortar or food processor. Add the five-spice, sugar, pepper, fish sauce and oil and work into a paste.

Coat the chicken in the lime leaf paste. Cover and marinate in the fridge for 4 hours.

When ready to cook, heat a chargrill or barbecue to medium. Place the chicken onto the hot grill, skin side down. When char lines appear, turn the bird over and continue cooking for a further 15 minutes, or until the juices run clear when a skewer is inserted into the thigh.

Cut the chicken into eight pieces and arrange on a platter. Serve with the dipping salt.

BRAISED PIGEON WITH ARTICHOKES AND LOTUS SEEDS

Chim bồ câu hầm ac ti sô và hạt sen

Hailing from the Central Highlands, this dish is usually prepared for special occasions such as Tet, the Lunar New Year. It is one of the few local dishes that uses artichokes — the Vietnamese mainly use artichokes for making tea.

55 G (2 OZ/⅓ CUP) DRIED CHESTNUTS

70 G (¼ OZ/⅓ CUP) DRIED LOTUS SEEDS

3 RED ASIAN SHALLOTS, FINELY DICED

VEGETABLE OIL, FOR PAN-FRYING

3 GLOBE ARTICHOKES, OUTER LEAVES AND HAIRY CHOKE REMOVED, HEARTS QUARTERED

2 TEASPOONS DRIED GOJI BERRIES

2 TEASPOONS FISH SAUCE

⅓ TEASPOON SICHUAN PEPPERCORNS

¼ TEASPOON FRESHLY GROUND BLACK PEPPER

3 SPRING ONIONS (SCALLIONS), SLICED

2 LARGE SQUAB PIGEONS, ABOUT 450 G (1 LB) EACH

½ TEASPOON SALT

80 ML (2½ FL OZ/⅓ CUP) RICE WINE

750 ML (25½ FL OZ/3 CUPS) CHICKEN STOCK OR WATER

STICKY RICE (SEE PAGE 26), TO SERVE

SERVES 6

Soak the chestnuts and lotus seeds for 2 hours in separate bowls of water.

Drain the chestnuts and lotus seeds and place in a small saucepan. Cover with cold water and bring to simmering point. Cook for 20 minutes, then drain well and set aside.

Sauté the shallot in 1 tablespoon of oil over medium heat until fragrant. Add the lotus seeds, chestnuts, artichokes and goji berries and cook for 2–3 minutes. Add the fish sauce, sichuan peppercorns, pepper and half the spring onion. Remove from the heat and leave to cool slightly.

Preheat the oven to 180°C (350°F). Wash the pigeons inside and out and pat dry with paper towel. Rub the salt onto the outside of the birds. Loosely fill the cavity of each pigeon with the artichoke mixture, then close each cavity with a bamboo skewer.

Heat 2 tablespoons of oil in a heavy-based frying pan over medium heat. When hot, place the pigeons in the pan, breast side down. Cook until golden underneath, before turning them over and browning the other side. Remove the pigeons and put them in a large clay pot or casserole dish.

Return the frying pan to the heat. Add the rice wine and cook until it has reduced by half, then pour in the stock or water and bring to the boil. Pour the liquid over the pigeons and sprinkle any leftover stuffing over the top.

Cover the dish, then transfer to the oven and bake for 10 minutes. Remove the lid and bake for a further 5–8 minutes. To test if the pigeon is cooked, insert a bamboo skewer into the thigh — the juices should run clear.

Sprinkle the pigeons with the remaining spring onion, if desired, and serve with sticky rice.

CHICKEN AND COCONUT ROLLS

Gà cuốn dừa

A good friend's father worked as a cook for the French at the end of the colonial era. This is a dish he created. It is a great example of how Vietnamese cooks invented variations of standard dishes to please the European palates of their French superiors — in this case turning a straightforward spring roll into a more refined poultry parcel by adding coconut and leaving out the rice wrapper.

1 x 1.6 kg (3½ lb) chicken
2 red Asian shallots, peeled
10 kaffir lime leaves
50g (1¾ oz/½ cup) roughly chopped fresh coconut
1 teaspoon fish sauce

½ teaspoon sesame oil
⅓ teaspoon freshly ground black pepper
vegetable oil, for pan-frying
lime and chilli dipping salt (see page 328)

Serves 6

Run a sharp knife along each side of the chicken's breast bone. Place your finger between the breast and the skin and gently lift the skin. Continue separating the skin from the flesh, taking care not to rip or tear the skin as you gently ease it off the meat. Set the skin aside for wrapping the rolls.

Remove the breast fillets from the bone and reserve for another use. Now remove the remaining meat from the chicken carcass, roughly chop and set aside.

Roughly chop the shallots and two of the lime leaves and place in a food processor. Add the coconut and process until you have a coarse mixture. Transfer to a large bowl.

Wipe out the processor, then process the chicken meat until minced (ground). Add the chicken to the coconut mixture, along with the fish sauce, sesame oil, pepper and a pinch of salt. Mix until combined.

To make the rolls, lay the reserved chicken skin flat on a chopping board, then cut it into 9 cm x 6 cm (3½ inch x 2½ inch) rectangles (1). Working with one piece at a time, lay a piece of the skin lengthways on the chopping board. Place a spoonful of the chicken mixture at the base of the skin, then roll up to cover the filling (2). Secure with toothpicks. Repeat with the remaining skins, then shape any leftover chicken mixture into patties.

Heat 2 tablespoons of vegetable oil in a frying pan over medium heat. Add the rolls and the remaining 8 whole lime leaves and fry for 7–8 minutes, or until the rolls are golden brown and cooked through (3).

Serve hot, with the dipping salt.

CHICKEN COOKED IN RICE WINE

Gà hầm rượu

A rustic dish from the Mekong Delta. The French introduced the concept of cooking with wine, and the Vietnamese adopted this method, characteristically putting their own spin on it and using the much stronger local rice wine.

VEGETABLE OIL, FOR PAN-FRYING

4 RED ASIAN SHALLOTS, DICED

3 CM (1¼ INCH) KNOB FRESH GINGER, THINLY SLICED

2 TEASPOONS ANNATTO OIL (SEE PAGE 320)

1 SMALL CHICKEN, ABOUT 1 KG (2 LB 3 OZ), LEFT ON THE BONE AND CUT INTO BITE-SIZED PIECES

2 TABLESPOONS RICE WINE

2 TEASPOONS CHILLI SAUCE (SEE PAGE 322)

2 TEASPOONS OYSTER SAUCE

60 ML (2 FL OZ/¼ CUP) COCONUT MILK

8 GARLIC CLOVES, PEELED BUT LEFT WHOLE

1 TABLESPOON SUGAR

1 TEASPOON SALT

1 HANDFUL THAI BASIL

BOILED RICE (SEE PAGE 18), TO SERVE

SERVES 6

Heat 2 tablespoons of vegetable oil in a large saucepan over medium heat. Add the shallot and fry until fragrant. Add the ginger and annatto oil and stir for 1 minute.

Place the chicken pieces in the saucepan and continue cooking for 8–10 minutes, or until the chicken is evenly coloured, turning the pieces so they brown evenly.

Pour in the rice wine, chilli sauce, oyster sauce, coconut milk and 125 ml (4 fl oz/½ cup) water. Add the garlic, sugar and salt. Bring to the boil, then reduce the heat and simmer for 15 minutes, or until the chicken is cooked through.

Mix the basil through. Serve in bowls, with boiled rice.

CHICKEN NOODLE SOUP

Phở Gà

Pho ga was invented during the Japanese occupation in the 1940s, when beef was very hard to come by — which might explain why this dish is sometimes considered the poor cousin of the more famous and glamorous beef noodle soup, *pho bo*.

We like it as a lighter, more summery variation of *pho*, and it has the added advantage of taking less time to prepare in a home kitchen.

8 RED ASIAN SHALLOTS, UNPEELED

4 CM (1½ INCH) KNOB FRESH GINGER, UNPEELED AND CUT IN HALF

1 x 1.6 KG (3½ LB) CHICKEN

1 TEASPOON SALT

1 CINNAMON STICK

4 STAR ANISE

1 TABLESPOON SUGAR

1 TABLESPOON FISH SAUCE, PLUS EXTRA TO SERVE

600 G (1 LB 5 OZ) FRESH PHO NOODLES

½ WHITE ONION, THINLY SLICED

6 SPRING ONIONS (SCALLIONS) — 3 SLICED, THE OTHER 3 CUT INTO STRIPS

1 HANDFUL CORIANDER (CILANTRO) LEAVES

4 KAFFIR LIME LEAVES, CUT INTO THIN STRIPS

1 LIME, CUT INTO WEDGES

1 LONG RED CHILLI, SLICED

SERVES 6

Chargrill the whole unpeeled shallots and ginger on a barbecue or gas burner over medium heat for 5 minutes, or until they are fragrant and the skin is lightly charred. Remove and cool slightly. Using your fingers, flake off the outer thin layer of skin.

Wash the chicken under cold running water. Place in a large saucepan, cover with cold water and add the salt. Slowly bring to the boil, skimming off any froth that rises to the surface. Immediately reduce the heat, then add the shallots, ginger, cinnamon stick and star anise. Gently simmer for 1 hour, skimming the surface regularly. To ensure a clear broth and moist, tender meat, it is important not to boil the chicken.

Remove the chicken from the broth. Test that it is cooked by inserting a skewer into the thigh — the juices should run clear. Set aside to rest while you finish preparing the broth.

Strain the broth through a fine sieve and discard the aromatics. Return the broth to the saucepan and add the sugar and fish sauce. Now keep the broth at a gentle simmer over low heat.

Cut the breasts and legs from the chicken. Remove all the meat from the bones and slice it into strips.

Bring a saucepan of water to the boil. Drop the noodles into the boiling water and stir with a chopstick for about 20 seconds to separate the noodles. Drain thoroughly and divide among six deep bowls.

Place the chicken on top of the noodles, then top with the onion, spring onion, coriander and lime leaves. Ladle in the hot broth.

Serve with the lime wedges, chilli and some extra fish sauce for diners to adjust the flavour, if desired.

CHICKEN WITH LEMONGRASS AND CHILLI

Gà xào sả ớt

This adaptable dish, originally from the centre of the country, is now commonly served in *bia hoi* eateries and restaurants throughout Vietnam. Instead of the chicken, it is often made with beef, pork, eel or frog's legs — and no, they don't taste like chicken!

5 BONELESS, SKINLESS CHICKEN THIGHS

2½ TABLESPOONS FISH SAUCE

1 TEASPOON FRESHLY GROUND BLACK PEPPER

1 TEASPOON SUGAR

2 LEMONGRASS STEMS, WHITE PART ONLY, FINELY CHOPPED

1 LONG RED CHILLI, CUT INTO THIN RINGS

2 GARLIC CLOVES, ROUGHLY CHOPPED

VEGETABLE OIL, FOR PAN-FRYING

10 SPRING ONIONS (SCALLIONS), SLICED

1 SMALL HANDFUL CORIANDER (CILANTRO) SPRIGS

LIME AND CHILLI DIPPING SALT (SEE PAGE 328), TO SERVE

SERVES 6

Cut the chicken into about six cubes per thigh. Marinate the pieces for 30 minutes in the fish sauce, pepper and sugar.

Fry the lemongrass, chilli and garlic in a lightly oiled hot wok, keeping the wok moving so they don't burn or stick. Once fragrant, add the chicken pieces and keep tossing the wok over medium–high heat to cook them evenly.

When the chicken is lightly coloured, add 80 ml (2½ fl oz/⅓ cup) water. Turn the heat up very high and finish cooking the chicken for another few minutes, until tender and just cooked through.

Add the spring onion and coriander and give the dish a final toss. Serve with the dipping salt.

CRISPY CHICKEN WINGS WITH FISH SAUCE

Cánh gà chiên mắm

With crispy skin on the outside and tender meat inside, these wings are a trusty *bia hoi* stand-by, and also very popular for family get-togethers.

9 CHICKEN WINGS

125 G (4½ OZ/1 CUP) CORNFLOUR (CORNSTARCH)

VEGETABLE OIL, FOR DEEP-FRYING

2 GARLIC CLOVES, FINELY CHOPPED

60 ML (2 FL OZ/¼ CUP) FISH SAUCE

55 G (2 OZ/¼ CUP) SUGAR

1 LONG RED CHILLI, CUT INTO THIN RINGS

1 HANDFUL CORIANDER (CILANTRO)

1 HANDFUL MINT

MARINADE

2 GARLIC CLOVES, FINELY CHOPPED

2 TABLESPOONS FISH SAUCE

½ TEASPOON FRESHLY GROUND BLACK PEPPER

SERVES 6

Cut each chicken wing through the joints into three pieces and place in a shallow tray. Mix together the marinade ingredients, pour over the chicken and toss to coat. Cover and place in the refrigerator for 1–2 hours to allow the flavours to develop.

Remove the chicken from the marinade and dry thoroughly with paper towel. Place on a tray and dust liberally with the cornflour. Toss the wings through the cornflour and shake to remove any excess.

Heat about 4 cm (1½ inches) of oil in a wok or frying pan over medium heat. Gently place the chicken pieces in the oil and fry for 8–10 minutes, until the skin is golden brown and crisp. Remove and drain on paper towel.

Carefully empty the oil into a container for later use and wipe the wok clean.

In a small bowl, mix together the garlic, fish sauce, sugar and 60 ml (2 fl oz/¼ cup) water, stirring to dissolve the sugar.

Return the wok to the heat, add the fish sauce mixture and reduce over medium heat for 4–5 minutes, until syrupy. Add the chilli and the chicken wings and toss to coat the wings with the hot, salty sauce.

Serve on a platter, scattered with the herbs.

THE OTHER FAST FOOD NATION

WHEN OUR DAUGHTER, FRANKA, WAS FOUR YEARS OLD, SHE SNUCK OUT OF THE HOUSE VERY EARLY ONE MORNING WHILE WE WERE STILL ASLEEP. SHE TOOK THE WALLET WITH THE WEEKLY HOUSEKEEPING MONEY FROM THE KITCHEN TABLE, MANAGED TO UNLOCK THE FRONT DOOR, INEXPLICABLY PERSUADED OUR SEPTUAGENARIAN LANDLORD LIVING IN THE BACK BUILDING TO OPEN THE FRONT GATE FOR HER, THEN MARCHED DOWN THE NARROW LANE TO OUR LOCAL STREET MARKET. HER DESTINATION: MS SAU'S STICKY RICE (*XOI*) STALL, FOR HER USUAL BREAKFAST OF *XOI* WITH MUNG BEAN SHAVINGS AND PEANUTS. FRANKA HANDED OVER THE WALLET AND MS SAU REMOVED 5000 DONG (ABOUT 50 CENTS), BEFORE RETURNING IT WITH HER BREAKFAST, AND THEN ORGANISED THE TOFU-SELLER WITH WHOM SHE SHARED HER STALL TO TAKE FRANKA BACK HOME.

Ms Sau's street stall is in many respects typical of the grassroots entrepreneurship of street-food vendors who are the commercial and social backbone of the numerous lanes and alleyways in Vietnam's cities. Like most stallholders, she plunged into self-employment on the back of one food item, based on a family recipe and prepared so often it is now as close to perfection as possible. But food stalls like hers are not just places to buy or eat. They are neighbourhood information exchanges, where patrons from all walks of life socialise and catch up on gossip cheek-by-jowl on blue plastic stools or wooden benches, over their favourite dish.

Street-food vendors turn the streets into an open-air kitchen and the pavement into a dining room. At every corner something tasty is being fried in a wok, simmered in a pot or barbecued on little hibachi-style grills, the cooking stations fuelled by the ubiquitous honeycomb coal briquettes delivered throughout the day by peddlers pushing impossibly overloaded bicycles.

Kerbside dining has become so much a part of everyday life in Vietnam that it is easy to overlook that this street-food revolution is a fairly recent phenomenon. In the first half of the 20th century, a 'takeaway' system was more common. Vendors would wander the streets with food and cooking utensils in baskets strung from bamboo poles, calling out to advertise their wares, and the locals would take their ready-made meals back into their homes. Thirty years of fighting for independence, from 1945 to 1975, followed by economic change and modernisation, caused a role reversal,

with many food vendors claiming a regular spot on the footpath, feeding people who were on the move.

The street-food scene follows a daily rhythm, like a giant tag team of vendors taking on different shifts. Breakfasts are hearty: lumps of delicious sticky rice, bowls of fragrant noodle soup (*pho*) and rice porridge (*chao*), or crunchy baguettes with egg and herbs. Lunches are either based on rice noodles, with meats like the marinated chargrilled pork patties in *bun cha*, or on steamed rice. At com binh dan shops, which are types of lunch buffets, patrons receive a plate with a mountain of rice, then select two or three accompanying side dishes from an array of trays. Other vendors target the after-work and after-school crowd, setting up shop in the afternoons to sell snack foods such as layered sweet soups (*che*) or fried dumplings with pork and quail egg filling (*banh goi*). And finally, there is dinner — the most social meal of the day, where groups of diners huddle around steamboats or kerosene-fired table barbecues, enjoying their meals while reviewing the day's events.

Although meeting their customers' needs for a bellyful of fast, fresh and cheap local fare, the economics of street vending can be difficult. Unlicensed and without legal status, vendors are often pitted against city planners and local authorities who are more concerned with traffic flow than taste sensations.

Luckily, out of economic necessity and tradition, the vendors persist in turning the city into a paradise for food grazers, and in doing so provide us with a window into Vietnam's unique culinary and cultural identity.

DUCK AND BAMBOO NOODLE SOUP

Bún măng vịt

Preparing dried bamboo is a labour of love. It requires overnight soaking, then boiling the following day, and the water needs to be changed at least once during cooking. Dried bamboo is usually only prepared at home on important occasions, such as Tet (Vietnamese New Year), ancestor days, or to farewell the kitchen god, Ong Tao.

Both fresh and dried bamboo have a musty, earthy flavour and perfume. The fresh variety adds crunch to this dish, while the dried one adds a chewy texture.

60 G (2 OZ) DRIED BAMBOO

120 G (4½ OZ) VACUUM-PACKED FRESH BAMBOO

600 G (1 LB 5 OZ) DRIED RICE VERMICELLI

1½ TABLESPOONS FISH SAUCE

3 CM (1¼ INCH) KNOB FRESH GINGER, CUT INTO THIN STRIPS

1 HANDFUL THAI BASIL SPRIGS

1 HANDFUL MINT SPRIGS

4 SPRING ONIONS (SCALLIONS), CUT INTO THIN STRIPS

60 G (2 OZ/⅔ CUP) FRIED SHALLOTS (SEE PAGE 326)

GINGER DIPPING SAUCE (SEE PAGE 327), TO SERVE (OPTIONAL)

BROTH

2 CHICKEN CARCASSES

1 X 2 KG (4 LB 6 OZ) DUCK

4 CM (1½ INCH) KNOB FRESH GINGER, CUT IN HALF

6 SPRING ONIONS (SCALLIONS), TRIMMED

2 LEMONGRASS STEMS, WHITE PART ONLY, CRUSHED

1 TEASPOON SALT

1 TEASPOON SUGAR

SERVES 6

Soak the dried bamboo in cold water overnight.

The next day, drain the bamboo, place in a saucepan and cover with cold water. Bring to the boil, then boil for 1 hour, topping up the water as needed.

Drain, then repeat the boiling process. The bamboo should now be tender, but still a little chewy. Drain and leave to cool, then cut the bamboo into pieces 4 cm (1½ inches) long.

Meanwhile, make the broth. Put the chicken carcasses and duck in a large saucepan and cover with cold water. Slowly bring to the boil, skimming off any froth that rises to the surface. Add the ginger, spring onions, lemongrass, salt and sugar. Reduce the heat and simmer for 1 hour. Transfer the duck to a chopping board and simmer the broth for a further 1 hour.

When the duck is cool enough to handle, use a cleaver to cut it into bite-sized pieces or slices.

Meanwhile, put the fresh bamboo in a saucepan and cover with cold water. Bring to the boil, then reduce the heat and simmer for 15 minutes. Drain and cool, then thinly slice the bamboo.

Soak the vermicelli in boiling water for 4–5 minutes. Gently stir to separate the noodles, then drain and refresh under cold water. Use kitchen scissors to cut the vermicelli into easy-to-manage lengths, then divide among six deep bowls.

Strain the broth through a fine sieve and discard the chicken bones and aromatics. Pour the broth into a clean saucepan. Bring to the boil, then add the fish sauce and ginger.

Arrange the fresh and dried bamboo, herbs, spring onion and duck pieces over the noodles.

Ladle the hot broth over the top. Serve sprinkled with the fried shallots, with dipping sauce on the side if desired.

DUCK RICE PORRIDGE

Cháo vịt

Chao is a popular winter warmer and can also be made with fish or chicken. If you don't have time to roast your own duck, purchase a Peking duck from your local Asian restaurant.

1 ROAST DUCK

6 RED ASIAN SHALLOTS, ROUGHLY CHOPPED

4 CM (1½ INCH) KNOB FRESH GINGER, ROUGHLY CHOPPED, PLUS AN EXTRA 2 CM (¾ INCH) KNOB FRESH GINGER, CUT INTO THIN STRIPS

200 G (7 OZ/1 CUP) LONG-GRAIN WHITE RICE

VEGETABLE OIL OR RENDERED CHICKEN FAT (SEE PAGE 337), FOR PAN-FRYING

1 TABLESPOON FISH SAUCE

1 TEASPOON SUGAR

½ TEASPOON SALT

½ TEASPOON FRESHLY GROUND BLACK PEPPER

4 SPRING ONIONS (SCALLIONS), SLICED

1 SMALL HANDFUL HOLY BASIL LEAVES, CHOPPED

1 SMALL HANDFUL PERILLA LEAVES, CHOPPED

4 SAW-TOOTH CORIANDER (CILANTRO) STEMS, SLICED

GINGER DIPPING SAUCE (SEE PAGE 327), TO SERVE

SERVES 6

Remove all the meat from the duck. Cut into bite-sized pieces and set aside.

Use a meat cleaver to chop the duck bones into pieces. Put the bones in a saucepan and cover with cold water. Slowly bring to the boil over medium heat, skimming off any froth that rises to the surface.

Meanwhile, put the shallot and the chopped ginger in a mortar and coarsely crush together using a pestle. Add the mixture to the stock and simmer gently for 2 hours. Strain the stock and discard the duck bones and aromatics.

Meanwhile, put the rice in a dry frying pan and cook over medium heat for 2–4 minutes, until lightly golden. Transfer to a food processor and blend for 5 seconds. Set aside.

Pour 1 litre (34 fl oz/4 cups) of the duck stock into a clean saucepan and bring to the boil.

In another saucepan, heat a little oil or chicken fat over medium heat and fry the toasted rice for 2–3 minutes, or until the grains start to look transparent. Pour in the boiling stock, then stir in the fish sauce, sugar, salt and pepper. Gently simmer for 20 minutes, stirring often.

Stir the duck meat and the ginger strips into the rice and simmer for 5 minutes, or until the rice is cooked. Remove from the heat and stir in the spring onion and herbs.

Spoon the rice porridge into six bowls and sprinkle with extra pepper, if desired. Serve with the dipping sauce.

GINGER CHICKEN

Gà rang gừng

It is best to use young ginger in this succulent dish, as the flavour of older ginger can be too strong. The idea is to retain the subtle perfume of the ginger throughout the cooking process, and then balance it with the delicate, fresh flavour of the lime leaf, added just prior to serving.

1 x 1.6 KG (3½ LB) CHICKEN

2 TABLESPOONS FISH SAUCE

1 TEASPOON CASTER (SUPERFINE) SUGAR

½ TEASPOON FRESHLY GROUND BLACK PEPPER

VEGETABLE OIL, FOR PAN-FRYING

6 GARLIC CLOVES, CHOPPED

1 TABLESPOON ANNATTO OIL (SEE PAGE 320)

5 CM (2 INCH) KNOB FRESH GINGER, CUT INTO THIN STRIPS

3 KAFFIR LIME LEAVES, CUT INTO THIN STRIPS

SOY CHILLI DIPPING SAUCE (SEE PAGE 340), TO SERVE

SERVES 6

Carefully cut the chicken into pieces small enough to be easily picked up with chopsticks. Marinate the chicken for 30 minutes in the fish sauce, sugar and pepper.

Heat 1 tablespoon of vegetable oil in a wok over medium heat and fry the garlic until fragrant, keeping the garlic moving so it doesn't burn or stick.

Add the annatto oil, ginger and chicken pieces and stir-fry until the chicken is evenly coloured. Pour in 125 ml (4 fl oz/ ½ cup) water, increase the heat and cook for 5–9 minutes, or until the chicken is cooked through.

Toss the lime leaves through and serve immediately, with the dipping sauce.

HOI AN CHICKEN AND RICE

Cơm gà Hội An

This is a Vietnamese version of the classic dish Hainan chicken, originally brought to Hoi An by Chinese traders. The addition of Vietnamese mint gives it that local twist.

1 X 1.6 KG (3½ LB) CHICKEN

3 CM (1¼ INCH) KNOB FRESH GINGER, THINLY SLICED

1 ONION, ROUGHLY CHOPPED

2 SPRING ONIONS (SCALLIONS), CUT INTO THIRDS

1 TEASPOON SUGAR

1 TEASPOON SALT

6 WHOLE BLACK PEPPERCORNS

2 TABLESPOONS FISH SAUCE

400 G (14 OZ/2 CUPS) JASMINE RICE

2 TABLESPOONS RENDERED CHICKEN FAT (SEE PAGE 337) OR VEGETABLE OIL

3 RED ASIAN SHALLOTS, FINELY DICED

2 GARLIC CLOVES, FINELY DICED

TO SERVE

1 CUCUMBER, SLICED

1 SMALL HANDFUL VIETNAMESE MINT

1 SMALL HANDFUL MINT

2 TABLESPOONS FRIED SHALLOTS (SEE PAGE 326)

1 LIME, CUT INTO 6 WEDGES

SOY CHILLI DIPPING SAUCE (SEE PAGE 340)

CHILLI SAUCE (SEE PAGE 322)

SERVES 6

Wash the chicken and pat dry with paper towel. Place the ginger, onion and spring onion into the cavity of the chicken.

Place the chicken in a large saucepan and cover with cold water. Add the sugar, salt and peppercorns. Bring to the boil, then reduce the heat and simmer for 45–50 minutes, skimming off any froth that rises to the surface. Test whether the chicken is cooked by inserting a skewer into the thigh — the juices will run clear.

Remove the chicken from the stock and leave to cool slightly. Take the chicken meat from the bone and cut or tear into strips. Cover and keep warm.

Remove any fat from the surface of the stock and reserve for cooking the rice. Add the fish sauce to the stock and place back over the heat. Reduce the stock by approximately one-third to intensify the flavour. Strain the stock through a colander lined with a piece of fine muslin (cheesecloth).

Rinse the rice under cold running water until the water runs clear. Run your hand through the rice to get rid of any excess water. Set aside.

In a saucepan, heat the chicken fat or oil over medium heat, then sauté the shallot and garlic until fragrant. Add the rice and stir. Continue cooking for 2–3 minutes, or until the rice grains are hot to touch — this will help the rice readily absorb the flavours from the aromatics and the stock.

Pour in 625 ml (21 fl oz/2½ cups) of the stock, standing back from the pan as it will bubble and spit a little. Stir the rice, then cover the pan and reduce to a simmer. Allow to cook for 15 minutes.

Turn off the heat, but leave the lid on for a further 10 minutes to let the cooking process finish.

To serve the chicken and rice, place a mound of rice on six individual plates. Arrange the cucumber and herbs beside the rice. Place a small pile of chicken next to the rice and drizzle with a teaspoon of hot stock to keep it moist.

Top the rice with the fried shallots. Serve with the lime wedges and the two dipping sauces.

PIGEON OVER STICKY RICE

Xôi chim

This dish is common in northern Vietnam, along the border to Laos — obviously taking its inspiration from the Laotian dish, *lahp*. You can use quail, duck or even chicken in place of the pigeon if it is unavailable, or if you don't have the time to bone it.

3 LARGE SQUAB PIGEONS, ABOUT 450 G (1 LB) EACH

VEGETABLE OIL, FOR PAN-FRYING

2 RED ASIAN SHALLOTS, FINELY DICED

2 GARLIC CLOVES, FINELY CHOPPED

2 LEMONGRASS STEMS, WHITE PART ONLY, FINELY CHOPPED

1/3 TEASPOON SUGAR

1/2 TEASPOON SALT

1/3 TEASPOON FRESHLY GROUND BLACK PEPPER

1/2 LONG RED CHILLI, CUT INTO THIN RINGS

3 SPRING ONIONS (SCALLIONS), THINLY SLICED

1 SMALL HANDFUL CORIANDER (CILANTRO)

2 TEASPOONS FISH SAUCE

STICKY RICE (SEE PAGE 26), TO SERVE

SERVES 6

Debone the pigeons using a sharp knife. To do this, place the bird on a chopping board, breast side down. Run the knife down both sides of the backbone, cutting through the skin and flesh. Hook your finger in the neck opening, then gently remove the backbone by pulling it towards you. Next, cut around the rib cage, removing the delicate breast meat. You should now be able to remove the breast bone by placing your finger on each side and pulling it towards you. Run the knife along the leg and wing bones and pull out the bones. Now very finely dice the pigeon meat and skin. Place in the refrigerator as you repeat the process with the remaining two birds. (You can freeze the bones for later use in a stock.)

Heat 2 tablespoons oil in a wok or frying pan. When hot, add the shallot, garlic and lemongrass and cook over high heat until fragrant.

Add the pigeon meat, sugar, salt and pepper and stir-fry for 2–3 minutes, ensuring that the ingredients are constantly moving so they will cook evenly and won't stick to the wok.

Lastly, add the chilli, spring onion, coriander and fish sauce and toss to combine.

Remove from the wok and serve with sticky rice.

ROAST CHICKEN

Gà rô ti

A Vietnamese take on a classic dish. This dish is particularly tasty in Vietnam, as most chickens you buy in the old-fashioned 'wet markets' are truly free range. For a southern Vietnamese variation, add lemongrass when pounding the garlic and shallots.

1 x 1.6 KG (3½ LB) CHICKEN
2 GARLIC CLOVES, ROUGHLY CHOPPED
2 RED ASIAN SHALLOTS, ROUGHLY CHOPPED
2 STAR ANISE
1 CINNAMON STICK
2 TABLESPOONS SOY SAUCE
1 TABLESPOON FISH SAUCE

1 TABLESPOON HONEY
1 TEASPOON ANNATTO OIL (SEE PAGE 320)
½ TEASPOON SESAME OIL
STICKY RICE (SEE PAGE 26), TO SERVE
LIME AND CHILLI DIPPING SALT (SEE PAGE 328), TO SERVE

SERVES 6

Rinse the chicken inside and out; pat dry with paper towel.

Place the garlic, shallot, star anise and cinnamon stick in a mortar and pound to a fine paste. Transfer to a bowl, then add the soy sauce, fish sauce, honey, annatto oil and sesame oil and mix to combine.

Pour the mixture over the chicken and massage it into the skin, inside and out. Cover the chicken and refrigerate for 4–6 hours to allow the flavours to develop.

Preheat the oven to 220°C (430°F). Place the chicken on its side in a baking dish. Transfer to the hot oven and roast for 20 minutes. Turn the bird over onto the other side and roast for a further 20 minutes.

Now turn the bird breast side up, and spoon over any juices from the bottom of the dish. Roast for a final 20 minutes. Check whether the chicken is cooked by inserting a bamboo skewer into the thigh — the juices should run clear. Remove the chicken from the oven and leave to rest for 5 minutes.

Cut the chicken into pieces, using a cleaver or poultry shears. Arrange on a platter and serve with the sticky rice and dipping salt.

ROAST DUCK

Vịt nướng

In Vietnam the ducks are usually prepared in street rotisseries over burning charcoal, which gives them a distinct smoky flavour. Instead of roasting the duck in the oven, you can cook it on a rotisserie for about 1 hour, if your barbecue has one.

This is a street food that people take home to eat with rice and steamed greens. We have also been known to make a risotto out of it.

1 x 2 KG (4 lb 6 OZ) DUCK	2 TABLESPOONS FISH SAUCE
2 STAR ANISE	1 TABLESPOON ANNATTO OIL (SEE PAGE 320)
1 CINNAMON STICK	1 TABLESPOON HONEY
1 TEASPOON SICHUAN PEPPERCORNS	2 TEASPOONS SOY SAUCE
4 CLOVES	6 GARLIC CLOVES, ROUGHLY CHOPPED
½ TEASPOON GROUND GINGER	1 LONG RED CHILLI, CUT IN HALF LENGTHWAYS
½ TEASPOON FENNEL SEEDS	4 SPRING ONIONS (SCALLIONS), CUT INTO THIRDS
3 CM (1¼ INCH) KNOB FRESH GINGER, ROUGHLY CHOPPED	**SERVES 6**

Preheat the oven to 160°C (320°F).

Meanwhile, remove the neck and giblets from the duck and cut off any excess fat. Wash the duck under cold running water, then pat dry with paper towel. Using your hand, carefully separate the duck skin from the flesh, taking care not to tear the skin, and leaving it still attached. Set the duck aside.

Put the star anise, cinnamon stick, sichuan peppercorns, cloves, ground ginger and fennel seeds on a baking tray and roast for 5 minutes, or until fragrant. Transfer the spices to a mortar and grind together using a pestle. Stir in the chopped ginger, then rub the spices into the duck flesh under the skin, as well as inside the cavity.

Refrigerate the duck overnight, without covering it. This allows the skin of the duck to dry out, which will help it become crisp during roasting.

When you're ready to roast the duck, preheat the oven to 220°C (430°F).

Combine the fish sauce, annatto oil, honey and soy sauce in a bowl. Rub the mixture into the duck skin and inside the cavity. Put the garlic, chilli and spring onion inside the duck and secure with a bamboo skewer.

Place the duck on its side in a baking dish and roast for 30 minutes, basting with the pan juices. Turn the duck over onto the other side and roast for a further 30 minutes.

Reduce the oven temperature to 200°C (400°F). Turn the duck breast side up, then roast for a final 20 minutes, or until the juices run clear when a skewer is inserted into the thigh.

SOY-POACHED CHICKEN

Gà kho xì dầu

The stock from this dish will keep for up to 3 months in the refrigerator. Use the stock to make this dish again, or to poach chicken for use in salads or baguettes, or to poach chicken wings or drumsticks that you can then fry until crispy-skinned. Just be sure to boil the stock for 10 minutes before and after each use and then strain it.

1 X 1.6 KG (3½ LB) CHICKEN
BOILED RICE (SEE PAGE 18), TO SERVE

STOCK
1 LITRE (34 FL OZ/4 CUPS) SOY SAUCE
60 ML (2 FL OZ/¼ CUP) RICE VINEGAR
125 ML (4 FL OZ/½ CUP) FISH SAUCE
2 TABLESPOONS SUGAR
2 TABLESPOONS SESAME OIL

1 TEASPOON FIVE-SPICE
3 STAR ANISE
1 CINNAMON STICK
4 CM (1½ INCH) KNOB FRESH GINGER, SLICED
4 GARLIC CLOVES, PEELED
6 SPRING ONIONS (SCALLIONS), CUT IN HALF
2 LONG RED CHILLIES, CUT IN HALF LENGTHWAYS

SERVES 6

Combine all the stock ingredients and 2.5 litres (85 fl oz/ 10 cups) water in a saucepan large enough to hold the chicken. Bring to the boil, then reduce the heat and simmer for 10 minutes.

Gently lower the chicken into the stock. Place a small plate on top to ensure the entire bird is completely covered by the liquid. Slowly bring back to simmering point and cook for 25 minutes.

Remove the pan from the heat. Allow the chicken to remain in the stock for a further 2 hours for maximum flavour.

Remove the chicken from the stock and cut into serving pieces.

Strain the stock into a clean saucepan. Bring back to the boil, then reduce the heat and leave to simmer for 10 minutes. Transfer the stock to a storage container, leave to cool, then refrigerate for later use.

Serve the chicken at room temperature, with boiled rice and your favourite vegetable. We particularly like it with the Cabbage with egg and fish sauce recipe (see page 40).

PORK, BEEF AND GOAT

ARTICHOKE AND PORK RIB SOUP

Canh ac ti sô và sườn lợn

A hearty dish from Dalat in the Central Highlands. The French introduced artichokes to the market gardens surrounding the town, but there are only a few local dishes featuring this vegetable, as it is mostly used to make tea.

VEGETABLE OIL, FOR PAN-FRYING

1 KG (2 LB 3 OZ) PORK RIBS, CUT INTO 3–4 CM (1¼–1½ INCH) LENGTHS BY YOUR BUTCHER

3 GLOBE ARTICHOKES

1 LEMON, CUT IN HALF

2 TABLESPOONS FISH SAUCE

½ TEASPOON SALT

½ TEASPOON FRESHLY GROUND BLACK PEPPER

1 HANDFUL RICE PADDY HERB

BOILED RICE (SEE PAGE 18), TO SERVE

SERVES 6

Heat 1 tablespoon of oil in a large saucepan over medium heat. When hot, add the pork and cook for 5–8 minutes, until the ribs are evenly coloured.

Pour in 2 litres (68 fl oz/8 cups) water and add the salt. Slowly bring to the boil, skimming off any froth that rises to the surface. Reduce the heat and simmer for 1 hour.

Meanwhile, prepare the artichokes. Trim the stems and remove any tough outer leaves, rubbing the lemon juice over any cut areas to prevent discolouration. Cut off and discard the top third of the artichokes.

Cut the artichokes in half lengthways and remove the hairy centre, if they are older artichokes. Drop the prepared artichokes into a saucepan, then pour in enough boiling water to cover them. Weigh the artichokes down with an upturned plate so they are fully submerged in the water and will cook evenly. Reduce the heat and simmer for 15–20 minutes, or until tender.

Add the cooked artichokes and half their cooking liquid to the pork broth. Season with the fish sauce, pepper and rice paddy herb. Taste to check if any additional seasoning is required before ladling into large bowls.

Serve with boiled rice.

BAGUETTE WITH PÂTÉ AND COLD CUTS

Bánh mì pa tê

As fillings for Vietnamese baguettes, we particularly like roast pork or char siu pork, which can be purchased at Asian cafes. Alternatively, for a simple lunch, ham or poached chicken are also possible. Fried tofu can be added for some extra crunch.

6 SMALL VIETNAMESE BAGUETTES (SEE PAGE 28)

125 G (4½ OZ/½ CUP) MAYONNAISE (SEE PAGE 329)

180 G (6½ OZ) CHICKEN LIVER PÂTÉ

12 SLICES OF YOUR FAVOURITE COOKED MEAT, SUCH AS PORK LOAF (SEE PAGE 302)

3 LONG RED CHILLIES, SEEDED AND SLICED

1 HANDUL CORIANDER (CILANTRO) SPRIGS

3 LEBANESE (SHORT) CUCUMBERS, SLICED

200 G (7 OZ) CARROT AND DAIKON PICKLE (SEE PAGE 321)

30 ML (1 FL OZ) CLASSIC DIPPING SAUCE (SEE PAGE 323)

SERVES 6

Heat the baguettes in a hot oven for 1 minute, then cut each in half and remove some of the soft centre (reserve these for making breadcrumbs).

Spread the mayonnaise on the top half of the baguettes, and spread the pâté on the bottom.

Fill the centres with the sliced meat, chilli, coriander, cucumber and pickles.

Drizzle the dipping sauce onto the sandwich fillings and serve immediately.

BARBECUED PORK TWO WAYS ON RICE VERMICELLI

Bún chả

Bun cha was traditionally sold by roving vendors, who carried it in baskets hanging on poles and served it on round bamboo trays. It is now offered by countless street stalls.

This is a very popular lunchtime dish in Hanoi, where stallholders start to fan their charcoal burners mid-morning, not only to increase the heat of the embers, but also to entice customers with the smoky aroma of the chargrilled, marinated meat.

25 ml (¾ fl oz) fish sauce
3 garlic cloves, chopped
8 red Asian shallots, finely chopped
1 tablespoon sugar
1 x 300 g (10½ oz) portion pork belly
350 g (12½ oz) pork shoulder, roughly chopped
1 egg
10 garlic chives, sliced

600 g (1 lb 5 oz) dried rice vermicelli
Bun cha dipping sauce (see page 321), to serve
150 g (5½ oz) bean sprouts
1 butter lettuce or stem lettuce, leaves separated
1 handful coriander (cilantro) sprigs
1 handful perilla

Serves 6

Combine the fish sauce, garlic, shallot and sugar, stirring to dissolve the sugar.

Cut the pork belly into slices 2 cm (¾ inch) thick. Cover with half the fish sauce mixture and marinate in the refrigerator for 2 hours.

Meanwhile, mince the pork shoulder in a food processor until finely ground. Place in a large bowl with the egg, garlic chives and remaining fish sauce mixture. Cover and marinate in the refrigerator for 2 hours.

Soak the vermicelli in boiling water for 4–5 minutes. Gently stir to separate the noodles, then drain and refresh under cold water. Use kitchen scissors to cut the vermicelli into easy-to-manage lengths.

Heat a chargrill or barbecue to medium–high. Using damp fingers, form the pork into patties about 3 cm (1¼ inches) in diameter. Cook the pork patties and pork belly slices on the hot grill for 3–5 minutes, or until they are cooked through and grill lines appear.

To serve, divide the dipping sauce among six small bowls. Add three patties and four pieces of barbecued pork to each large serving bowl, and put the remaining pork on a platter in the centre of the table.

Arrange the noodles, bean sprouts, lettuce leaves and herbs on another platter and place within easy chopstick reach.

Diners dip the noodles and salad ingredients into their dipping sauce before eating with the pork.

BARBECUED PORK RIBS

Sườn nướng

This dish has always been a crowd-pleaser, and has the added advantage of being fairly easy to prepare — great for lazy summer Sundays. It is full of robust flavours, and barbecuing the ribs releases a truly mouthwatering aroma.

Ask your butcher to cut the pork ribs into manageable pieces for you.

1.5 kg (3 lb 5 oz) pork ribs, chopped by your butcher
50 ml (1¾ fl oz) soy sauce
1 tablespoon fish sauce
3 teaspoons annatto oil (see page 320)
6 garlic cloves, roughly chopped
3 cm (1¼ inch) knob fresh ginger, roughly chopped
4 red Asian shallots, roughly chopped
1 long red chilli, chopped

1 tablespoon brown sugar
2 teaspoons five-spice
½ teaspoon freshly ground black pepper
2 star anise, crushed
1 cinnamon stick, crushed
boiled rice (see page 18), to serve

SERVES 6

Place the pork in a shallow tray. Combine all the remaining ingredients in a bowl, then pour over the ribs and toss to coat (1). Cover with plastic wrap and marinate in the refrigerator for 8 hours, or overnight.

Remove the ribs from the refrigerator 30 minutes before you wish to cook them.

Steam the ribs on a steaming rack set over a saucepan of boiling water for 45 minutes (2).

Meanwhile, heat a barbecue or charcoal grill to medium–high. Grill the ribs for 15 minutes, or until grill lines appear and the meat takes on a deep golden colour (3).

Serve with boiled rice.

BARBECUED LEMONGRASS-MARINATED PORK WITH RICE VERMICELLI

Bún thịt nướng

Among the three broad food regions of the south, centre and north, you can find variations of the same culinary theme. This dish, for example, is Hue's answer to Hanoi's bun cha.

350 G (12½ OZ) PORK SHOULDER

4 GARLIC CLOVES, ROUGHLY CHOPPED

3 LEMONGRASS STEMS, WHITE PART ONLY, ROUGHLY CHOPPED

2 TEASPOONS SUGAR

½ TEASPOON SALT

1 TEASPOON FRESHLY GROUND BLACK PEPPER

2 TABLESPOONS FISH SAUCE

1 TABLESPOON SESAME SEEDS

PEANUT SAUCE

4 RED ASIAN SHALLOTS, FINELY DICED

2 GARLIC CLOVES, FINELY CHOPPED

VEGETABLE OIL, FOR PAN-FRYING

4 TABLESPOONS UNSALTED PEANUTS, ROASTED

4 TABLESPOONS SESAME SEEDS, TOASTED

2 TEASPOONS PEANUT BUTTER

1 TEASPOON SALT

1 TEASPOON SUGAR

TO SERVE

600 G (1 LB 5 OZ) DRIED RICE VERMICELLI

1 SMALL BUTTER LETTUCE, THINLY SLICED

100 G (3½ OZ) BEAN SPROUTS

1 SMALL HANDFUL THAI BASIL

1 SMALL HANDFUL MINT

SERVES 6

Cut the pork into slices about 1 cm (½ inch) thick, so they are easy to pick up with chopsticks.

Using a mortar and pestle or a food processor, form a paste out of the garlic, lemongrass, sugar, salt, pepper and fish sauce. Add the sesame seeds and slightly crush them. Rub the paste into the sliced pork and let it sit for about 1 hour for the flavours to develop.

To make the peanut sauce, sauté the shallot and garlic in 1 tablespoon of oil until fragrant. Add 250 ml (8½ fl oz/1 cup) water and the remaining peanut sauce ingredients and stir until well combined. Slowly bring to the boil, then remove from the heat.

Soak the vermicelli in boiling water for 4–5 minutes. Gently stir to separate the noodles, then drain and refresh under cold water. Use kitchen scissors to cut the vermicelli into easy-to-manage lengths, then divide among six bowls.

Heat a chargrill or barbecue to medium–high. Chargrill the pork for approximately 1–2 minutes on each side.

To serve, top the noodles with the lettuce, bean sprouts and herbs. Arrange the pork over the top and ladle the warm peanut sauce over each dish.

BARBECUED PORK RIBS WITH SESAME SEEDS AND GREEN CHILLI DIPPING SALT

Sườn lợn tẩm vừng nướng

Tracey and I enjoyed a wonderful version of this dish in Buon Ma Thuot in the Central Highlands, where the green chilli, which gives the dipping sauce that special edge, is grown.

Ask your butcher to cut the pork ribs through the bone into 5 cm (2 inch) pieces.

1.5 KG (3 LB 5 OZ) PORK RIBS, CUT INTO 5 CM (2 INCH) PIECES
1 SMALL HANDFUL MINT
GREEN CHILLI DIPPING SALT (SEE PAGE 327), TO SERVE
STICKY RICE (SEE PAGE 26), TO SERVE

MARINADE
2 GARLIC CLOVES, ROUGHLY CHOPPED
2 RED ASIAN SHALLOTS, ROUGHLY CHOPPED
3 LEMONGRASS STEMS, WHITE PART ONLY, ROUGHLY CHOPPED

2 TABLESPOONS FISH SAUCE
1 TABLESPOON SOY SAUCE
1 TABLESPOON HONEY
1 TEASPOON FIVE-SPICE
1 TEASPOON SUGAR
½ TEASPOON FRESHLY GROUND BLACK PEPPER
1½ TABLESPOONS SESAME SEEDS

SERVES 6

Place the pork in a shallow tray.

Combine the marinade ingredients in a bowl, stirring to dissolve the sugar. Coat the ribs with the marinade, cover with plastic wrap and marinate in the refrigerator for 8 hours, or overnight.

Remove the ribs from the refrigerator about 30 minutes before you wish to cook them.

Heat a barbecue or chargrill to medium. Cook the ribs for 8–10 minutes on each side, until they are cooked through and a deep golden colour.

Serve the ribs scattered with the mint, with the dipping salt and sticky rice on the side.

BEEF AND GREEN PEPPERCORNS IN BANANA LEAF WITH RICE PAPER

Bò cuốn lá chuối

Most Vietnamese like their meat well done, but for this dish we prefer it cooked medium to medium–rare so it stays tender. Always rest the beef before serving, so you don't lose the precious juices when you slice it. Fresh green peppercorns feature in the cuisines of Vietnam, Cambodia and Thailand; in Australia, they are available fresh from July to August. You can instead use green peppercorns in brine.

400 G (14 OZ) PORTERHOUSE OR FILLET STEAK

1 SMALL BANANA LEAF, FOR WRAPPING

2 GREEN BANANAS

600 G (1 LB 5 OZ) DRIED RICE VERMICELLI, SOAKED AS DIRECTED ON PAGE 250

1 PINEAPPLE, NOT TOO RIPE, FLESH CUT INTO BATONS

1 LEMONGRASS STEM, WHITE PART ONLY, THINLY SLICED

1 LONG RED CHILLI, SEEDED AND CUT INTO THIN STRIPS

1 SMALL HANDFUL CORIANDER (CILANTRO) LEAVES

1 SMALL HANDFUL MINT

1 SMALL HANDFUL RICE PADDY HERB

18 RICE PAPER SHEETS, ABOUT 18 CM (7 INCHES) IN SIZE

CLASSIC DIPPING SAUCE (SEE PAGE 323), TO SERVE

MARINADE

2 LEMONGRASS STEMS, WHITE PART ONLY, FINELY CHOPPED

2 STEMS FRESH GREEN PEPPERCORNS, CRUSHED

PINCH OF FRESHLY CRACKED BLACK PEPPERCORNS

1 TABLESPOON FISH SAUCE

SERVES 6

Combine the marinade ingredients and mix through the beef. Leave to sit for 30 minutes, then wrap the marinated beef mixture in the banana leaf, securing the parcel with skewers (1).

Meanwhile, heat a barbecue or chargrill to high. Using a sharp knife, peel off the outer layer of skin from each banana, leaving on a thin layer of the skin for texture (2). Thinly slice the banana lengthways and arrange on a platter with the noodles, pineapple, lemongrass, chilli and herbs.

Cook the beef parcel on the hot grill for 5–6 minutes on each side, or until medium–rare. Remove from the heat and leave

to rest, wrapped, for 10 minutes. Then unwrap the banana leaf, thinly slice the beef and arrange on a serving platter.

Soften the rice paper sheets by dipping them one at a time into warm water for 1 second. Place on a flat surface, wait for 20 seconds, then soak up any excess water with a clean cloth.

Invite your guests to take a rice paper sheet and roll their own spring rolls. To do this, they put a strip of beef and small portions of the fruit, lemongrass, chilli, noodles and herbs on the bottom third of the sheet, bring the bottom of the wrapper up over the filling, then fold in the sides and roll up (3).

BEEF AND MUSTARD LEAF ROLLS

Bò cuốn cải

Wasabi has recently become fashionable, and the dipping sauce is a good example of the Vietnamese taking what they like from another culture and making it their own. This dish is from Ho Chi Minh City.

Mustard leaf, also called mustard greens, is a herb used in many Asian cuisines, including those from China, India and Japan. Its flavour is reminiscent of pepper, horseradish and, as the name suggests, mustard. If you can't obtain mustard leaves, just use crisp lettuce leaves instead.

200 G (7OZ) BEEF FILLET, THINLY SLICED

1 TABLESPOON VEGETABLE OIL

12 SPRING ONIONS (SCALLIONS), GREEN PART ONLY

300 G (10½ OZ) DRIED RICE VERMICELLI

12 MUSTARD LEAVES

½ UNRIPE PINEAPPLE, PEELED AND CUT INTO 4 CM (1½ INCH) BATONS

1 SMALL HANDFUL MINT

OYSTER AND WASABI DIPPING SAUCE (SEE PAGE 329), TO SERVE

MARINADE

3 GARLIC CLOVES, FINELY CHOPPED

3 RED ASIAN SHALLOTS, FINELY CHOPPED

PINCH OF SUGAR

¼ TEASPOON FRESHLY GROUND BLACK PEPPER

2 TEASPOONS FISH SAUCE

1 TEASPOON VEGETABLE OIL

SERVES 6

Combine the marinade ingredients, stirring to dissolve the sugar. Pour the marinade over the beef and toss to coat. Set aside for 15 minutes to allow the flavours to develop.

Heat a wok over high heat, add the oil and stir-fry the beef for 2–3 minutes, until browned. Remove from the wok; set aside.

Blanch the spring onions in a saucepan of boiling salted water for a few seconds, until they have wilted; this will make them pliable enough to tie up the rolls without them tearing. Plunge the spring onions into iced water so they retain their colour. Remove the chilled spring onions and drain well.

Soak the vermicelli in boiling water for 4–5 minutes. Stir to separate the noodles, then drain and refresh under cold water. Use kitchen scissors to cut the vermicelli into easy-to-manage lengths.

Trim the mustard leaves to roughly 10 cm (4 inch) lengths, then place on a chopping board, vein side up. Put a small pile of noodles, a pineapple baton, some beef and mint onto the bottom third of the leaf. Fold the leaf over to enclose the filling and keep rolling. To secure the roll, place the spring onion around the roll and tie with a knot. Repeat with the remaining ingredients.

Serve with the dipping sauce.

BEEF AND PORK LIVER IN CAUL FAT

Bò cuốn mỡ chài

Caul fat keeps the meat moist during cooking, and also crisps up nicely, adding texture to this dish.
Soak it overnight in salted water to remove any residue or blood; use as directed, or freeze for later use.

1 x 100 g (3½ oz) pork liver
1 x 250 g (9 oz) beef rump, cut into 9 pieces
½ lap cheong sausage
200 g (7 oz) caul fat, cut into nine 8 cm (3¼ inch) squares
vegetable oil, for pan-frying
2 red Asian shallots, finely chopped
2 garlic cloves, finely chopped
1 lemongrass stem, white part only, finely chopped
2 tablespoons roasted peanuts, pounded to a paste
1 handful coriander (cilantro)
1 handful mint
peanut, garlic and shallot dipping sauce (see page 335)

MARINADE

4 cm (1½ inch) knob fresh ginger, finely chopped
1 lemongrass stem, white part only, finely chopped
6 garlic cloves, finely chopped
3 red Asian shallots, finely chopped
2 tablespoons roasted peanuts, roughly chopped
1 tablespoon oyster sauce
½ teaspoon sugar
¼ teaspoon salt
⅓ teaspoon freshly ground black pepper

SERVES 6

Remove and discard membrane from the liver. Place the liver in a saucepan with cold water, bring to simmering point and cook for 3 minutes. Remove the liver from the liquid and leave to cool. Slice into nine pieces and place in a shallow tray with the beef (1). Combine the marinade ingredients, spoon over the meats and toss to coat (2). Leave to marinate for 15 minutes.

Meanwhile, fry the lap cheong sausage in a hot wok or frying pan for 3–4 minutes, then remove and cut into nine slices.

Place a slice of beef on a chopping board. Top with a piece of liver and sausage, then fold the beef over to encase the filling. Continue with the remaining beef, liver and sausage.

Heat about 1 cm (½ inch) of oil in a frying pan over medium–high heat. Heat a chargrill or barbecue to medium–high. Lay the caul fat squares on a board, then put the beef rolls on top. Fold the caul over the beef rolls, tucking in the sides (3).

Fry the beef rolls in the hot pan for 2 minutes on both sides. Drain well on paper towel, then char on the hot grill on both sides for 3–4 minutes. Transfer to a platter and keep warm.

Sauté the shallot, garlic and lemongrass in 1 tablespoon of oil until fragrant. Add the peanuts and cook for 1 minute, then spoon the mixture over the warm beef parcels. Serve with the herbs and dipping sauce.

BEEF IN BETEL LEAF

Bò lá lốt

This dish was one of my earliest introductions to Vietnamese street food. The wonderful aroma of the betel leaf charring on the outdoor charcoal burners holds a dear place in my culinary memory.

Though commonly known as betel leaf, this ingredient is actually not part of the betel nut tree! The tree is just the host to the special vine that produces this leaf.

250 G (9 OZ) MINCED (GROUND) BEEF FILLET

80 G (2¾ OZ) MINCED (GROUND) PORK FAT

2 TABLESPOONS PEANUTS, ROASTED AND CHOPPED

1 LEMONGRASS STEM, WHITE PART ONLY, FINELY CHOPPED

¾ TEASPOON SUGAR

1 TEASPOON FISH SAUCE

⅓ TEASPOON FIVE-SPICE

⅓ TEASPOON SESAME OIL

18 WHOLE BETEL NUT LEAVES, WITHOUT ANY TEARS

VEGETABLE OIL, FOR BRUSHING

TO SERVE

300 G (10½ OZ) DRIED RICE VERMICELLI

1 BUTTER LETTUCE, SEPARATED INTO CUPS

1 LARGE HANDFUL CORIANDER (CILANTRO) LEAVES

1 LARGE HANDFUL MINT

1 LARGE HANDFUL THAI BASIL

30 G (1 OZ) PEANUTS, ROASTED AND CHOPPED

CLASSIC DIPPING SAUCE (SEE PAGE 323)

SERVES 6

Soak six bamboo skewers in cold water for 30 minutes.

Meanwhile, heat a chargrill or barbecue to medium–high.

Combine the beef, pork fat, peanuts, lemongrass, sugar, fish sauce, five-spice and sesame oil in a bowl and mix thoroughly.

Prepare the betel leaves by removing any tough stems and wiping the leaves with a damp cloth. Place the leaves on a work surface, smooth side down, with the point of the leaf furthest away from you. Divide the beef mixture equally among the leaves, placing it just below the centre of the leaf (1). Roll each leaf up, taking care to fold in the sides (2,3).

Thread three rolls onto each skewer. Brush the rolls with oil and chargrill for a few minutes on each side, until the leaves are nicely charred and the beef is just cooked through.

Meanwhile, soak the vermicelli in boiling water for 4–5 minutes. Gently stir to separate the noodles, then drain and refresh under cold water. Use kitchen scissors to cut the vermicelli into easy-to-manage lengths.

Arrange the noodles, lettuce cups and herbs on a platter. Top with the beef parcels then scatter with the peanuts. Serve with the dipping sauce.

BEEF NOODLE SOUP

Phở bò

A true Vietnamese classic! *Pho* is a well-balanced meal with plenty of broth to ward off dehydration in the hot, humid summer months, and to warm body and soul in the cool and drizzly winters. Hanoians like to slurp the noodles first so they don't become soft and mushy from sitting in the broth too long.

BROTH

2 KG (4 LB 6 OZ) BEEF BONES

6 RED ASIAN SHALLOTS, LEFT WHOLE

1.5 CM (½ INCH) KNOB FRESH GINGER, UNPEELED, CUT INTO CHUNKS

1 PIG'S TROTTER, SAWN IN HALF BY YOUR BUTCHER

500 G (1 LB 2 OZ) BEEF BRISKET

1 STAR ANISE

4 CM (1½ INCH) PIECE OF CASSIA BARK, OR 1 CINNAMON STICK

1 TEASPOON SALT

TO SERVE

200 G (7 OZ) SCOTCH FILLET, THINLY SLICED

1 TABLESPOON FISH SAUCE, PLUS EXTRA TO TASTE

600 G (1 LB 5 OZ) FRESH PHO NOODLES

½ ONION, THINLY SLICED

4 SPRING ONIONS (SCALLIONS), 2 THINLY SLICED LENGTHWAYS, AND 2 CUT INTO RINGS

1 SMALL HANDFUL CORIANDER (CILANTRO) LEAVES

1 SMALL HANDFUL BASIL

1 LEMON, CUT INTO 6 WEDGES

1 LONG RED CHILLI, SLICED

SERVES 6

Preheat the oven to 200°C (400°F). Place the beef bones on a baking tray and roast for 20 minutes. Turn the bones over and roast for a further 20 minutes.

Meanwhile, chargrill the whole unpeeled shallots and ginger on a barbecue or gas burner over medium heat for 5 minutes, until they are fragrant and the skin is lightly charred (1). Leave to cool slightly. Using your fingers, flake off the thin outer skin.

Place the roasted bones in a large saucepan with the trotter. Cover with cold water and slowly bring to a simmer, skimming off any froth. Add the chargrilled shallots, ginger, brisket, spices and salt. Simmer gently for 30 minutes, taking care not

to boil the stock. Remove and reserve the brisket, then simmer the stock for a further 4 hours. Strain the stock and discard the solids.

When ready to serve, marinate the scotch fillet in the fish sauce and set aside. Slice the brisket and set aside. Ensure the broth is at simmering point.

Drop the noodles into a pan of boiling water and stir with a chopstick for 20 seconds. Drain and divide among six bowls (2). Top with the meats, onion, spring onion and herbs. Ladle the hot broth over (3). Serve with lemon, chilli and extra fish sauce.

PHO: VIETNAM
IN A BOWL

PHỞ GIA TRUYEN IN BAT DAN STREET, HANOI, MIGHT WELL BE THE ONLY PLACE IN VIETNAM WHERE LOCALS FORM AN ORDERLY QUEUE RATHER THAN SOMETHING RESEMBLING A RUGBY SCRUM. THE TRADITIONAL *PHỞ* RESTAURANT, NOW RUN BY ITS THIRD-GENERATION OWNER, STARTED THE QUEUING SYSTEM DURING THE LEAN YEARS FOLLOWING THE VIETNAM WAR, AS THIS MADE IT EASIER TO CHECK RATIONING CARDS. NOW, AFTER DECADES OF ECONOMIC LIBERALISATION, THE PUNTERS ARE STILL PATIENTLY LINING UP FOR WHAT IS RUMOURED TO BE THE BEST *PHỞ BO* IN THE CITY. IT IS THE FEAR OF NOT BEING SERVED THEIR DAILY FIX OF BEEF NOODLE SOUP THAT KEEPS THEM IN LINE.

This fragrant soup, in principle, is a rather simple dish: a clear, aromatic beef broth, with chewy rice noodles, and featuring beef cooked *à la minute* (*phở tai*) or boiled or some dried beef (*phở chin*), and rounded off with spring onions, cumquat juice and chilli sauce.

But in reality *phở* is anything but simple: there are myriad variations and philosophies on how to achieve that perfect balance of tastes and textures.

The Vietnamese are passionate about *phở*. Where to eat it? How to cook it? Questions which are mulled over in ways that border on the obsessive. More than any other dish, this soup has come to embody the essence of Vietnamese cuisine.

The status of this iconic soup is even more astonishing when one considers that it has been around for only a century. The earliest record of this dish seems to be by the author Jean Marquet, who claimed he heard a beef noodle soup seller yell 'Yoc pheu' on the streets of Hanoi in 1919. It is also known that a villager from the Nam Dinh province opened the first *phở* stall in Hanoi in 1925.

'The history of Vietnam lies in this bowl,' exclaims a character in Camilla Gibb's Vietnam novel, *The Beauty of Humanity Movement*. This sentiment is more than just hyperbole, as the dish does indeed marry Chinese and French influences to create something uniquely Vietnamese.

Until the early 20th century, chicken or duck soups with either wheat or rice noodles were a common offering by Vietnamese and Chinese food vendors. *Phở* started its victory march through the stomachs of the country in Nam Dinh province, the centre of the French colonial textile industry. The French introduced beef to the local diet when bones and beef scraps from their butchers found their way into local soup kitchens.

Another departure from traditional Vietnamese cooking was charring the onions and ginger before adding them to the stock — a French cooking technique that adds colour and sweetness to the broth.

Although not partial to most Vietnamese food, the French colonisers eagerly embraced *phở*, calling it 'soupe tonkinoise'. They played up the French influence, even claiming that its name might have been a phonetic copy of the French dish *pot-au-feu*. However, this seems to be drawing a very long bow, given that the name is most likely derived from the rice noodles *banh phở*, which over time became shorthand for the entire dish.

After the French left, the Vietnamese reclaimed *phở* as their very own, and by some it was imbued with potent political symbolism and commentary. Writer Nguyen Tuan published a famous article in 1957, for example, in which he played with the image of the meatless *phở*, implicitly criticising the food policy of the government at the time. The essay landed the author in such trouble that the magazine was taken off the shelves, and Nguyen Tuan was made to publicly apologise for using the national dish in such a scandalous way.

Today, *phở* remains one of the most recognised Vietnamese dishes. It can be eaten any time of the day,

but in Vietnam makes a perfect breakfast — offering both a balance of protein and carbohydrates to provide energy for a busy day, and a salty broth to rehydrate after sweating through a sultry summer night.

In any case, it is definitely best eaten at street level, rubbing shoulders with fellow punters, hunched over steaming bowls, slurping the noodles first before they become soggy, then picking at the beef.

Not part of a fancy banquet, *phở* is a quintessentially Vietnamese pleasure, available to all.

BRAISED BEEF WITH LEMONGRASS AND STAR ANISE

Bò kho

Despite being a hearty stew, *bo kho* is a surprisingly popular breakfast in the tropical south, and particularly in Ho Chi Minh City, where it is served with a crusty baguette. It also works well as an evening meal, served with noodles or rice.

1 KG (2 LB 3 OZ) BEEF TOPSIDE, DICED

1 TABLESPOON ANNATTO OIL (SEE PAGE 320)

2 LEMONGRASS STEMS, WHITE PART ONLY, ROUGHLY CHOPPED

1 LONG RED CHILLI, SEEDED AND CHOPPED

3 CM (1¼ INCH) KNOB FRESH GINGER, CHOPPED

5 RED ASIAN SHALLOTS, CHOPPED

4 GARLIC CLOVES, CHOPPED

VEGETABLE OIL, FOR PAN-FRYING

4 STAR ANISE

1 TEASPOON FIVE-SPICE

⅓ TEASPOON GROUND CINNAMON

5 TOMATOES, PEELED, SEEDED AND CHOPPED

1½ TABLESPOONS FISH SAUCE

1 TABLESPOON SUGAR

½ TEASPOON SALT

2 LARGE CARROTS, CUT INTO CHUNKS

3 POTATOES, CUT INTO CHUNKS

SERVES 6

Toss the beef with the annatto oil and set aside.

Using a mortar and pestle, pound the lemongrass, chilli, ginger, shallot and garlic to a paste. Heat 2 tablespoons of vegetable oil in a saucepan over medium heat and fry the paste for 2–3 minutes, or until aromatic.

Add the beef to the pan and cook, stirring frequently, for 8–10 minutes, until browned all over. Stir in the star anise, five-spice and cinnamon, then add the tomatoes, fish sauce, sugar, salt and 1 litre (34 fl oz/4 cups) water.

Bring to the boil, then reduce the heat and simmer for 1½ hours, or until the beef is tender.

Add the carrot and potato and simmer for a further 20 minutes, or until the vegetables are tender.

Serve with crusty baguettes, noodles or rice.

BRAISED GOAT WITH FERMENTED TOFU

Dê nấu chao

Fermented tofu is sold in jars in Asian supermarkets. It can be quite pungent, and works best with strongly flavoured meats such as goat.

2 TABLESPOONS FERMENTED TOFU

1 TABLESPOON SUGAR

2 TABLESPOONS VEGETABLE OIL

1 KG (2 LB 3 OZ) DICED GOAT, PREFERABLY FROM THE SHOULDER

5 GARLIC CLOVES, CHOPPED

3 CM (1¼ INCH) KNOB FRESH GINGER, CHOPPED

1 LONG RED CHILLI, SEEDED AND FINELY CHOPPED

1 LITRES (34 FL OZ/4 CUPS) COCONUT JUICE

500 G (1 LB 2 OZ) TARO, PEELED AND DICED

SERVES 6

Put the fermented tofu in a small bowl. Mash it up with a fork, then combine with the sugar and 1 tablespoon of the oil to form a paste. Rub the mixture into the goat and leave to sit for 30 minutes to allow the flavours to develop.

Heat the remaining 1 tablespoon oil in a saucepan, then add the garlic, ginger and chilli and stir over medium heat for 1 minute, or until fragrant.

Add the marinated goat and continue cooking for 4–5 minutes, stirring occasionally. When the meat has coloured, stir in the coconut juice. You might need to top up the liquid with a little bit of water to ensure all the goat pieces are submerged. Bring to the boil, then reduce the heat and simmer for 1 hour.

Lastly, add the taro and cook for a final 5–8 minutes, until the taro is tender.

BROKEN RICE WITH GRILLED PORK AND EGG, SUNNY SIDE UP

Cơm tấm sườn nướng

A popular worker's lunch or dinner from Ho Chi Minh City, this dish is strangely uncommon in the north. For best results, marinate the pork overnight before cooking.

This is an individually plated dish, which is not shared.

6 SMALL PORK CHOPS

VEGETABLE OIL, FOR PAN-FRYING

6 EGGS

1/3 TEASPOON SALT

1/4 TEASPOON FRESHLY GROUND BLACK PEPPER

BROKEN RICE (SEE PAGE 19), TO SERVE

1/2 CUCUMBER, SLICED

125 G (41/2 OZ/11/2 CUPS) PICKLED CABBAGE (SEE PAGE 336)

SPRING ONION OIL (SEE PAGE 341)

CLASSIC DIPPING SAUCE (SEE PAGE 323), TO SERVE

MARINADE

3 GARLIC CLOVES, FINELY CHOPPED

2 RED ASIAN SHALLOTS, FINELY CHOPPED

1 TABLESPOON SOY SAUCE

1 TABLESPOON FISH SAUCE

2 TEASPOONS PEANUT OIL

1 TEASPOON HONEY

1/2 TABLESPOON SUGAR

1 TEASPOON FIVE-SPICE

1/3 TEASPOON FRESHLY GROUND BLACK PEPPERCORNS

SERVES 6

Combine all the marinade ingredients in a small bowl, stirring to dissolve the sugar. Place the pork chops in a shallow tray and coat with the marinade. Cover and refrigerate for 6 hours, or overnight.

Heat a barbecue or chargrill to medium. Cook the chops for about 3–4 minutes on each side, then remove from the grill.

To cook the eggs, heat two non-stick frying pans and coat with a light film of oil. Break the eggs into individual cups. When the oil is hot, ease three eggs into each pan. Sprinkle with the salt and pepper and reduce the heat to low. Fry for 2–3 minutes, until the white is set, but the yolk is still soft.

To serve, fill a small bowl with rice and turn out onto six individual plates. Next to the rice, place the sliced cucumber and a small amount of the pickled cabbage.

Lastly, put a pork chop and egg on each plate and drizzle with the spring onion oil.

Serve with the dipping sauce.

HUE BEEF NOODLE SOUP

Bún bò Huế

The classic noodle soup from the old imperial capital. Extra *mam tom* (fermented shrimp paste) may be added to the broth at the table, although many Westerners can find this condiment a little too pungent, so you could offer some fish sauce instead.

2 TABLESPOONS ANNATTO OIL (SEE PAGE 320)

2 LEMONGRASS STEMS, WHITE PART ONLY, FINELY CHOPPED

1 TABLESPOON CHILLI SAUCE (SEE PAGE 322)

1 TABLESPOON MAM TOM (FERMENTED SHRIMP PASTE)

BROTH

6 RED ASIAN SHALLOTS

3 CM (1¼ INCH) KNOB FRESH GINGER, UNPEELED

2 PIG'S TROTTERS

1.5 KG (3 LB 5 OZ) BEEF BONES

2/3 TEASPOON SALT

1 TEASPOON SUGAR

500 G (1 LB 2 OZ) BEEF SHANK

4 LEMONGRASS STEMS, WHITE PART ONLY, CRUSHED

TO SERVE

600 G (1 LB 5 OZ) DRIED RICE VERMICELLI

½ ONION, THINLY SLICED

1 SMALL HANDFUL PERILLA

1 SMALL HANDFUL CORIANDER (CILANTRO) LEAVES

1 HANDFUL BEAN SPROUTS

2 RED BIRD'S EYE CHILLIES, SLICED

1 LIME, CUT INTO 6 WEDGES

SERVES 6

To make the broth, first chargrill the whole unpeeled shallots and ginger on a barbecue or gas burner over medium heat for about 5 minutes, until they are fragrant and the skin is lightly charred. Remove and cool slightly. Using your fingers, flake off the outer thin layer of skin.

Meanwhile, place the trotters and beef bones in a large saucepan and cover with cold water.

Add the salt, sugar and the chargrilled shallots and ginger to the pan and slowly bring to simmering point, skimming off any froth that rises to the surface. Simmer for 2 hours, skimming off any more froth. Add the beef shank and the crushed lemongrass and cook for a further 1 hour.

Remove the shank and set aside. Strain the broth and discard the ginger, shallots and lemongrass. Pick any meat from the bones and add to the broth.

When the shank is cool enough to handle, remove the meat from the bone and cut into pieces 5 mm (¼ inch) thick.

Heat the annatto oil in a clean saucepan. Add the chopped lemongrass and cook over medium heat for 1 minute. Add the chilli sauce and mam tom and cook for a few seconds, then pour in the broth and bring back to the boil.

Meanwhile, soak the vermicelli in boiling water for 4–5 minutes. Gently stir to separate the noodles, then drain and refresh under cold water. Use kitchen scissors to cut the vermicelli into easy-to-manage lengths.

Divide the noodles and the meats among six deep bowls, then ladle the hot broth over. Scatter with the onion and some of the herbs.

Serve the remaining herbs, bean sprouts, chilli and lime wedges on the side.

CABBAGE ROLLS

Bắp cải cuốn thịt

❀

These rolls are a hearty comfort food from the countryside of chef Duyen, from the Hanoi Cooking Centre — and a favourite for staff lunches.

3 DRIED BLACK FUNGUS (WOOD EARS)
3 DRIED CHINESE MUSHROOMS
12 SMALL CABBAGE LEAVES
300 G (10½ OZ) MINCED (GROUND) PORK
4 RED ASIAN SHALLOTS, DICED

3 SPRING ONIONS (SCALLIONS), SLICED
3 TEASPOONS FISH SAUCE
TOMATO DIPPING SAUCE (SEE PAGE 342), TO SERVE

SERVES 6

Soak the mushrooms in warm water for 20 minutes.

Meanwhile, bring a saucepan of salted water to the boil. Place a cup of ice cubes and cold water into a large bowl. Lower the cabbage leaves into the boiling water and blanch for 1 minute. Remove the leaves with tongs and place in the iced water. When the leaves are cool, remove from the water and drain off any excess. Pat dry with paper towel.

Drain the mushrooms and squeeze out any excess water. Discard the stems. Thinly slice the caps, then place in a bowl with the pork, shallot, spring onion, fish sauce and a generous pinch of freshly ground black pepper. Mix together well, then divide into 12 equal portions.

Place a cabbage leaf on a work surface, vein side down. Put a portion of the pork mixture on the bottom third of the leaf (1). Roll the bottom part of the leaf over the filling, then fold the sides in and continue rolling (2). Repeat with the remaining pork mixture and cabbage leaves.

Place the rolls in a steamer, seam side down (3). Set the steamer over a saucepan of boiling water and cook for 15 minutes.

Serve warm, with the dipping sauce.

CLAY POT PORK WITH QUAIL EGGS AND DAIKON

Thịt kho tàu

This is a Vietnamese classic: a typical worker's lunch at *com binh dan* eateries, and a regular at family meals. If using your clay pot for the first time, soak it in cold water overnight so it won't crack in the oven.

1 x 800 g (1 lb 12 oz) pork belly
6 quail eggs
1 tablespoon sugar
vegetable oil, for deep-frying
60 ml (2 fl oz/¼ cup) fish sauce
100 ml (3½ fl oz) coconut milk
¼ daikon, peeled and diced

MARINADE
40 ml (1¼ fl oz) fish sauce
2 garlic cloves, chopped
2 red Asian shallots, chopped
⅓ teaspoon freshly ground black pepper

SERVES 6

Slice the pork belly into 2 cm (¾ inch) strips and place in a shallow tray. Combine the marinade ingredients and spread over the pork belly, tossing to coat. Set aside to infuse for 20 minutes.

Meanwhile, bring a saucepan of water to the boil. Gently lower the eggs into the water and boil for 5 minutes. Remove with a slotted spoon and plunge into cold water to stop the cooking process. Cool, then peel and set aside.

Place the sugar and 1½ tablespoons water in a heavy-based saucepan over medium heat and stir until the sugar has dissolved. Bring to the boil and cook for about 5 minutes, until the sugar is a rich golden colour.

Standing away from the pan, pour in 250 ml (8½ fl oz/1 cup) water. When the spluttering has stopped, stir until you have a smooth caramel sauce.

Preheat the oven to 160°C (320°F) and place a clay pot in the oven to heat up.

Heat 1 tablespoon of oil in a wok and stir-fry the pork over medium heat until browned all over.

Add the caramel sauce, fish sauce, coconut milk, daikon and enough water to cover the pork. Transfer to the heated clay pot, then cover and bake in the oven for 40 minutes.

Meanwhile, deep-fry the quail eggs in about 4 cm (1½ inches) of oil until lightly golden.

Add the eggs to the clay pot and bake, uncovered, for a final 15 minutes.

FRIED SPRING ROLLS

Nem rán Hà Nội

The humble spring roll is sometimes used as a metaphor for a good marriage. Wedding speeches, particularly in the south, refer to the recipe in all kinds of symbolic ways. For example, ingredients have to stick together to make both a marriage and a spring roll work. Even the frying oil is made to stand in as an image for romantic passion: if it is too hot, it will burn what it touches — both literally and figuratively! Corny as this may sound, it is also a wonderful indication of how central food is within Vietnamese culture.

4 DRIED BLACK FUNGUS (WOOD EARS)
50 G (1¾ OZ) DRIED CELLOPHANE NOODLES
1 SMALL JICAMA
400 G (14 OZ) MINCED (GROUND) PORK
100 G (3½ OZ) CRABMEAT
2 RED ASIAN SHALLOTS, FINELY DICED

1 EGG
1 TEASPOON FRESHLY GROUND BLACK PEPPER
12 LARGE OR 24 SMALL RICE PAPER SHEETS
VEGETABLE OIL, FOR DEEP-FRYING
CLASSIC DIPPING SAUCE (SEE PAGE 323), TO SERVE
SERVES 6

Soak the mushrooms in warm water for 20 minutes. Drain the mushrooms and squeeze out any excess water. Discard the stems. Thinly slice the caps and place in a bowl (1).

Soak the noodles in hot water for 1 minute, then drain and refresh under cold running water. Drain the noodles, then cut into 4 cm (1½ inch) lengths using kitchen scissors. Add to the mushrooms.

Peel and grate the jicama, then pat dry with paper towel to remove excess moisture. Add to the mushrooms with the pork, crabmeat, shallot, egg and pepper. Mix until well combined.

Soften the rice paper sheets by dipping them one at a time into warm water for 1 second. Do not soak the sheets as they will become too soft and tear when rolled. Place on a flat surface, wait for 20 seconds, then soak up any excess water with a clean cloth.

Put two tablespoons of the pork mixture on the bottom third of the sheet (2). Lightly squeeze the mixture to expel any air bubbles, then form the mixture into a cylinder. Bring the bottom of the sheet up over the filling, then fold in the sides and then roll up (3). Set aside, seam side down, while you prepare the remaining spring rolls.

Heat 10–12 cm (4–4¾ inches) of oil in a deep frying pan or wok. Deep-fry the spring rolls in batches over medium heat for 3–4 minutes, until golden and crispy. Drain thoroughly on paper towel.

Serve hot, with the dipping sauce.

FRIED TOFU FILLED WITH PORK

Đậu phụ nhồi thịt heo

The best place to enjoy this dish is at one of the many eateries at the central market in Dalat, where you can observe the frenzied pace of market life from your table while savouring these tasty flavours.

50 G (1¾ OZ) CELLOPHANE NOODLES

VEGETABLE OIL, FOR DEEP-FRYING

4 x 150 G (5½ OZ) BLOCKS FIRM TOFU

500 G (1 LB 2 OZ) MINCED (GROUND) PORK

4 RED ASIAN SHALLOTS, FINELY CHOPPED

¼ TEASPOON SUGAR

1 TEASPOON SALT

½ TEASPOON FRESHLY GROUND BLACK PEPPER

2 SPRING ONIONS (SCALLIONS), THINLY SLICED

SOY CHILLI DIPPING SAUCE (SEE PAGE 340), TO SERVE

TOMATO SAUCE

1 BROWN ONION, FINELY CHOPPED

2 GARLIC CLOVES, CRUSHED

1 TABLESPOON VEGETABLE OIL

4 TOMATOES, PEELED, SEEDED AND ROUGHLY CHOPPED

1 TEASPOON CASTER (SUPERFINE) SUGAR

1 TABLESPOON FISH SAUCE

½ TEASPOON FRESHLY GROUND BLACK PEPPER

SERVES 6

Soak the noodles in hot water for 1 minute, then drain and refresh under cold running water. Drain the noodles, then cut into 3 cm (1¼ inch) lengths using kitchen scissors.

Heat about 2 cm (¾ inch) of oil in a wok or deep frying pan. To test the oil, place the tip of a wooden chopstick into the oil — when bubbles slowly rise to the surface, the oil is hot enough to use.

Cut each tofu block in half, then dry thoroughly with paper towel. Carefully lower half the tofu into the oil and cook for 3–4 minutes, until lightly golden. Remove from the oil with a slotted spoon and drain on paper towel. Repeat with the remaining tofu.

When cool enough to handle, make a slit in each tofu piece with the tip of a sharp knife. Enlarge this pocket by using a spoon to remove a third of the tofu inside and placing it in a bowl. Add the noodles, pork, shallot, sugar, salt and pepper

to the tofu in the bowl and mix together well. Insert the mixture into the tofu pockets, taking care not to tear the tofu.

Return the filled tofu to the hot oil and cook for a further 5–6 minutes, or until a deep golden colour. Remove and drain well on paper towel.

To make the tomato sauce, sauté the onion and garlic in the oil over medium heat for 3–4 minutes, until translucent. Stir in the tomatoes, sugar, fish sauce and pepper and simmer for 5–6 minutes. If the mixture is too dry, add a small amount of water to achieve a sauce-like consistency.

Add the tofu to the tomato sauce and cook for 1 minute to heat through. Sprinkle with the spring onion and serve with the dipping sauce.

GOAT CURRY

Cà ri dê

This big-flavoured curry is a variation of a dish by famous Vietnamese chef Ms Nguyen Dzoan Cam Van. Goat is a strong-tasting meat, available from many Asian and Middle-Eastern butchers. If you can't get goat, try duck and replace the eggplant with sweet potato.

Serve with Boiled rice (see page 18) or crusty bread.

1 KG (2 LB 3 OZ) DICED GOAT, PREFERABLY FROM THE SHOULDER

VEGETABLE OIL, FOR PAN-FRYING

2 ONIONS, FINELY DICED

¾ TEASPOON SALT

750 ML (25½ FL OZ/3 CUPS) MILK

800 ML (27 FL OZ) COCONUT MILK

5 LEMONGRASS STEMS, WHITE PART ONLY, CUT IN HALF LENGTHWAYS

2 EGGPLANTS (AUBERGINES)

150 G (5½ OZ) BUTTER

1 SMALL HANDFUL CORIANDER (CILANTRO) SPRIGS

CURRY PASTE

4 LEMONGRASS STEMS, WHITE PART ONLY, FINELY CHOPPED

1 LONG RED CHILLI, SEEDED AND FINELY CHOPPED

VEGETABLE OIL, FOR FRYING

35 G (1¼ OZ/⅓ CUP) CURRY POWDER

250 ML (8½ FL OZ/1 CUP) MILK

2 TABLESPOONS SUGAR

SERVES 6

To make the curry paste, fry the lemongrass and chilli in 1 tablespoon of oil over medium heat until fragrant. Add the curry powder and stir for 1 minute, ensuring the spices don't burn as they will become bitter. Add the milk and sugar and bring to the boil. Remove from the heat and allow to cool.

Put the goat in a bowl, pour over the curry paste and toss to coat. Allow to marinate for 30 minutes.

Heat 1 tablespoon of oil in a large saucepan and sauté the onion over medium heat for 3–4 minutes, until soft and translucent. Add the goat and sprinkle with the salt. Stirring regularly, cook for 4–5 minutes, until the meat has browned.

Pour in 500 ml (17 fl oz/2 cups) of the milk, then add the coconut milk and lemongrass. Simmer for about 1 hour, or until the meat is tender.

Meanwhile, cut the eggplants into 3 cm (1¼ inch) chunks. Place in a colander and sprinkle with extra salt. Leave to sit for 30 minutes to remove the bitter tannin. Wash the salt from the eggplant and pat dry with paper towel.

Heat 2 tablespoons of oil in a frying pan. Cook the eggplant in batches over medium heat until golden brown all over, adding more oil to the pan to cook each batch. Drain on paper towel to remove any excess oil.

When the goat is tender, stir in the eggplant and the remaining milk and butter. After the butter has melted, transfer the curry to a serving bowl. Scatter with the coriander and serve.

GRILLED RICE PAPER WITH PORK, DRIED SHRIMP AND QUAIL EGG

Bánh đa nướng

This dish is a relatively new addition to the Ho Chi Minh City street-food scene. The vendors appear mid-afternoon to catch the children after school. The rice paper is folded in half like a taco — a great snack that can be eaten with one hand while riding home on the back of a motorbike.

2 RED ASIAN SHALLOTS, FINELY DICED

1 GARLIC CLOVE, FINELY CHOPPED

1 TABLESPOON VEGETABLE OIL

300 G (10½ OZ) MINCED (GROUND) PORK

¼ TEASPOON SUGAR

⅓ TEASPOON SALT

⅓ TEASPOON FRESHLY GROUND BLACK PEPPER

1 TEASPOON FISH SAUCE

12 RICE PAPER SHEETS, ABOUT 18 CM (7 INCHES) IN SIZE

3 SPRING ONIONS (SCALLIONS), THINLY SLICED

100 G (3½ OZ) SMALL DRIED SHRIMP

12 QUAIL EGGS

60 G (2 OZ) BUTTER

CHILLI SAUCE (SEE PAGE 322), FOR DRIZZLING

MAKES 12

Sauté the shallot and garlic in the oil over medium heat until fragrant. Add the pork, sugar, salt and pepper and cook, stirring, for 3–4 minutes, until the meat is coloured. Lastly, stir in the fish sauce and cook for a further 1 minute. Remove the mixture from the heat and allow to cool slightly.

Heat a small chargrill and assemble all your other ingredients.

Take one sheet of rice paper and place 1 heaped tablespoon of the pork mixture, 1 teaspoon of dried shrimp and 1 teaspoon of spring onion on top (1). Break a quail egg into the centre and lightly spread it over the rice paper (2).

Place the rice paper sheet onto the chargrill and start stirring the topping around, breaking the egg yolk as you go, and mixing the ingredients. Add 1 teaspoon of butter to the mix and stir that through. Lastly, add a small drizzle of chilli sauce in a zig-zag pattern, then fold the sheet in half (3).

Remove from the chargrill and eat while hot.

Repeat with the remaining ingredients.

HANOI BRAISED BEEF WITH RED WINE

Sốt vang

A real winter warmer from the capital, where the temperature can drop to single digits in the months of December to February. The use of red wine in this dish clearly shows the French influence on food from what was, in colonial times, the region known as Tonkin.

Serve with crusty Vietnamese baguettes (see page 28) or rice vermicelli.

1 KG (2 LB 3 OZ) BEEF TOPSIDE, DICED

5 GARLIC CLOVES, FINELY CHOPPED

2 TABLESPOONS FISH SAUCE

1 TABLESPOON VEGETABLE OIL

1 ONION, FINELY DICED

3 CM (1¼ INCH) KNOB FRESH GINGER, THINLY SLICED

150 ML (5 FL OZ) RED WINE

1 CINNAMON STICK

5 TOMATOES, PEELED, SEEDED AND CHOPPED

½ TEASPOON SALT

⅓ TEASPOON FRESHLY CRACKED BLACK PEPPER

3 CARROTS, CUT INTO CHUNKS

CHILLI SAUCE (SEE PAGE 322), TO SERVE

SERVES 6

Marinate the beef in the garlic and half the fish sauce for about 30 minutes.

Heat the oil in a large frying pan over medium heat. Sauté the onion for 3–4 minutes, or until translucent. Add the beef and ginger and cook for 8–10 minutes, until browned all over. Pour in the wine and simmer until the liquid has reduced by two-thirds.

Now stir in the remaining 1 tablespoon fish sauce, the cinnamon stick, tomatoes, salt, pepper and 1 litre (34 fl oz/ 4 cups) water. Bring back to the boil, then reduce the heat and simmer for 1½ hours, or until the beef is tender.

Add the carrot and cook for a further 20 minutes, or until the carrot is tender.

Serve with the chilli sauce on the side.

MEATBALL BAGUETTE

Bánh mì xá xíu

Here's Dalat's answer to New York's meatball sub. These delicious meatballs can be served in a baguette, as here, or with a baguette or rice on the side to mop up the homemade tomato sauce.

MEATBALLS

500 G (1 LB 2 OZ) MINCED (GROUND) PORK

2 RED ASIAN SHALLOTS, FINELY DICED

1 EGG

25 G (1 OZ/⅓ CUP) FRESH BREADCRUMBS

1 TEASPOON FISH SAUCE

⅓ TEASPOON SALT

⅓ TEASPOON FRESHLY GROUND BLACK PEPPER

TOMATO SAUCE

VEGETABLE OIL, FOR PAN-FRYING

4 RED ASIAN SHALLOTS, FINELY DICED

4 GARLIC CLOVES, FINELY CHOPPED

8 TOMATOES, PEELED, SEEDED AND ROUGHLY CHOPPED

1 LONG RED CHILLI, CUT IN HALF

1 TABLESPOON FISH SAUCE

1 TEASPOON SUGAR

½ TEASPOON SALT

½ TEASPOON FRESHLY GROUND BLACK PEPPER

TO SERVE

6 SMALL VIETNAMESE BAGUETTES (SEE PAGE 28)

BUTTER, FOR SPREADING OVER THE BAGUETTES

CARROT AND DAIKON PICKLE (SEE PAGE 321)

1 HANDFUL CORIANDER (CILANTRO)

1 LONG RED CHILLI, SEEDED AND CUT INTO RINGS

SERVES 6

Combine all the meatball ingredients in a large bowl and mix thoroughly. With lightly oiled fingers, form the mixture into meatballs the size of golf balls. Cover and set aside for the flavours to develop while you make the tomato sauce.

Heat 2 tablespoons of oil in a heavy-based saucepan over medium heat. Add the shallot and garlic and sauté until fragrant. Stir in the tomatoes, chilli, fish sauce, sugar, salt and pepper and simmer for 15 minutes. If the sauce is too dry after this time, add a little water.

To cook the meatballs, heat about 2 tablespoons of oil in a frying pan. Working in batches, brown the meatballs on all sides. Pour the tomato sauce over and simmer for a further 10 minutes, or until the meatballs are cooked through.

To serve, cut the baguettes open along one side, then spread with a little butter. Fill them with the meatballs, some of the tomato sauce, the pickles, coriander and chilli.

Enjoy straight away.

MY QUANG NOODLES WITH PRAWN AND PORK

Mỳ Quảng

A soup from Quang Nam province, which is popular along the south-central coastline. It has less liquid than its cousins *pho bo* from the north and *bun bo Hue* from the centre, with noodles, pork belly and prawns poking out of the broth. Traditionally, the soup is prepared with turmeric noodles, but if these are unavailable you can use the plain variety.

1 KG (2 LB 3 OZ) PORK BONES, PREFERABLY FROM THE TAIL

3 LEMONGRASS STEMS, WHITE PART ONLY

300 G (10½ OZ) PORK BELLY, CUT INTO 18 SLICES

12 QUAIL EGGS

VEGETABLE OIL, FOR PAN-FRYING

6 RED ASIAN SHALLOTS, FINELY CHOPPED

6 GARLIC CLOVES, FINELY CHOPPED

250 G (9 OZ) PRAWNS (SHRIMP), PEELED AND DEVEINED

1 TABLESPOON CHILLI SAUCE (SEE PAGE 322)

125 ML (4 FL OZ/½ CUP) SOY SAUCE

6 TOMATOES, PEELED, CORED AND ROUGHLY DICED

MARINADE

2 TABLESPOONS FISH SAUCE

6 RED ASIAN SHALLOTS, FINELY CHOPPED

4 GARLIC CLOVES, FINELY CHOPPED

TO SERVE

500 G (1 LB 2 OZ) FRESH EGG OR RICE NOODLES

1 SMALL HANDFUL PERILLA

1 SMALL HANDFUL MINT

1 SMALL HANDFUL THAI BASIL

100 G (3½ OZ) BEAN SPROUTS

3 SPRING ONIONS (SCALLIONS), SLICED

3 TABLESPOONS ROASTED PEANUTS, CHOPPED

2 LARGE RICE CRACKERS, BROKEN INTO SHARDS

CHILLI SAUCE (SEE PAGE 322), TO SERVE

VINEGAR SHALLOTS (SEE PAGE 342), TO SERVE

SERVES 6

Put the pork bones and lemongrass in a large saucepan. Cover with about 1.5 litres (51 fl oz/6 cups) cold water and slowly bring to the boil, skimming off any froth that rises to the surface. Reduce the heat and simmer for 1½ hours.

Meanwhile, marinate the pork belly in the marinade ingredients for 20 minutes. Cook the quail eggs in a saucepan of boiling water for 4 minutes, then cool, peel and set aside.

Heat 1 tablespoon of oil in a large frying pan over medium heat and sauté the shallot and two-thirds of the garlic. When fragrant, add the prawns and cook for 3–4 minutes. Remove the mixture from the pan and set aside.

Clean out the pan, then heat 1 tablespoon of oil in the pan. Cook the marinated pork over medium heat until golden brown. Now add the chilli sauce, soy sauce, quail eggs and prawns. Cook for a further 30 minutes over low heat, until all the sauce has evaporated. Remove the mixture from the pan.

Strain the pork stock and discard the bones and lemongrass.

In a large saucepan, sauté the remaining garlic in a little oil over medium heat until fragrant. Add the tomatoes and cook for 5 minutes, until soft. Pour in the stock and simmer for 15 minutes, then add the meat mixture and return to the boil.

To serve, blanch the noodles and divide among six bowls, placing them in one half of the bowl. In the other half place the herbs, bean sprouts and spring onion.

Ladle the soup over the noodles, distributing the pork, prawns and quail eggs evenly. Scatter with the peanuts, then rest some rice cracker shards at the back of each bowl. Serve with chilli sauce and vinegar shallots.

PORK AND MUSHROOM PASTRIES

Bánh gối

Small kerbside stalls pop up in Hanoi during the cold winter months, selling a variety of fried snacks. These pork and mushroom pastries are the most popular.

8 DRIED BLACK FUNGUS (WOOD EARS)
50 G (1¾ OZ) CELLOPHANE NOODLES
300 G (10½ OZ) MINCED (GROUND) PORK
3 SPRING ONIONS (SCALLIONS), THINLY SLICED
2 TEASPOONS FISH SAUCE
¼ TEASPOON SALT
VEGETABLE OIL, FOR DEEP-FRYING
CLASSIC DIPPING SAUCE (SEE PAGE 323), TO SERVE

DOUGH
150 G (5½ OZ/1 CUP) PLAIN (ALL-PURPOSE) FLOUR
¼ TEASPOON SALT
1 TEASPOON DRIED YEAST
90 ML (3 FL OZ) LUKEWARM MILK

MAKES 12

To make the dough, place the flour and salt in a bowl and make a well in the centre. Whisk the yeast into the lukewarm milk, then pour the mixture into the well. Make small circular motions with your fingers, incorporating the milk into the flour.

When the milk and flour have come together, place the dough on a floured bench. Using the heel of your hand, knead the dough for 8–10 minutes, until it becomes smooth and elastic.

Place the dough in a clean bowl, cover with a damp cloth and leave in a warm, draught-free spot to rise for about 1 hour.

Meanwhile, prepare the filling. Soak the mushrooms in warm water for 20 minutes. Drain the mushrooms and squeeze out any excess water. Discard the stems. Thinly slice the caps and place in a bowl.

Cook the noodles in boiling water for 2 minutes, then drain and refresh in cold water. Drain and add to the mushrooms, along with the pork, spring onion, fish sauce, salt and a pinch of freshly ground black pepper.

Divide the dough into 12 portions and roll each out into a 12 cm (4¾ inch) disc. Spoon 2 tablespoons of the filling onto one half of the disc. Dampen the edges of the dough, fold the other half over to enclose the filling, then pinch the edges together to seal. Repeat with the remaining dough and filling.

Heat about 12 cm (4¾ inches) of oil in a deep frying pan or wok. To test the oil, place the tip of a wooden chopstick into the oil — when bubbles slowly rise to the surface, the oil is hot enough to use. Cook the pastries in batches for 4–5 minutes, until golden. Drain on paper towel.

Serve hot as a snack, with the dipping sauce.

PORK BROTH WITH NOODLES

Bánh canh Trảng Bàng

A southern variation of the famous *pho*, this rice noodle soup originated in Tay Ninh province, some 60 kilometres north of Ho Chi Minh City. In Tay Ninh, the noodles are thicker, resembling the Japanese udon noodles. However if you can't get them, use the more common, thinner variety.

3 KG (6 LB 10 OZ) PIG'S TROTTERS, SAWN IN HALF LENGTHWAYS BY YOUR BUTCHER

1 TEASPOON SALT

8 RED ASIAN SHALLOTS, UNPEELED

1 x 300 G (10½ OZ) PIECE PORK LEG OR SHOULDER

1 HANDFUL BEAN SPROUTS

1 HANDFUL THAI BASIL

1 LONG RED CHILLI, CUT INTO RINGS

1 LIME, CUT INTO 6 WEDGES

100 ML (3½ FL OZ) FISH SAUCE

¾ TEASPOON FRESHLY GROUND BLACK PEPPER

600 G (1 LB 5 OZ) FRESH THICK RICE NOODLES

5 SPRING ONIONS (SCALLIONS), THINLY SLICED

2 TABLESPOONS FRIED SHALLOTS (SEE PAGE 326)

SERVES 6

Wash the trotters under running water, then place in a large saucepan and cover with cold water. Add the salt and slowly bring to simmering point, skimming off any froth that rises to the surface.

Chargrill the whole unpeeled shallots on a barbecue or gas burner over medium heat for about 5 minutes, until they are fragrant and the skin is lightly charred. Leave to cool slightly. Using your fingers, flake off the outer thin layer of skin.

Add the shallots to the stock and simmer for a further 3½ hours. Be careful not to boil the stock, or the end result will be very cloudy.

Add the pork to the broth and continue to simmer for a further 20 minutes, or until the pork is cooked.

Remove the pork from the broth and leave to rest for 10 minutes before thinly slicing it. Strain the broth and discard the trotters.

Arrange the bean sprouts, basil, chilli and lime wedges on a platter. Divide the fish sauce among six dipping bowls and sprinkle with the pepper.

When ready to serve, reheat the broth. Quickly blanch the noodles in boiling water, then drain and divide among six serving bowls.

Arrange the sliced pork and spring onion over the noodles. Ladle the hot broth over and top with the fried shallots. Diners can now add the fish sauce, herbs, chilli and lime to suit their own taste.

PORK LOAF

Giò lợn

Ask your butcher to put the pork through the mincer twice, for an extra-fine texture.

Common variations to this recipe are adding ½ teaspoon freshly ground cinnamon or 200 g (7oz) young green rice to the pork mixture before cooking the loaf.

2 RED ASIAN SHALLOTS, ROUGHLY CHOPPED

3 GARLIC CLOVES, ROUGHLY CHOPPED

1 KG (2 LB 3 OZ) MINCED (GROUND) PORK LEG

2 TABLESPOONS FISH SAUCE

½ TEASPOON SUGAR

½ TABLESPOON SALT

⅓ TEASPOON FRESHLY GROUND BLACK PEPPER

1 BANANA LEAF

SERVES 6; MAKES ABOUT 1 KG (2 LB 3 OZ)

Using a mortar and pestle, grind the shallot and garlic to a fine paste.

Combine all the remaining ingredients, except the banana leaf, in a large bowl. Using a food processor, blend the mixture to form a fine paste.

Remove the mixture to a clean bowl, then cover and refrigerate for 4 hours to allow the flavours to develop.

When ready to cook the pork loaf, bring a saucepan of water to the boil. Cut the banana leaf into 45 cm (18 inch) lengths and drop them into the boiling water for a few seconds to soften. Remove with tongs and pat dry. The leaf portions should now be pliable enough to roll without cracking or breaking.

Place two pieces of banana leaf, shiny side down, in a cross pattern on a work surface. Put the pork mixture in the centre of the cross and form into a loaf shape. Fold the banana leaf over to cover the pork mixture, then secure with kitchen string.

Gently lower the loaf into the boiling water. Reduce the heat and simmer for 45 minutes.

Remove the loaf from the water and leave to cool before peeling away the banana leaf.

Slice off pieces of the loaf and serve as desired, such as in a crusty Vietnamese baguette or in rice paper rolls. The loaf will keep covered in the fridge for several days.

PORK RIBS BRAISED WITH PEANUTS AND LEMONGRASS

Xôi thịt hòn

We found this dish at a tiny breakfast stall in Hue. Very popular with the locals, the stall sold out by 8 am. These rich, heavily scented pork ribs were a great start to a long day touring the Perfume River.

1.5 KG (3 LB 5 OZ) PORK RIBS, CUT BY YOUR BUTCHER INTO 5 CM (2 INCH) LENGTHS

2 TABLESPOONS FISH SAUCE

1 TEASPOON SUGAR

½ TEASPOON FRESHLY GROUND BLACK PEPPER

4 LEMONGRASS STEMS, WHITE PART ONLY

VEGETABLE OIL, FOR PAN-FRYING

6 RED ASIAN SHALLOTS, FINELY DICED

3 CM (1¼ INCH) KNOB FRESH GALANGAL, FINELY CHOPPED

1 TABLESPOON RICE WINE

1 TABLESPOON RICE VINEGAR

60 ML (2 FL OZ/¼ CUP) SOY SAUCE

160 G (5½ OZ/1 CUP) UNSALTED PEANUTS, ROASTED AND CRUSHED

STICKY RICE (SEE PAGE 26), TO SERVE

SERVES 6

Place the pork in a shallow tray. Combine the fish sauce, sugar and pepper and pour over the ribs, tossing to coat. Leave to marinate for 30 minutes.

Crush two of the lemongrass stems and set aside. Finely chop the remaining two lemongrass stems and set aside.

Heat about 2 tablespoons of oil in a large heavy-based saucepan over medium heat and sauté the shallot for 2 minutes. Add the chopped lemongrass and galangal and cook for a further 1 minute, until fragrant.

In a separate frying pan, heat another 2 tablespoons of oil over medium heat and brown the ribs in batches. Add the ribs to the shallot mixture.

Deglaze the frying pan the ribs were browned in by adding the rice wine and vinegar, stirring to loosen any cooked-on bits. Add this mixture to the saucepan, along with the soy sauce, crushed peanuts and the reserved crushed lemongrass.

Add enough water to cover the ribs. Bring to the boil, then reduce the heat and simmer for 45 minutes, or until the meat is tender.

Serve with sticky rice.

PORK SKEWERS IN RICE PAPER

Nem nướng

These Nha Trang-style pork skewers go into spring rolls that your guests can roll for themselves at the table. Green banana, pineapple or carambola (star fruit) can be served as additional rice paper fillings.

The pork mixture can also be formed into little patties and used as a filling for crusty baguettes.

1 SHEET TOFU SKIN

VEGETABLE OIL, FOR PAN-FRYING

600 G (1 LB 5 OZ) DRIED RICE VERMICELLI

2 SMALL LETTUCES, SEPARATED INTO CUPS

1 SMALL HANDFUL VIETNAMESE MINT

3 TABLESPOONS ROASTED UNSALTED PEANUTS, CHOPPED

1 QUANTITY CARROT AND DAIKON PICKLE (SEE PAGE 321)

24 RICE PAPER SHEETS, ABOUT 18 CM (7 INCHES) IN SIZE

CLASSIC DIPPING SAUCE (SEE PAGE 323), TO SERVE

PATTIES

600 G (1 LB 5 OZ) MINCED (GROUND) PORK

2 TABLESPOONS ROASTED RICE FLOUR (SEE PAGE 337)

3 GARLIC CLOVES, CHOPPED

2 RED ASIAN SHALLOTS, CHOPPED

20 ML (¾ FL OZ) FISH SAUCE

1 TEASPOON ANNATTO OIL (SEE PAGE 320)

½ TEASPOON SUGAR

¼ TEASPOON SALT

½ TEASPOON FRESHLY GROUND BLACK PEPPER

MAKES 24

In a bowl, combine all the patty ingredients. Mix well, then cover and set aside for 30 minutes for the flavours to develop.

Meanwhile, soak 12 bamboo skewers in cold water for 20 minutes.

Cut the tofu skin into strips about 2.5 cm (1 inch) wide and 5–6 cm (2–2½ inches) long with a pair of scissors.

Heat 2 cm (¾ inch) of oil in a wok over medium heat and fry the tofu skins in batches for 40–60 seconds, until golden brown. Drain well on paper towel.

With lightly oiled fingers, divide the pork mixture into 12 portions. Take one portion and form into a long sausage shape around one of the bamboo skewers. Repeat with the remaining pork mixture and skewers.

Soak the vermicelli in boiling water for 4–5 minutes. Gently stir to separate the noodles, then drain and refresh under cold water. Use kitchen scissors to cut the vermicelli into easy-to-manage lengths.

On platters, assemble the noodles, tofu skin, lettuce, mint, peanuts and pickles.

Heat a chargrill pan or barbecue to high. When hot, cook the skewers for 2–3 minutes on each side, then place on a platter.

Prepare the rice paper by taking one sheet and dipping it into warm water for 1 second. Do not allow to soak as the paper will continue to take in water and will tear when rolled. Remove and place on a flat surface for 20 seconds, removing any excess water with a clean cloth, then place on a serving platter. Continue with the remaining rice paper.

Invite diners to prepare their own rolls. To do this, place some lettuce, tofu skin, noodles, mint, pickles, peanuts and the meat from one skewer onto a sheet of rice paper, bring the bottom end over to encase the filling, then fold in the two sides and roll up.

Serve with the dipping sauce.

RICE DUMPLING STEAMED IN BANANA LEAF

Bánh nậm

This is a typical dish of Hue royal cuisine, and one of the very few to be eaten with a fork or spoon, as the dumplings are too difficult to pick up with chopsticks. Traditionally, the dumplings are steamed in galangal leaves, but outside Vietnam you can substitute banana leaves.

15 PRAWNS (SHRIMP), PEELED AND DEVEINED

200 G (7 OZ) MINCED (GROUND) PORK

1 TABLESPOON ANNATTO OIL (SEE PAGE 320)

2 RED ASIAN SHALLOTS, FINELY DICED

1 TEASPOON SUGAR

½ TEASPOON SALT

1 TEASPOON FRESHLY GROUND BLACK PEPPER

2 TEASPOONS FISH SAUCE

18 BANANA LEAF RECTANGLES, EACH MEASURING ABOUT 15 CM X 20 CM (6 INCHES X 8 INCHES)

BANH NAM DIPPING SAUCE (SEE PAGE 320), TO SERVE

RICE PASTE

250 G (9 OZ/1⅓ CUPS) RICE FLOUR

2 TEASPOONS SUGAR

½ TEASPOON SALT

MAKES 18

To make the rice paste, mix the rice flour, sugar and salt with 400 ml (13½ fl oz) water to form a thick paste. Leave to sit for 15 minutes while preparing the topping.

Using a mortar and pestle or food processor, grind the prawns into a fine paste (1). Transfer to a bowl and mix the pork through.

Heat the annatto oil in a frying pan. When hot, add the shallot and cook over medium heat until fragrant. Now add the pork mixture, sugar, salt and pepper and cook for 3–4 minutes, until the meat is coloured. Lastly add the fish sauce and cook for a further 1 minute (2). Remove from the heat and leave to cool slightly before making the dumplings.

Take one piece of banana leaf, non-shiny side up. Evenly spread ½ tablespoon of the rice paste in a rectangle shape in the centre. Place ½ tablespoon of the prawn mixture over the top (3). Fold the sides of the leaf over to cover the dumpling, then tuck the ends in underneath. Secure with a toothpick or small skewer.

Repeat with the remaining ingredients.

Place the dumplings in a steamer set over a saucepan of boiling water and cook for 10 minutes.

Serve the dumplings in the banana leaves. Diners unwrap their dumplings, drizzle a small amount of dipping sauce over the dumplings, then enjoy straight from the leaf using a spoon or fork.

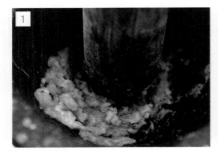

RICE NOODLES IN PORK BROTH WITH CHICKEN, PRAWNS AND OMELETTE

Bún thang

Thang is a loan word from the Chinese, meaning 'broth', pointing to the Chinese culinary influence on this northern noodle soup. This is considered a very sophisticated, subtle dish, often prepared on special occasions such as lunar new year (Tet), weddings and anniversaries. Traditionally, the qualities of a good *bun thang* have been likened to characteristics attributed to Vietnamese women: beauty, modesty and intelligence.

Gio lon is a pork loaf with fish sauce that is steamed in banana leaf. You can make it yourself (see recipe on page 302), or buy commercially produced *cha lua* from most Asian grocers. Alternatively, you can use good-quality ham instead.

3 KG (6 LB 10 OZ) PORK BONES

1 TEASPOON SALT

6 RED ASIAN SHALLOTS

6 DRIED SHRIMP

2 TEASPOONS SUGAR

20 ML (3⁄4 FL OZ) FISH SAUCE

1 CHICKEN BREAST, STILL ON THE BONE

4 EGGS

VEGETABLE OIL, FOR PAN-FRYING

600 G (1 LB 5 OZ) DRIED RICE VERMICELLI

12 COOKED PRAWNS (SHRIMP), PEELED AND DEVEINED

200 G (7 OZ) PORK LOAF (SEE PAGE 302), SLICED

4 SPRING ONIONS (SCALLIONS), SLICED

1 HANDFUL CORIANDER (CILANTRO), ROUGHLY CHOPPED

1½ TABLESPOONS FRIED SHALLOTS (SEE PAGE 326)

1 LIME, CUT INTO 6 WEDGES

SERVES 6

To prepare the broth, wash the bones under cold water, then place in a large saucepan and cover with cold water. Add the salt and slowly bring to simmering point, skimming off any froth that rises to the surface.

Meanwhile, chargrill the whole unpeeled shallots on a barbecue or gas burner over medium heat for about 5 minutes, until they are fragrant and the skin is lightly charred. Remove and cool slightly. Using your fingers, flake off the outer thin layer of skin.

Add the chargrilled shallots to the broth along with the dried shrimp, sugar and fish sauce. Simmer for 2 hours, skimming regularly to ensure you have a clear broth.

Add the chicken breast to the broth and simmer for a further 20 minutes. Remove the chicken, then strain the broth and discard the solids. When the chicken is cool enough to handle, remove the meat from the bone and thinly slice.

Pour the broth into a clean saucepan and return to a simmer. Bring a separate saucepan of water to the boil.

Meanwhile, break two eggs into a small bowl and whisk. Pour into a hot lightly oiled frying pan and gently stir for 5 seconds. Ensure the base of the pan is covered in the egg, and allow to cook until set. Remove from the pan and repeat with the remaining eggs. When the omelettes have cooled, cut them into strips about 5 mm (¼ inch) wide.

Soak the vermicelli in boiling water for 4–5 minutes. Gently stir to separate the noodles, then drain and refresh under cold water. Use kitchen scissors to cut the vermicelli into easy-to-manage lengths. Divide among six bowls.

Top the noodles with the shredded egg, prawns, pork, spring onion and coriander. Ladle the hot broth over and sprinkle with the fried shallots. Serve straight away, with the lime wedges.

SPRING ROLLS WITH CHINESE SAUSAGE, JICAMA AND OMELETTE

Bò bía

Roaming street vendors peddle these spring rolls from their carts in Ho Chi Minh City. This dish is a legacy of the migration of ethnic Chinese to southern Vietnam, many of whom settled in the Cholon district. Traditionally, the Chinese would have made these rolls with wheat-based wrappers, but the Vietnamese have adapted the recipe to suit local tastes and now use rice paper wrappers.

Lap cheong is a dry pork sausage with a slightly sweet taste and a hint of cassia. It is readily available from Asian grocers.

48 SMALL DRIED SHRIMP

3 LAP CHEONG SAUSAGES

8 EGGS

VEGETABLE OIL, FOR PAN-FRYING

3 GARLIC CLOVES, CHOPPED

24 RICE PAPER SHEETS, ABOUT 18 CM (7 INCHES) IN SIZE

1 BUTTER LETTUCE, SEPARATED INTO CUPS

1 JICAMA, PEELED AND CUT INTO MATCHSTICKS

1 HANDFUL THAI BASIL

HOISIN DIPPING SAUCE (SEE PAGE 328), TO SERVE

MAKES 24

Cover the dried shrimp with warm water and allow to soak while preparing the remaining ingredients.

Cook the whole sausages in a frying pan on all sides over medium heat for 5–6 minutes, then drain well on paper towel. When cool enough to handle, cut the sausages at an angle into slices 3 mm (⅛ inch) thick.

Break two eggs into a small bowl and whisk. Pour into a lightly oiled hot frying pan and gently stir for 5 seconds. Ensure the base of the pan is covered in the egg, and allow to cook until set. Remove from the pan and repeat with the remaining eggs. When the omelettes have cooled, cut them into strips about 5 mm (¼ inch) wide.

Drain the shrimp and reserve the liquid for the dipping sauce.

Heat 1 tablespoon of oil in a frying pan and sauté the garlic over medium heat until fragrant. Add the shrimp and cook for a further 3–4 minutes. Remove from the pan and set aside.

When all the cooked ingredients have cooled, you can begin rolling the spring rolls.

Take one sheet of rice paper and dip it into warm water for 1 second. Do not allow to soak, as the paper will tear when rolled. Place on a flat surface, wait for 20 seconds, then soak up any excess water with a clean cloth.

On the bottom third of the sheet, place a lettuce cup, some omelette strips, jicama, basil, sausage and two shrimp. Bring the bottom of the wrapper up over the filling, then fold in the sides and roll up. Set aside, seam side down.

Continue with the remaining ingredients, then serve with the dipping sauce.

STICKY RICE FROM THE COUNTRYSIDE WITH PORK AND MUNG BEANS

Bánh khúc

Traditionally this dish from the northern provinces was eaten after the rice harvest, when *khuc* leaf was available. As the leaf is rare, this family recipe has been adapted to use spinach and pandan instead.

9 RED ASIAN SHALLOTS, THINLY SLICED

1 TABLESPOON VEGETABLE OIL

500 G (1 LB 2 OZ) SPINACH LEAVES

150 G (5½ OZ) DRIED MUNG BEANS, SOAKED FOR 2 HOURS

110 G (4 OZ) PORK BELLY, CUT INTO 5 MM (¼ INCH) PIECES

1 TEASPOON FRESHLY CRACKED BLACK PEPPER

2½ TEASPOONS SALT

2 PANDAN LEAVES, CUT INTO THIN STRIPS USING SCISSORS

250 G (9 OZ/1⅓ CUPS) GLUTINOUS RICE FLOUR

1 KG (2 LB 3 OZ) GLUTINOUS RICE, SOAKED FOR 2 HOURS

1 BANANA LEAF

PEANUT AND SESAME MIX (SEE PAGE 334), TO SERVE

SERVES 6

Sauté the shallot in the oil over medium heat for 3–4 minutes, until soft and translucent. Remove from the heat and set aside.

In another pan, cook the spinach without any oil or water until wilted, then place in iced water to keep its colour. When cool, drain the spinach and squeeze out as much water as possible.

Drain the soaked mung beans and place in a bowl with the sautéed shallot, pork, pepper and ½ teaspoon of the salt. Mix well, then form into balls the size of golf balls. Set aside.

For the dough, put the pandan leaves in a mortar with the spinach and 2 tablespoons of the rice flour, then pound together until you have a smooth mixture (1).

Remove the spinach mixture from the mortar, then divide into six portions. Divide the remaining rice flour into six portions.

Return one portion of the spinach mixture to the mortar.

Slowly add one portion of the rice flour and 1 tablespoon water. Pound until the mixture reaches the consistency of pasta dough. Form into a flat disc, set aside and repeat with the remaining spinach mixture and rice flour portions.

Take a dough disc and place a mung bean ball in the centre. Bring up the sides of the dough to seal the filling and form a ball (2). Repeat with the remaining dough and mung bean balls.

Drain the sticky rice and stir in the remaining 2 teaspoons salt. Place half the rice into a prepared steamer. Nestle the six mung bean balls into the rice and top with the rest of the sticky rice (3). Cover with the banana leaf, cutting it to size if needed, then cover with a tight-fitting lid. Cook for 45 minutes.

Remove the mung bean balls, covered in the sticky rice, and serve warm, with the peanut and sesame mix.

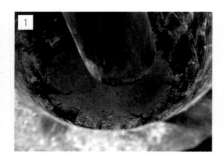

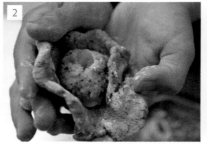

TAPIOCA DUMPLINGS WITH PRAWN AND PORK

Bánh bột lọc

Tapioca makes for a lovely chewy and sticky dumpling, but is not the easiest flour to use. We did a lot of research trying to work out how the street vendors in Hue achieve the tapioca dumpling's translucent look, and it seems this is due to the addition of borax, which is not yet banned as a food additive in Vietnam. Needless to say, borax is not included in this recipe, which preserves the taste and texture of the original dumpling. However, it doesn't have the same appearance you may be familiar with from visiting Hue.

1 TABLESPOON VEGETABLE OIL

2 RED ASIAN SHALLOTS, DICED

150 G (5½ OZ) MINCED (GROUND) PORK

8 PRAWNS (SHRIMP), PEELED AND DEVEINED, CUT INTO THIRDS

1 TABLESPOON SUGAR

1 TABLESPOON OYSTER SAUCE

½ TABLESPOON FISH SAUCE

½ TEASPOON SALT

⅓ TEASPOON FRESHLY GROUND BLACK PEPPER

CLASSIC DIPPING SAUCE (SEE PAGE 323), TO SERVE

DOUGH

150 G (5½ OZ/1 CUP) TAPIOCA FLOUR, PLUS EXTRA FOR DUSTING

½ TABLESPOON VEGETABLE OIL

⅓ TEASPOON SUGAR

½ TEASPOON SALT

MAKES 24 DUMPLINGS

To make the dough, place the tapioca flour in a bowl and add the oil, sugar and salt. Pour in 190 ml (6½ fl oz/¾ cup) boiling water and combine with a spoon.

When the dough is cool enough to handle, remove to a lightly floured work surface and knead for 5–7 minutes, until smooth. Cover with a damp cloth and allow to rest for 20 minutes, so it will be easier to handle.

For the filling, heat the oil in a frying pan over medium heat and sauté the shallot for about 1 minute. Add the pork and cook for 2–3 minutes, until the meat is evenly coloured. Now add the prawns and cook for a further 1 minute. Remove and drain on paper towel.

Wipe the pan clean and return to the heat. Sprinkle the sugar on the base of the pan and allow to caramelise until it is a deep golden colour.

Standing away from the pan, pour in 100 ml (3½ fl oz) water. When the spluttering has stopped, add the oyster sauce, fish sauce, salt and pepper and stir to combine. Add the prawn

mixture and reduce the heat to a simmer. Continue cooking until all the liquid has been absorbed, then remove from the heat and leave to cool.

Bring a large saucepan of water to the boil.

Meanwhile, divide the dough into 24 balls, then cover with a damp cloth so they don't dry out. Using a rolling pin, flatten one ball into a 5–6 cm (2–2½ inch) disc.

On one half of the disc, place a teaspoon of the filling, making sure a piece of prawn is sitting on top. Fold the dough over and seal with your fingers, making sure no air is trapped inside, as the dumpling will otherwise burst when cooking.

Place the dumpling on a lightly oiled tray and continue with the remaining ingredients.

Boil the dumplings in batches for 2 minutes. Remove with a slotted spoon and place in cold water for 30 seconds to stop the cooking process. Remove from the water and drain well.

Serve warm, with the dipping sauce.

CONDIMENTS

ANNATTO OIL

Dầu điều

Annatto seeds are small seeds grown on trees originating from South America. They are used mainly for colouring, as they have very little flavour.

250 ML (8½ FL OZ/1 CUP) VEGETABLE OR CANOLA OIL
1 TABLESPOON ANNATTO SEEDS

MAKES 250 ML (8½ FL OZ/1 CUP)

Put the oil and annatto seeds in a saucepan and gently heat for 1 hour, until the oil takes on a deep red colour. Do not allow the oil to boil or become too hot, or it will taste bitter.

Remove from the heat and leave to cool completely. Strain the oil through a fine sieve and discard the annatto seeds.

Store the oil in a sealed jar for up to 4 weeks.

BANH NAM DIPPING SAUCE

Nước chấm bánh nậm

1½ TABLESPOONS SUGAR
60 ML (2 FL OZ/¼ CUP) FISH SAUCE
2 GARLIC CLOVES, FINELY CHOPPED

1 LONG RED CHILLI, SEEDED AND CHOPPED

SERVES 6

Combine the sugar and 60 ml (2 fl oz/¼ cup) water in a small bowl and stir until the sugar has completely dissolved.

Stir in the fish sauce, garlic and chilli and divide among six dipping bowls.

BUN CHA DIPPING SAUCE

Nước chấm bún chả

200 G (7 OZ) SUGAR

200 ML (7 FL OZ) WATER OR PORK STOCK

100 ML (3½ FL OZ) FISH SAUCE

100 ML (3½ FL OZ) RICE VINEGAR

100 ML (3½ FL OZ) LIME JUICE

1 LONG RED CHILLI, SEEDED AND CHOPPED

3 GARLIC CLOVES, CHOPPED

½ SMALL CARROT, THINLY SLICED

60 G (2 OZ/½ CUP) THINLY SLICED GREEN PAPAYA FLESH

MAKES ABOUT 500 ML (17 FL OZ/2 CUPS)

Combine the sugar and the water or stock in a saucepan and heat until the sugar has completely dissolved. Remove from the heat.

Stir in the remaining ingredients and divide among six dipping bowls.

CARROT AND DAIKON PICKLE

Dưa góp

1 CARROT

½ DAIKON

250 ML (8½ FL OZ/1 CUP) RICE VINEGAR

2 TEASPOONS SALT

100 G (3½ OZ) SUGAR

MAKES ABOUT 500 ML (17 FL OZ/2 CUPS)

Peel the carrot and daikon and cut into 5 cm (2 inch) batons. Place in a container or large screw-top jar.

To make the pickling liquid, heat the vinegar, salt, sugar and 190 ml (6½ fl oz/¾ cup) water in a small saucepan until the sugar has completely dissolved. Allow to cool until lukewarm.

Pour the liquid over the vegetables and leave to pickle for at least 1 hour before eating.

The pickled vegetables will keep covered in the fridge for 2 weeks.

CHILLI SAUCE

Sốt ớt

1 KG (2 LB 3 OZ) LONG RED CHILLIES
500 G (1 LB 2 OZ) TOMATOES
165 G (6 OZ/¾ CUP) SUGAR
3 GARLIC CLOVES, CUT IN HALF

2 TEASPOONS SALT
2 TEASPOONS VINEGAR
MAKES 750 ML (25½ FL OZ/3 CUPS)

Cut the chillies in half lengthways. Remove the seeds, then place the seeds in a small saucepan. Put the chilli halves in a separate saucepan.

Remove the seeds from the tomatoes by cutting the tomatoes in half, then scooping out the seeds with a teaspoon. Add the tomato seeds to the same pan as the chilli seeds. Roughly chop the tomatoes and place them in the same pan as the chilli halves.

Add the sugar, garlic and 250 ml (8½ fl oz/1 cup) water to the pan containing the tomato seeds and chilli seeds. Bring to the boil, then reduce the heat and simmer for 2 minutes. Remove from the heat.

Strain the seed liquid into the pan containing the chillies and tomatoes, discarding the seeds. Stir in the salt, vinegar and 310 ml (10½ fl oz/1¼ cups) cold water and slowly bring to the boil. Now reduce the heat and simmer for 8–10 minutes, until the chillies are soft.

Remove from the heat and purée the mixture in a food processor. Strain the sauce through a fine sieve, into an airtight container, discarding the skins.

The sauce will keep in an airtight container in the refrigerator for up to 1 month.

CHILLI AND LEMONGRASS DIPPING SALT

Chấm muối ớt, sả

1½ TABLESPOONS SEA SALT
½ LONG RED CHILLI, SEEDED AND FINELY CHOPPED

1 LEMONGRASS STEM, WHITE PART ONLY, FINELY CHOPPED
SERVES 6

Place the salt, chilli and lemongrass on a chopping board and chop for about 10 seconds to combine the flavours.

Divide among six dipping bowls.

CLASSIC DIPPING SAUCE

Nước chấm truyền thống

100 ML (3½ FL OZ) LIME JUICE

1 TEASPOON RICE VINEGAR

110 G (4 OZ/½ CUP) SUGAR

60 ML (2 FL OZ/¼ CUP) FISH SAUCE

2 GARLIC CLOVES, FINELY CHOPPED

1 LONG RED CHILLI, FINELY CHOPPED

SERVES 6

Combine the lime juice, vinegar and sugar in a small bowl. Stir until the sugar has completely dissolved.

Stir in the fish sauce, garlic and chilli and divide among six dipping bowls.

FISH SAUCE AND COCONUT DIPPING SAUCE

Nước chấm dừa

80 ML (2½ FL OZ/⅓ CUP) COCONUT JUICE

80 ML (2½ FL OZ/⅓ CUP) RICE VINEGAR

110 G (4 OZ/½ CUP) SUGAR

80 ML (2½ FL OZ/⅓ CUP) FISH SAUCE

2 GARLIC CLOVES, FINELY CHOPPED

1 LONG RED CHILLI, SEEDED AND FINELY CHOPPED

SERVES 6

Put the coconut juice, vinegar and sugar in a bowl and whisk until the sugar has dissolved.

Stir in the fish sauce, garlic and chilli and divide among six dipping bowls.

DIPPING SAUCES

LEFT TO RIGHT (1) Prawn dipping sauce (Sốt tom chua), (2) Soy Chilli dipping sauce (Xì dầu ớt), (3) Tomato dipping sauce (Sốt cà chua), (4) Vegan dipping sauce (Nước chấm chay), (5) Annatto oil (Dầu điều), (6) Classic dipping sauce (Nước chấm truyền thống), (7) Chilli sauce (Sốt ớt), (8) Tamarind water (Sốt me), (9) Oyster and wasabi (Sốt hao va mu tạc), (10) Fish sauce and coconut dipping sauce (Nước chấm dừa), (11) Spring onion oil (Dầu hanh), (12) Hoisin dipping sauce (Dầu hao), (13) Ginger dipping sauce (Nước chấm gừng), (14) Spicy satay sauce (Sốt satay cay)

FRIED GARLIC

Tỏi phi

4 GARLIC CLOVES

VEGETABLE OIL, FOR DEEP-FRYING

MAKES ABOUT 2 TABLESPOONS

Peel the garlic and thinly slice lengthways, ensuring the slices are all the same thickness so they will cook evenly.

Heat about 4 cm (1½ inches) of oil in a wok or deep frying pan over high heat. To test the oil, place the tip of a wooden chopstick into the oil — when bubbles slowly rise to the surface, the oil is hot enough to use.

Cook the garlic in two batches, using a slotted spoon to keep the garlic moving, and to remove when the garlic is golden brown. Drain well on paper towel.

The fried garlic chips will keep for up to 3 days in an airtight container.

FRIED SHALLOTS

Hành phi

6 RED ASIAN SHALLOTS, PEELED

VEGETABLE OR PEANUT OIL, FOR DEEP-FRYING

MAKES ABOUT 2 TABLESPOONS

Finely slice the shallots lengthways, ensuring the slices are all the same thickness so they will cook evenly.

Heat about 4 cm (1½ inches) of oil in a wok or deep frying pan over high heat until it is hot, but not smoking. To test the oil, drop in a shallot slice — it should sizzle when it hits the oil.

When the oil is ready, add half the shallot. Carefully move the pieces around in the oil using a metal spoon to ensure they colour evenly. When the shallot is golden brown, remove

with a slotted spoon and drain well on paper towel. Repeat with the remaining shallot.

Leave to cool, then store in a sealed bottle.

For maximum crispness, fried shallots are best eaten on the day they are cooked.

GINGER DIPPING SAUCE

Nước chấm gừng

125 ml (4 fl oz/½ cup) fish sauce

1 teaspoon sugar

2 cm (¾ inch) knob fresh ginger, thinly sliced

3 garlic cloves, chopped

1 long red chilli, chopped

SERVES 6

Combine the fish sauce and sugar in a small bowl. Stir until the sugar has completely dissolved.

Stir in the ginger, garlic and chilli and divide among six dipping bowls.

GREEN CHILLI DIPPING SALT

Chấm ớt xanh

1 long green chilli, roughly chopped

3 teaspoons sea salt

1 lime, cut into 6 wedges

SERVES 6

Place the chilli in a mortar and pound to a coarse texture. Add the salt and pound until combined. Do not overwork the mixture, as larger pieces of chilli and salt enhance the flavour of this dipping salt.

Divide among six dipping bowls. Just before serving, squeeze a wedge of lime over each bowl.

HOISIN DIPPING SAUCE

Dầu hào

40 G (1½ OZ/¼ CUP) ROASTED UNSALTED PEANUTS, CHOPPED

1 TABLESPOON VEGETABLE OIL

2 GARLIC CLOVES, CHOPPED

60 ML (2 FL OZ/¼ CUP) HOISIN SAUCE

1½ TABLESPOONS WATER RESERVED FROM SOAKING DRIED SHRIMP, OR JUST USE PLAIN WATER

1 RED BIRD'S EYE CHILLI, SEEDED AND CHOPPED

SERVES 6

Place half the peanuts in a mortar and grind to a coarse powder. Set aside.

Heat the oil in a wok or frying pan over medium heat and cook the garlic until fragrant. Add the ground peanuts and toss together.

Stir in the hoisin sauce, the water and half the chilli, then cook for a further 2 minutes. If the sauce is too thick after this time, add a little more water to obtain the desired dipping consistency.

Remove from the heat and divide among six dipping bowls. When cool, scatter the remaining peanuts and chilli on top.

LIME AND CHILLI DIPPING SALT

Lá chanh muối ớt

½ TEASPOON SEA SALT

1 KAFFIR LIME LEAF, SLICED INTO THIN STRIPS (OPTIONAL)

2–3 THIN RED CHILLI RINGS (SEE NOTE)

¼ SMALL LIME, CUT INTO A WEDGE

SERVES 1

Place a little mound of the salt in a dipping bowl. Next to the salt place the lime leaf, if using, and the chilli, and beside that the lime wedge.

Just before serving, squeeze the lime juice into the centre of the dipping bowl and stir with a chopstick to incorporate the flavours.

Note: Instead of chilli rings, you can use some freshly ground black pepper.

MAYONNAISE

May ơ nais

2 EGG YOLKS

3 TEASPOONS LIME JUICE OR RICE VINEGAR

½ TEASPOON SALT

¼ TEASPOON FRESHLY GROUND BLACK PEPPER

200 ML (7 FL OZ) VEGETABLE OIL

MAKES ABOUT 250 ML (8½ FL OZ/1 CUP)

Before you start, ensure all the ingredients are at room temperature, as this will result in a more stable mayonnaise.

Place the egg yolks, lime juice, salt and pepper in a bowl and beat with a wire whisk for 40–60 seconds, until the eggs slightly thicken.

Keep whisking, and in a slow steady stream pour in the oil, ensuring it is fully emulsified into the egg yolks. This should take 4–5 minutes, or will happen more quickly if using an electric mixer or food processor.

Use immediately, or cover and store in the refrigerator for up to 1 week.

OYSTER AND WASABI DIPPING SAUCE

Sốt hào và mù tạc

100 ML (3½ FL OZ) OYSTER SAUCE

JUICE OF ½ LEMON

½ TEASPOON CASTER (SUPERFINE) SUGAR

¼ TEASPOON WASABI PASTE, OR TO TASTE

SERVES 6

Combine the oyster sauce, lemon juice and sugar in a small bowl, mixing until the sugar has completely dissolved.

Divide the sauce among six dipping bowls and add a small portion of wasabi to each.

PHU QUOC'S TREASURES: FISH SAUCE & PEPPER

THE ANNOUNCEMENT CAME THROUGH 15 MINUTES BEFORE BOARDING: 'MS LISTER, MR POHL, REPORT TO THE CUSTOMS OFFICE IMMEDIATELY!' THE CUSTOMS OFFICERS STERNLY ORDERED US TO OPEN OUR SUITCASE. IT TOOK THEM LESS THAN A MINUTE TO REMOVE THE OFFENDING ITEMS: TWO BOTTLES OF PHU QUOC'S FINEST FISH SAUCE. UNBEKNOWN TO US, THE AIRLINE DIDN'T ALLOW THIS LOCAL SPECIALTY TO BE CARRIED TO THE MAINLAND, LEST THE CARGO HOLD BE FOULED BY THE SAUCE'S PUNGENT ODOUR FROM BOTTLES BREAKING IN TRANSIT.

Phu Quoc, in the Gulf of Thailand, is Vietnam's largest island, and resonates with Khmer, Chinese and Vietnamese influences. Through history, the Khmer have been the island's main inhabitants, with the Vietnamese and Chinese settling during the 18th and 19th centuries. Despite its proximity to Cambodia (which on a clear day can be seen from its northern shore), the French colonial authorities gave the island to Vietnam, although Cambodia continues to claim it as theirs, calling it Koh Tral. Despite efforts by the French to establish coconut and rubber plantations, the island's inhabitants stuck with two main industries: making fish sauce (*nuoc mam*), and growing pepper.

Our confiscated bottles were souvenirs from a visit to one of the hundred or so fish sauce distilleries on Phu Quoc. Overwhelmed by the aroma of fermenting fish that hung thickly in the tropical air, we had walked along rows of wooden vats, each holding in excess of 10,000 litres of the condiment on which, along with rice and herbs, an entire

cuisine is built. A rich source of the protein lacking in rice and herbs, fish sauce also contains amino acids, nitrates, vitamins and minerals. It is easy to see its importance to a diet in which throughout history, fish or meat was reserved for village feasts and other special occasions.

For centuries the fish sauce of Phu Quoc has been reputed to be the best in the country, if not the region. In the early 19th century, Trihn Hoai Duc, governor of Vietnam's southern provinces, likened its aroma to the sweetness of cinnamon, and it was so sought after that it had to be shipped under guard to the mainland.

Good fish sauce has a dark colour, yet remains transparent. One way to test its quality is to dip a finger in it, then into clean water: if the scent disappears, the sauce is of lower quality. However, there was no dipping fingers with our guide. He made us slurp the fish sauce straight from tasting spoons, and while we probably wouldn't have settled for cinnamon, there was a complex, savoury and mouth-filling richness of maritime flavours just beneath that first taste of saltiness.

The basics of making fish sauce appear deceptively simple: three parts fish and one part salt are packed in layers into the vats and weighed down by a heavy lid; it is then left to nature to run its course. The salt preserves the fish and assists in separating liquids from solids during fermentation. The fish is kept in the vats for at least 12 months, and every day during that time, the liquid from the bottom of the vat is poured back over the fish and salt mixture. Yet within this straightforward procedure, a skilled artisan can turn fermenting fish into liquid gold.

The locals claim three things set their *nuoc mam* apart. First, the fish: a variety of anchovies called *ca com*, found only in the waters around the island. Second, using wooden vats instead of the earthenware ones employed elsewhere is said to contribute to the taste, in the same way oak does with wine. (Traditionally, wood from the *boi loi* tree native to Phu Quoc was used to make the vats, but the tree is now considered endangered and the vats are now made with other wood, or in more industrial operations with concrete.) Finally, many Phu Quoc fish sauce artisans add a little of the local pepper to the salt mixture.

Phu Quoc's climate and soil are particularly suited to growing this spice, and there are almost 400 hectares of pepper gardens on the island. Historically, Vietnam imported pepper from China, but in the 19th century it decided that importing pepper farmers instead might be more lucrative in the long term.

Settlers from Hainan started the island's pepper industry. Phu Quoc pepper is a big seed with a thin skin, harvested from February to early July when the corns start to turn a reddish colour. Hand-picked from vines growing up to 10 metres in height, the green seeds are briefly cooked in hot water to tear the skin, speeding up the drying process. They are then laid out under the sun on every available surface — be they front yards, roofs or the side of the roads — until they have shrivelled into hard black corns, ready to be cracked to release their aromatic, spicy flavour.

PEANUT AND SESAME MIX

Muối vừng lạc

50 G (1¾ OZ/⅓ CUP) ROASTED UNSALTED PEANUTS
40 G (1½ OZ/¼ CUP) TOASTED SESAME SEEDS
PINCH OF CASTER (SUPERFINE) SUGAR

⅔ TEASPOON SALT

SERVES 6

Pound the peanuts and sesame seeds to crumbs using a mortar and pestle. Stir the sugar and salt through.

Divide among six dipping bowls and serve.

PEANUT SAUCE

Sốt lạc

1 TABLESPOON VEGETABLE OIL
2 GARLIC CLOVES, FINELY CHOPPED
1 RED BIRD'S EYE CHILLI, FINELY CHOPPED
160 G (5½ OZ/1 CUP) ROASTED, UNSALTED PEANUTS,
CHOPPED, PLUS EXTRA TO GARNISH
1 TABLESPOON SESAME SEEDS, TOASTED
½ LEMONGRASS STEM, WHITE PART ONLY, FINELY CHOPPED

125 ML (4 FL OZ/½ CUP) COCONUT MILK
2 TABLESPOONS HOISIN SAUCE
1 TABLESPOON FISH SAUCE
1 TABLESPOON CASTER (SUPERFINE) SUGAR

SERVES 6

Heat the oil in a wok or frying pan over medium heat. Add the garlic and chilli and fry for 1–2 minutes, until fragrant.

Add the peanuts, sesame seeds and lemongrass and toss.

Add the coconut milk, 125 ml (4 fl oz/½ cup) water, and the remaining ingredients, except the extra peanuts.

Bring to the boil, then reduce the heat and simmer for 3–5 minutes, or until the sauce thickens. Remove from the heat and allow to cool.

Divide the sauce among small dipping bowls and serve with a sprinkling of extra peanuts. This sauce is best served on the day it is made.

PEANUT, GARLIC AND SHALLOT DIPPING SAUCE

Nước chấm tỏi ớt

100 ML (3½ FL OZ) LIME JUICE
1 TEASPOON RICE VINEGAR
110 G (4 OZ/½ CUP) SUGAR
60 ML (2 FL OZ/¼ CUP) FISH SAUCE
1 LONG RED CHILLI, CHOPPED
50 G (1¾ OZ/⅓ CUP) PEANUTS

1 TABLESPOON VEGETABLE OIL
3 GARLIC CLOVES, FINELY CHOPPED
2 RED ASIAN SHALLOTS, FINELY DICED
1 LEMONGRASS STEM, WHITE PART ONLY, FINELY CHOPPED
SERVES 6

Combine the lime juice, vinegar and sugar in a small bowl and mix until the sugar has dissolved. Stir in the fish sauce and chilli and set aside.

Pound the peanuts to a coarse texture in a mortar. Set aside.

Heat the oil in a wok or frying pan over medium heat. Sauté the garlic, shallot and lemongrass until fragrant. Add the peanuts and continue cooking for 1–2 minutes, keeping the wok moving to stop the peanuts burning.

Stir the peanut mixture through the fish sauce mixture, then divide among six dipping bowls.

PICKLED BEAN SPROUTS

Dưa giá

125 ML (4 FL OZ/½ CUP) RICE VINEGAR
2 TEASPOONS SALT
¼ TEASPOON CASTER (SUPERFINE) SUGAR
100 G (3½ OZ) BEAN SPROUTS, SCRAGGLY ENDS REMOVED
1 TELEGRAPH (LONG) CUCUMBER, PEELED AND CUT INTO 5 CM (2 INCH) BATONS

½ PINEAPPLE, PEELED AND CUT INTO 5 CM (2 INCH) BATONS
1 LONG RED CHILLI, SEEDED AND CHOPPED
SERVES 6

To make the pickling liquid, heat the vinegar, salt and sugar in a small saucepan until the sugar has completely dissolved. Allow to cool until lukewarm.

Combine the bean sprouts, cucumber, pineapple and chilli in a bowl.

Pour the cooled pickling liquid over and lightly toss through. Allow to pickle for 30 minutes before serving.

This pickle is best served on the day it is made.

PICKLED CABBAGE

Dưa muối

2 CARROTS, THINLY SLICED

¼ CABBAGE, THINLY SLICED

2 TABLESPOONS SALT

2 TABLESPOONS SUGAR

125 ML (4 FL OZ/½ CUP) RICE VINEGAR

3 CM (1¼ INCH) KNOB FRESH GINGER, FINELY CHOPPED

2 LONG RED CHILLIES, SEEDED AND FINELY CHOPPED

4 GARLIC CLOVES, ROUGHLY CHOPPED

MAKES ABOUT 900 G (2 LB/4 CUPS)

Put the carrot and cabbage in a bowl and cover with cold water. Add the salt and leave to sit for 30 minutes. Drain the vegetables and return to the bowl.

In another small bowl, combine the sugar and vinegar. Stir until the sugar has completely dissolved, then add the ginger, chilli and garlic.

Pour the pickling liquid over the vegetables and evenly mix through.

Store in an airtight container in the refrigerator for 24 hours before use.

This pickle will keep for up to 2 weeks in the refrigerator.

PRAWN DIPPING SAUCE

Sốt tôm chua

A Hue specialty, pickled shrimp is sold in jars at Asian grocers. The liquid from the pickled shrimp, used in this dipping sauce below, is a souring agent like vinegar, but more complex in flavour.

1 TABLESPOON VEGETABLE OIL

2 CM (¾ INCH) KNOB FRESH GINGER, FINELY CHOPPED

2 GARLIC CLOVES, FINELY CHOPPED

100 G (3½ OZ) RAW PRAWNS (SHRIMP), PEELED AND DEVEINED, FINELY CHOPPED

2 TABLESPOONS OYSTER SAUCE

1 TABLESPOON PICKLING LIQUID FROM HUE PICKLED SHRIMP

SERVES 6

Heat the oil in a small frying pan over medium heat and add the ginger and garlic. Stir continually to ensure they don't burn. When fragrant, add the prawn and continue frying for 1 minute, or until cooked through.

Reduce the heat and stir in the oyster sauce and pickling liquid. Remove from the heat and season to taste with salt and freshly ground black pepper.

Add a little water if needed to achieve the right consistency for dipping, then divide among six dipping bowls.

RENDERED CHICKEN FAT

Mỡ gà

Your butcher will usually have the excess skin and fat from chickens, and will probably be happy to give it to you at no cost.

250 G (9 OZ) EXCESS CHICKEN FAT   **MAKES ABOUT 80 ML (2½ FL OZ/⅓ CUP)**

Place the chicken fat in a heavy-based saucepan. Add a small amount of water — 1–2 tablespoons depending on the amount of fat.

Place over low heat and slowly bring to simmering point. Cook for 4–5 minutes, or until the fat is clear. Strain through a fine sieve, discarding any solids.

The rendered fat can be refrigerated in an airtight container for up to 1 month.

ROASTED RICE FLOUR

Thính

100 G (3½ OZ/½ CUP) LONG-GRAIN WHITE RICE   **MAKES ABOUT 100 G (3½ OZ/½ CUP)**

Heat a wok or heavy-based frying pan over high heat. Add the rice and reduce the heat to medium.

Using a wooden spoon, keep the rice moving in the wok for 4–5 minutes, until lightly golden all over.

Remove from the heat and pound the rice to a fine powder using a mortar and pestle.

Store in an airtight container in a cool, dark place for up to 2 months.

CONDIMENTS

LEFT TO RIGHT (1) Fried shallots (Hanh phi), (2) Lime and chilli dipping salt (La chanh muối ớt), (3) Vegetable pickle (Dưa chua), (4) Vinegar shallots (Hanh muối), (5) Mayonnaise (May ơ nais), (6) Chilli and lemongrass dipping salt (Chấm muối ớt, sả), (7) Carrot and daikon pickle (Dưa gop), (8) Peanut and sesame mix (Muối vừng lạc), (9) Green chilli dipping sauce (Chấm ớt xanh), (10) Bun cha dipping sauce (Nước chấm bbn chả), (11) Pickled bean sprouts (Dưa gia), (12) Roasted rice flour (Thinh), (13) Pickled cabbage (Dưa muối), (14) Fried garlic (Tỏi phi)

SOY CHILLI DIPPING SAUCE

Xì dầu ớt

100 ML (3½ FL OZ) SOY SAUCE

JUICE OF ½ LIME

¼ TEASPOON SUGAR

½ LONG RED CHILLI, CUT INTO THIN RINGS

SERVES 6

Combine the soy sauce, lime juice and sugar in a small bowl. Stir until the sugar has completely dissolved.

Divide the sauce among six dipping bowls. Add the chilli and serve.

SPICY SATAY SAUCE

Sốt satay cay

6 DRIED SHRIMP

190 ML (6½ FL OZ/¾ CUP) PEANUT OIL

8 GARLIC CLOVES, FINELY CHOPPED

3 RED ASIAN SHALLOTS, FINELY CHOPPED

2 LONG RED CHILLIES, FINELY CHOPPED

3 TEASPOONS SUGAR

1 TABLESPOON SOY SAUCE

2 TABLESPOONS FISH SAUCE

MAKES ABOUT 250 ML (8½ FL OZ/1 CUP)

Soak the dried shrimp in cold water for 1 hour. Drain the shrimp, then pound in a mortar or finely chop. Set aside.

Heat the oil in a heavy-based saucepan over medium heat, then add the garlic and shallot and cook until fragrant.

Add the pounded shrimp and chilli. Reduce the heat and cook for a further 8–10 minutes, stirring occasionally.

Stir in the sugar, soy and fish sauce. Cook for a further 2–3 minutes for the flavours to develop, and until the mixture assumes the consistency of a paste.

Remove from the heat and allow to cool before using.

The sauce can be refrigerated in an airtight container for up to 2 weeks.

SPRING ONION OIL

Dầu hành

6 SPRING ONIONS (SCALLIONS)
80 ML (2½ FL OZ/⅓ CUP) PEANUT OIL

SERVES 6

Thinly slice the green part of the spring onions. Set aside the white and pale green ends for use in another dish.

Heat the peanut oil in a frying pan or wok over medium heat. Add the spring onion greens and keep them moving with a wooden spoon for a few seconds. As soon as the spring onion wilts, remove from the pan.

Divide the oil and spring onion among six dipping bowls.

SWEET COCONUT SAUCE

Sốt nước dừa

250 ML (8½ FL OZ/1 CUP) COCONUT MILK
2 TEASPOONS SUGAR
1 PANDAN LEAF, CRUSHED

2 TEASPOONS CORNFLOUR (CORNSTARCH), MIXED TO A SMOOTH PASTE WITH 1 TABLESPOON COLD WATER

MAKES ABOUT 250 ML (8½ FL OZ/1 CUP)

Put the coconut milk, sugar and pandan in a small pan with a pinch of salt. Slowly bring to simmering point. Remove from the heat and infuse for 20 minutes. Strain into a clean pan.

Bring the sauce back to simmering point. Add the cornflour mixture and stir for 1 minute, until the sauce thickens, and the raw cornflour taste has cooked out. Serve warm.

TAMARIND WATER

Sốt mè

200 G (7 OZ) TAMARIND PULP, BROKEN INTO SMALL PIECES

MAKES ABOUT 150 ML (5 FL OZ/⅔ CUP)

Soak the tamarind in 100 ml (3½ fl oz) warm water for 15 minutes, mashing the pulp now and then with a spoon. Pass the mixture through a sieve, discarding the seeds. The tamarind water can be refrigerated in a sealed jar for 3 weeks.

TOMATO DIPPING SAUCE

Sốt cà chua

6 TOMATOES, PEELED, SEEDED AND ROUGHLY CHOPPED
8 GARLIC CLOVES, FINELY CHOPPED
2 LONG RED CHILLIES, FINELY CHOPPED
55 G (2 OZ/¼ CUP) SUGAR
2 TABLESPOONS FISH SAUCE
1 TEASPOON CORNFLOUR (CORNSTARCH)
SERVES 6

Combine the tomatoes, garlic, chilli, sugar and fish sauce in a saucepan. Stir in 60 ml (2 fl oz/¼ cup) water. Bring to a gentle simmer and cook slowly for 15 minutes, or until the tomatoes are soft.

Pass the tomatoes through a fine sieve, into a clean saucepan, and return to the heat.

Mix the cornflour and a small amount of water to a smooth paste, then add to the tomato sauce, stirring continuously. Bring to the boil and cook for 3 minutes to remove any raw cornflour taste.

Remove from the heat and divide among six dipping bowls.

The sauce can be refrigerated in an airtight container for up to 1 week. Reheat before serving.

VINEGAR SHALLOTS

Hành muối

200 G (7 OZ) RED ASIAN SHALLOTS (THE SMALLER THE BETTER)
300 ML (10 FL OZ) RICE VINEGAR
MAKES ABOUT 500 G (1 LB 2 OZ/2 CUPS)

Peel the shallots, leaving the bulbs whole. Place in a bowl or container.

Gently heat the vinegar in a small saucepan, but do not allow to boil. Pour the hot vinegar over the shallots. Leave to cool, then cover.

Leave to steep for 24 hours before using.

The shallots can be refrigerated in an airtight container for up to 1 month.

VEGAN DIPPING SAUCE

Nước chấm chay

2 TABLESPOONS SOY SAUCE

1 TABLESPOON RICE VINEGAR

1 TABLESPOON LEMON JUICE

½ RED CHILLI, SEEDED AND CHOPPED

2 GARLIC CLOVES, CHOPPED

50 G (1¾ OZ/⅓ CUP) GREEN PAPAYA, PEELED AND THINLY SLICED INTO 2 CM (¾ INCH) LENGTHS

SERVES 6

Combine the soy sauce, vinegar and lemon juice in a small bowl. Add a pinch of sugar, a pinch of salt and 60 ml (2 fl oz/ ¼ cup) water. Whisk to combine.

Add the remaining ingredients and divide among six dipping bowls.

VEGETABLE PICKLE

Dưa chua

1 CARROT, THINLY SLICED

200 G (7 OZ) GREEN PAPAYA, FLESH THINLY SLICED

½ TEASPOON SALT

55 G (2 OZ/¼ CUP) SUGAR

60 ML (2 FL OZ/¼ CUP) RICE VINEGAR

2 TABLESPOONS FISH SAUCE

2 GARLIC CLOVES, CHOPPED

1 CHILLI, SEEDED AND CHOPPED

SERVES 6

Place the carrot and papaya in a bowl and sprinkle with the salt. Leave to sit for 5 minutes.

In another bowl, whisk together the sugar and vinegar until the sugar has completely dissolved. Add the fish sauce, garlic and chilli.

Wash the salt off the carrot and papaya, pat dry with paper towel and add to the fish sauce mixture.

The pickle can be refrigerated in an airtight container for up to 2 days.

SWEETS

AVOCADO SMOOTHIE

Sinh tố bơ

We were just as surprised to find out that the Vietnamese use avocado in smoothies, as they were on learning that we put it into salads — or even more strangely, on toast!

You can also use other fruits to make this smoothie: mango or dragon fruit are our favourites.

1 RIPE AVOCADO

70 G (2½ OZ/½ CUP) ICE CUBES, SLIGHTLY BROKEN UP USING A MORTAR AND PESTLE

60 ML (2 FL OZ/¼ CUP) CONDENSED MILK

190 ML (6½ FL OZ/¾ CUP) MILK OR SOY MILK

SERVES 2

Peel the avocado and purée the flesh in a blender. Add the remaining ingredients and pulse until combined and chilled.

Serve in two glasses, with long spoons to reach all the goodness at the bottom of the glass.

BANANA CAKE

Bánh chuối

A dessert for people with very sweet teeth! Like many Vietnamese desserts, it contains sweetened condensed milk, which was introduced by the French in the early 20th century and has maintained its popularity ever since.

9 RIPE BANANAS

BUTTER, FOR GREASING

2 TABLESPOONS SUGAR

5 EGGS, LIGHTLY WHISKED

250 ML (8½ FL OZ/1 CUP) CONDENSED MILK

125 ML (4 FL OZ/½ CUP) COCONUT MILK

200 G (7 OZ/1⅓ CUPS) PLAIN (ALL-PURPOSE) FLOUR

SERVES 10–12

Preheat the oven to 180°C (350°F). Generously butter a 24 cm (9½ inch) diameter round cake tin.

Peel the bananas and thinly slice them on the diagonal. Place on a tray, cut side up, and sprinkle with half the sugar. Set aside.

Put the remaining sugar in a large bowl. Add the eggs, condensed milk and coconut milk and stir together.

Add the flour and stir until just combined, taking care to not overwork the mixture or the cake will be tough. Lastly, add the sliced bananas and carefully coat them in the batter.

Pour the mixture into the cake tin. Bake for 50–60 minutes, or until a skewer inserted in the centre of the cake comes out clean.

Remove from the oven and let the cake cool in the tin for about 10 minutes before removing it.

Cut into wedges and enjoy with coffee or green tea.

This cake is best eaten on the day it is made.

COCONUT CRÈME CARAMEL

Ca ra men dừa

The coconut is a Vietnamese twist on the classic baked French custard. For best results use individual ceramic baking dishes or ramekins.

250 G CASTER (SUPERFINE) SUGAR, PLUS 1½ TABLESPOONS EXTRA, FOR THE CUSTARDS
3 EGGS, PLUS 2 EXTRA EGG YOLKS

250 ML (8½ FL OZ/1 CUP) MILK
75 ML (2½ FL OZ) COCONUT MILK

SERVES 6

Preheat the oven to 160°C (320°F).

To make the caramel, place the sugar and 125 ml (4 fl oz/ ½ cup) water in a small saucepan over gentle heat. Stir, while heating, until the sugar has completely dissolved. Once dissolved, increase the heat and boil for 8–10 minutes, until the water has evaporated and the sugar turns a deep golden colour. Remove from the heat.

When the caramel stops bubbling, pour it into six 150 ml (5 fl oz) ramekins. Pick up the ramekins and turn them carefully to coat the sides with the caramel.

For the custard, whisk together the eggs, egg yolks and extra sugar. Pour in the milk and coconut milk and mix until combined. Evenly pour the mixture into the six ramekins.

Place the ramekins in a deep baking dish lined with a tea towel (dish towel). Pour boiling water into the baking dish until it comes halfway up the side of the ramekins. Cover with foil and bake for 35 minutes.

Remove the ramekins from the hot water and allow to cool, then refrigerate overnight.

To serve, carefully run a palette knife around each custard, then invert the ramekin onto an individual serving plate. Remove the ramekin and allow the caramel to flow down the mound of custard.

COCONUT ICE CREAM

Kem dừa

If you don't have an ice-cream maker, you can follow the method for the Coffee yoghurt ice cream recipe below. However, please note that non-churned ice creams need to be eaten within 24 hours.

6 EGG YOLKS
125 ML (4 FL OZ/½ CUP) CONDENSED MILK
250 ML (8½ FL OZ/1 CUP) MILK

250 ML (8½ FL OZ/1 CUP) POURING (SINGLE/LIGHT) CREAM (35% FAT)
250 ML (8½ FL OZ/1 CUP) COCONUT CREAM

MAKES ABOUT 1 LITRE (34 FL OZ/ 4 CUPS)

Whisk together the egg yolks and condensed milk.

Gently heat the milk, cream and coconut cream in a small saucepan over low heat. Whisk in the egg yolk mixture and stir constantly with a wooden spoon until the mixture thickens and coats the back of the spoon. This will take about 8–10 minutes.

Immediately remove from the heat and pour into a chilled bowl. Leave to cool.

When cool, transfer to an ice-cream maker and follow the manufacturer's instructions for making ice cream.

You can keep the ice cream in the freezer for up to 1 week — if you don't eat it all first!

COFFEE YOGHURT ICE CREAM

Kem cà phê sữa chua

This ice cream is best eaten within 24 hours of making, as ice will form if left in the freezer too long.

45 G (1½ OZ/½ CUP) GROUND VIETNAMESE COFFEE, OR OTHER FINELY GROUND COFFEE
125 ML (4 FL OZ/½ CUP) CONDENSED MILK

250 G (9 OZ/1 CUP) PLAIN YOGHURT
250 ML (8½ FL OZ/1 CUP) CREAM (40% FAT)

MAKES ABOUT 750 ML (25½ FL OZ/3 CUPS)

Put the ground coffee into the bottom of a Vietnamese coffee filter, then screw the upper filter on top. Don't screw too tightly as you don't want to compact the coffee.

Place the filter on top of a coffee cup or mug and pour 80 ml (2½ fl oz/⅓ cup) boiling water into the filter. Leave to sit for a few minutes to soften the ground coffee. Now completely fill the filter with boiling water and wait for 4–5 minutes for the water to drip through.

Transfer to a bowl and chill in the refrigerator, then add the condensed milk and yoghurt and mix together using a spoon. Fold the cream through.

Transfer the mixture to a 1 litre (34 fl oz/4 cup) container lined with plastic. Cover and place in the freezer for 6 hours.

Remove from the freezer 10 minutes before serving, to allow the ice cream to soften slightly.

COFFEE WITH YOGHURT

Cà phê sữa chua

Here's a wonderful version of the ubiquitous iced coffee with condensed milk. It is a refreshing summer drink, in which the slightly sour yoghurt perfectly complements the rich dark coffee and the sweetness of the condensed milk.

2 TEASPOONS GROUND VIETNAMESE COFFEE, OR OTHER FINELY GROUND COFFEE

70 G (2½ OZ/½ CUP) ICE CUBES

100 G (3½ OZ) SWEETENED YOGHURT

1 TEASPOON CONDENSED MILK

SERVES 1

Put the ground coffee into the bottom of a Vietnamese coffee filter, then screw the upper filter on top. Don't screw too tightly as you don't want to compact the coffee.

Place the filter on top of a coffee cup or mug and pour 80 ml (2½ fl oz/⅓ cup) boiling water into the filter. Leave to sit for a few minutes to soften the ground coffee. Now completely fill the filter with boiling water and wait for 4–5 minutes for the water to drip through.

Place the ice cubes in a tall glass and pour the coffee over. Top with the yoghurt and drizzle with the condensed milk.

COFFEE WITH EGG

Cà phê trứng

The egg cream in this Hanoi specialty is reminiscent of zabaglione and adds protein and sugar to the caffeine. This sweet and bitter pick-me-up is particularly suited to the colder winter months.

4 TEASPOONS GROUND VIETNAMESE COFFEE, OR OTHER FINELY GROUND COFFEE

1 EGG, SEPARATED

1 TEASPOON CONDENSED MILK

1 TEASPOON SUGAR

SERVES 1

Filter the coffee as described in the recipe above.

Put the egg yolk and egg white in two separate bowls.

Add the condensed milk to the egg yolk and whisk by hand until the mixture turns a pale lemon colour. Set aside.

Add the sugar to the egg white and whisk by hand until soft peaks form, then gently fold into the egg yolk mixture.

Pour all but 1 tablespoon of the coffee into a cup. Top with the egg mixture, then drizzle the remaining tablespoon of coffee over the top.

LADY FINGER BANANAS IN STICKY RICE

Xôi cuốn chuối nướng

This wonderfully tropical snack is widely available on the streets of Ho Chi Minh City. Be sure to use small sweet bananas for this dish. If banana leaf is unavailable, you can use foil instead.

400 G (14 OZ/2 CUPS) GLUTINOUS RICE
250 ML (8½ FL OZ/1 CUP) COCONUT MILK
½ TEASPOON SALT
2 TABLESPOONS SUGAR

6 LADY FINGER BANANAS
1 BANANA LEAF, CUT INTO 6 PIECES
SWEET COCONUT SAUCE (SEE PAGE 341), OPTIONAL

SERVES 6

Soak the rice overnight in cold water.

The next day, drain and rinse the rice, then place in a rice cooker or saucepan. Mix together the coconut milk, salt and 375 ml (12½ fl oz/1½ cups) water, then pour the mixture onto the rice.

If using a rice cooker, cook the rice according to the rice cooker's instructions. If using a saucepan, cook over medium heat for 20 minutes, or until the rice is just tender. Using chopsticks, stir the sugar through, then allow to cool.

Meanwhile, heat a chargrill or barbecue to medium–high.

Divide the cooked rice into six portions. Take one portion and flatten it out with damp fingers to the size of your hand. Place one whole peeled banana in the centre, then encase it in the rice. Now wrap the banana leaf around it and secure the parcel with bamboo skewers.

Repeat with the remaining rice and bananas.

Chargrill or barbecue the parcels for about 5 minutes on each side, until heated through.

Serve warm, with sweet coconut sauce if desired.

PANDAN CREAM

Kem lá thơm

The pandan leaf adds subtle hints of hazelnut and grassy flavours to the cream, and also serves as a natural food colouring.

2 PANDAN LEAVES
5 EGG YOLKS
110 G (4 OZ/½ CUP) SUGAR

30 G (1 OZ/¼ CUP) CORNFLOUR (CORNSTARCH)
500 ML (17 FL OZ/2 CUPS) MILK

MAKES ABOUT 625 G (1 LB 6 OZ/2½ CUPS)

Cut the pandan leaves into small pieces using kitchen scissors, then place in a mortar. Add ½ teaspoon water and pound to extract the liquid from the leaf. Using your hands, squeeze out any further liquid and strain through a fine sieve.

Mix the egg yolks, sugar and cornflour together in a bowl.

In a saucepan, slowly bring the milk to simmering point, then whisk it into the egg mixture.

Pour the mixture back into a clean saucepan, then stir over low heat until the mixture boils and becomes smooth and shiny. Continue to cook for a further 2 minutes.

Remove from the heat and stir through 1 tablespoon of the pandan liquid. Tranfer to a bowl and cover with plastic wrap to prevent a skin forming. Allow to cool slightly, then refrigerate until cold.

When cold, use as a filling for profiteroles (see page 368), your favourite cake or biscuit (cookie) recipes. The mixture will keep for 3–4 days in the fridge.

OLD BLACK MAGIC: COFFEE CULTURE

THE TIES THAT BIND THE PHAM FAMILY MUST SURELY BE LACED WITH CAFFEINE. NGUYEN THI OANH, THE MATRIARCH OF THE FAMILY, OPENED HER FIRST COFFEE SHOP ON MAI HAC DE STREET IN 1936 TO SUPPLEMENT THE MEAGRE INCOME HER HUSBAND WAS EARNING FROM HIS MARTIAL ARTS SCHOOL. ALL HER EIGHT SONS AND DAUGHTERS HAVE BEEN INVOLVED IN THE COFFEE TRADE IN ONE WAY OR ANOTHER EVER SINCE.

The original café operated for nine years as a popular meeting spot for well-to-do Hanoians, before her husband participated in the 1945 uprising against the French. The family was forced to flee the capital and decamped to the north, which was still controlled by Ho Chi Minh's forces. They reopened the café in the small township of Viet Bac in Thanh Hoa province: a humble, open-sided shack with the thatched roof still proudly displaying the original sign salvaged from the Mai Hac De café.

When the French finally left Vietnam in 1954, the Phams moved back to the capital. A photo of the time shows the entire local People's Committee dressed in their Sunday best, posing in front of their new café on Pho Hue in 1955. In the early 1960s, the coffee shop moved once more to Le Van Huu Street, where it is still operating under the original name.

The oldest son, Pham Dyu Tri, was the last to make a living from those magic beans, when he started his own coffee shop after retiring from the army. His venture now joins Café Mai and Café Duy Dung, which are owned by his two brothers.

The French introduced coffee to Vietnam in the mid-19th century when they forced villagers to turn their small plots into large-scale plantations. Since the time Tri started waiting on tables at the tender age of six, he has witnessed the black brew transform itself from a luxury good to an everyday indulgence. These days, Vietnam is the second largest exporter of coffee behind Brazil.

Tri produces his own blend of robusta and arabica beans at his small factory close to the Red River. The beans are processed in the traditional French way, with a little bit of butter and chicory. The dark roast, high in caffeine and with a slight taste of chocolate, produces its richest flavour when prepared the old-fashioned way: by ever so slowly dripping through a stainless-steel filter, making a brew strong enough for a teaspoon to almost stand upright in the cup!

While the arabica beans come from the north, where the plantations are at a higher altitude and the soil is better suited to growing this delicate, aromatic variety, Tri sources his robusta beans from the central highlands.

Buon Ma Thuot is the coffee capital there — a small town with great ambitions, which are mainly driven by its favourite son, coffee baron Dang Le Nguyen Vu. The success story of this straight-talking, cigar-smoking tycoon is that of a local boy made good. Coming from a poor family in the countryside, Vu excelled at school and started medical studies at university, before packing it all in for a career in coffee.

In the late 1990s, he started out with one roasting machine in a rented shack. Now, more than 3000 employees produce one of the most recognised coffee brands in the nation, which is exported to over 60 countries worldwide. Vu's grand vision includes selling his Trung Nguyen brand in his very own chain of upmarket coffee shops.

There are no signs yet, though, that traditional independent coffee shops like Café Duy Tri are threatened by the big brand competitors. Wedged between two clothes shops, the narrow café with its low wooden tables and upturned beer crates covered with pillows serving as stools is crowded with loyal locals, still enjoying their *ca phe den* (black coffee), *ca phe sua da* (iced coffee with condensed milk), or the house specialty, *ca phe sua chua* (coffee with yoghurt).

PANDAN WAFFLES

Bánh kẹp lá dứa

Originally sold by street vendors in Saigon, these popular waffles have a delicate nutty flavour and a soft, green hue from the pandan leaf. The waffles can be individually frozen for up to two weeks, then reheated in a toaster or hot oven at a later date.

3 PANDAN LEAVES

2 EGGS, SEPARATED

300 G (10½ OZ/2 CUPS) PLAIN (ALL-PURPOSE) FLOUR

1½ TEASPOONS BAKING POWDER

¾ TEASPOON BICARBONATE OF SODA (BAKING SODA)

55 G (2 OZ/¼ CUP) SUGAR

½ TEASPOON SALT

50 G (1¾ OZ) BUTTER, MELTED AND COOLED, PLUS EXTRA FOR GREASING

125 ML (4 FL OZ/½ CUP) MILK

375 ML (12½ FL OZ/1½ CUPS) COCONUT MILK

SERVES 6

Cut the pandan leaves into small pieces using kitchen scissors, then place in a mortar. Add ½ teaspoon water and pound to extract the liquid from the leaf. Using your hands, squeeze out any further liquid and strain through a fine sieve.

Whisk the egg whites by hand until they form soft peaks.

Sift the flour, baking powder, bicarbonate of soda, sugar and salt into a bowl, then make a well in the centre. Add the egg yolks, butter, milk, coconut milk and 1 tablespoon of the pandan juice and mix until just combined. Be careful to not overwork the batter, or the waffles will be tough. Finally, use a metal spoon to fold in the whisked egg white.

Heat a waffle iron according to the manufacturer's instructions. When hot, add a little of the extra butter so the waffles won't stick. Now pour in 80 ml (2½ fl oz/⅓ cup) of the batter and cook for 4–5 minutes, until golden.

Remove the waffle and repeat with the remaining batter.

Serve hot with tea or coffee, or as a dessert with Coconut ice cream (see page 352).

PROFITEROLES

Bánh xu

The choux pastry for these profiteroles is of French culinary heritage. Profiteroles are an old stand-by at the traditional Kinh Do Café in Hanoi, famous for being the favourite haunt of French actress Catherine Deneuve when she stayed in Vietnam to shoot her movie *Indochine*.

⅓ TEASPOON SALT
80 G (2¾ OZ) BUTTER, ROUGHLY CHOPPED
150 G (5½ OZ/1 CUP) PLAIN (ALL-PURPOSE) FLOUR

4 EGGS
375 G (13 OZ/1½ CUPS) PANDAN CREAM (SEE PAGE 360)

MAKES ABOUT 20

Preheat the oven to 180°C (350°F).

Place the salt, butter and 250 ml (8½ fl oz/1 cup) water in a saucepan and slowly bring to the boil. Remove from the heat, add the flour and vigorously stir to combine.

Now cook over medium heat for 3–4 minutes, or until the paste starts to come away from the side of the pan, stirring occasionally.

Transfer to the bowl of an electric mixer and leave to cool slightly for 2–3 minutes. Using the paddle attachment, add the eggs one at a time, making sure they are fully incorporated before adding the next one. Continue mixing until the paste is smooth and shiny.

Line a baking tray with baking paper. Using a piping (icing) bag or two dessertspoons, place small mounds of the paste on the tray, spacing them evenly.

Bake the pastry for 30 minutes. Leaving the door closed, reduce the oven temperature to 160°C (320°F) and bake for a further 10 minutes.

Now turn off the oven and allow the pastry to sit in the oven for 10 minutes.

Remove the profiteroles and leave to cool on a wire rack.

When cool, pierce the bottom of each profiterole using a knife or the nozzle of a piping bag. Fill with the pandan cream and serve.

The profiteroles are best eaten on the day they are made.

RICE FLOUR DOUGHNUTS WITH A MUNG BEAN FILLING

Bánh rán lúc lắc

This recipe is from the Director of the Viet Way Centre, Hanoi chef Nguyen Phuong Hai, who recently released his own cookbook in Vietnam. The banana and sweet potato provide the necessary starch, which rice flour lacks, so the dough is strong enough to deep-fry.

100 G (3½ OZ/½ CUP) DRIED MUNG BEANS
140 G (5 OZ/⅔ CUP) SUGAR
A FEW DROPS OF VANILLA EXTRACT
1 SWEET POTATO
1 BANANA

180 G (6½ OZ) GLUTINOUS RICE FLOUR
40 G (1½ OZ/¼ CUP) SESAME SEEDS
VEGETABLE OIL, FOR DEEP-FRYING
MAKES 40

To make the doughnut filling, rinse the mung beans under cold running water and place in a bowl. Cover with cold water and allow to soak for 2 hours.

Drain the mung beans well. Place in a steamer set over a saucepan of boiling water and cook for 20 minutes, or until soft.

Transfer the mung beans to a dry wok or frying pan. Add half the sugar and dry-fry over low heat until the sugar has dissolved. Remove from the heat and stir in the vanilla. Divide the mixture into 40 portions and shape into small balls.

Peel the sweet potato and steam it whole for 15 minutes, or until soft.

Weigh out 120 g (4½ oz) of both the sweet potato and banana. Place in a mortar and pound until smooth.

Sift the flour into a bowl. Add the remaining sugar and 2½ tablespoons warm water and mix to combine. Now add the mashed sweet potato and banana and lightly knead for 3–4 minutes, until you have a smooth dough. Cover with a damp cloth and leave to rest for 20 minutes.

Divide the dough into 40 equal portions, roughly the size of golf balls. Take one piece of dough at a time and flatten it into a disc. Place a mung bean ball in the middle, then encase it in the dough (1). Roll in the palm of your hands to form a ball, then dip the doughnut in the sesame seeds (2).

Repeat with the remaining ingredients.

Heat about 10 cm (4 inches) of oil in a wok. To test the oil, place the tip of a wooden chopstick into the oil — when bubbles slowly rise to the surface, the oil is hot enough to use. Fry the doughnuts in batches for 4–5 minutes per batch, until golden brown (3).

Drain well on paper towel and eat while still warm.

SALTY PEANUT AND SESAME COOKIES

Bánh lạc vừng

The Vietnamese have always loved the combination of salty and sweet flavours, which in Western countries is now becoming fashionable as well.

185 G (6½ OZ/1¼ CUPS) PLAIN (ALL-PURPOSE) FLOUR

105 G (3½ OZ/¾ CUP) GROUND PEANUTS

80 G (2¾ OZ/⅓ CUP) CASTER (SUPERFINE) SUGAR

1 TEASPOON SALT

100 G (3½ OZ) BUTTER, AT ROOM TEMPERATURE

1 EGG YOLK, LIGHTLY WHISKED

1 TEASPOON WHITE SESAME SEEDS

1 TEASPOON BLACK SESAME SEEDS

MAKES 20

Sift the flour, ground peanuts, sugar and salt into a bowl. Using your fingertips, rub in the butter until combined. You may need to add a small amount of water if the mixture seems too dry. When combined, lightly knead the dough on a work surface, then leave to rest in the refrigerator for 20 minutes.

Roll the dough between two sheets of baking paper until it is 5 mm (¼ inch) thick. Cut into discs using a 5 cm (2 inch) biscuit cutter and place on a baking tray. Brush the cookies with the egg yolk and sprinkle with the sesame seeds. Place the tray of cookies in the fridge and chill for 10 minutes.

Meanwhile, preheat the oven to 180°C (350°F).

Take the tray directly from the fridge into the oven and bake for 15 minutes. Remove from the oven and leave to cool.

These cookies will keep for 1 week in an airtight container.

SPICED BAKED CUSTARD

Bánh gan

When baking an egg custard, it is best to cook it in a bain-marie, or water bath. This ensures an even, gentle heat around the custard, and protects it from the direct heat of the oven, so the eggs don't curdle. For the water bath, you'll need a roasting tin that is slightly larger than the baking dish the egg custard is cooked in.

125 ML (4 FL OZ/½ CUP) MILK
400 ML (13½ FL OZ) COCONUT MILK
275 G (9½ OZ/1¼ CUPS) SUGAR
1 CINNAMON STICK, GROUND
6 CLOVES

3 STAR ANISE
BUTTER, FOR GREASING
12 EGGS, AT ROOM TEMPERATURE
1 TEASPOON BAKING POWDER
SERVES 10–12

Combine the milk, coconut milk, sugar and spices in a small saucepan and slowly bring to simmering point. Stir to dissolve the sugar, then remove from the heat and leave to sit for 45 minutes for the flavours to develop.

Preheat the oven to 180°C (350°F). Butter a 22 cm (8¾ inch) baking dish, and line the base of a slightly larger roasting tin with a tea towel (dish towel). (The tea towel will stop the baking dish slipping once it has been placed in its water bath.)

Whisk the eggs in a large bowl. Stir in the coconut milk mixture and the baking powder. Strain the mixture through a sieve, into the baking dish, discarding the spices.

Place the baking dish in the roasting tin. Pour enough boiling water into the roasting tin to come two-thirds up the side of the baking dish.

Carefully transfer the roasting tin to the oven and bake for 35–40 minutes, or until the custard has just set.

Remove from the oven and leave to cool for at least 2 hours before cutting.

The custard will keep for 2–3 days in the refrigerator.

STICKY RICE WITH RED BEANS, COCONUT AND SESAME SEEDS

Xôi đậu đỏ

We love the rich colours of this rice dish. The red beans scattered throughout the rice provide a great contrast to the white coconut and golden sesame seeds. This makes a wonderful afternoon snack, or for a more decadent dessert, you could pour some Sweet coconut sauce (see page 341) over it.

80 G (2¾ OZ/½ CUP) DRIED RED BEANS
300 G (10½ OZ/1½ CUPS) GLUTINOUS RICE
75 G (2¾ OZ/⅓ CUP) SUGAR
¼ TEASPOON SALT

30 G (1 OZ/½ CUP) GRATED COCONUT
1 TABLESPOON TOASTED SESAME SEEDS

SERVES 6

Soak the beans and the rice overnight in separate bowls of cold water.

The next day, drain the beans, place in a saucepan and cover with cold water. Bring to the boil, then reduce the heat and simmer for 15 minutes. Drain and place in a bowl.

Drain the rice and rinse under cold water until the water runs clear. Add to the beans, then stir in the sugar and salt until combined.

Place the mixture in a steamer set over a saucepan of boiling water and steam for 45 minutes, or until the rice is cooked.

Remove from the heat and serve sprinkled with the coconut and sesame seeds.

This dish is best eaten the same day it is made.

SWEET CORN AND COCONUT SOUP

Chè ngô

A versatile sweet dish for all seasons, this soup can be served warm to ward off winter chills, or in a tall glass with crushed ice as a refreshing summer dessert.

150 G (5½ OZ/¾ CUP) GLUTINOUS RICE, SOAKED OVERNIGHT
2 PANDAN LEAVES, CRUSHED
3 CORN COBS, KERNELS REMOVED
190 ML (6½ FL OZ/¾ CUP) COCONUT MILK
½ TEASPOON SALT

75 G (2¾ OZ/⅓ CUP) SUGAR
SWEET COCONUT SAUCE (SEE RECIPE 341), TO SERVE
2 TABLESPOONS SESAME SEEDS, TOASTED
SERVES 6

Drain the rice and rinse until the water runs clear. Place in a pan with the pandan and 500 ml (17 fl oz/2 cups) cold water. Stir together, cover and cook over low heat for 15 minutes.

Meanwhile, break the corn kernels into small pieces, using a mortar and pestle or a food processor.

Stir the corn, coconut milk, salt and sugar through the rice and cook, uncovered, for a further 10 minutes.

Serve drizzled with sweet coconut sauce and sprinkled with the sesame seeds.

SWEET POTATO AND COCONUT SOUP

Chè bà ba

25 G (1 OZ/⅓ CUP) TAPIOCA STRIPS
2 TABLESPOONS DRIED MUNG BEANS
3 DRIED BLACK FUNGUS (WOOD EARS)
300 G (10½ OZ) SWEET POTATO, PEELED AND CUT INTO 1 CM (½ INCH) CUBES
50 G (1¾ OZ) RED DATES

50 G (1¾ OZ/⅓ CUP) PEANUTS
80 G (2¾ OZ) SUGAR
125 ML (4 FL OZ/½ CUP) COCONUT JUICE
500 ML (17 FL OZ/2 CUPS) COCONUT MILK
SERVES 6

Soak the tapioca and mung beans separately for 1 hour in cold water; soak the mushrooms in warm water for 20 minutes.

Put the sweet potato, dates and peanuts in a pan with 125 ml (4 fl oz/½ cup) cold water. Simmer for 5 minutes, until the sweet potato is tender. Add the drained tapioca and mung beans, the sugar and coconut juice and cook for 15 minutes.

Drain the mushrooms and squeeze dry. Thinly slice the caps and add to the soup with the coconut milk. Bring to the boil, skimming off any froth that rises to the surface.

Serve warm in small soup bowls, or in tall glasses over ice on a hot day.

Rice paddy herb
(Ngo om)

Coriander (cilantro)

Mint

Dill

Vietnamese mint

Thai basil

Chives

Sawtooth
coriander

Celery leaf

Perilla

Vietnamese balm

Spring onion (scallion)

Betel leaf

Lemongrass

Pandan

INDEX

Vietnamese recipe names are printed in *italics*. English recipe names have an initial capital letter; general topics are in lower case.

A

B

ABOUT THE AUTHORS

Australian chef **Tracey Lister** knows how to shop, cook and eat in Vietnam and through her successful cooking school, the Hanoi Cooking Centre near the capital's famous old quarter, she follows her passion to promote Vietnamese food in all its facets.

Tracey started to develop a deep appreciation of Vietnamese cuisine more than a decade ago when she helped to set up KOTO, a grassroots social enterprise training street kids in cooking and serving. She has been exploring the local fare at street stalls, private kitchens and fine dining restaurants ever since, talking to vendors, home cooks and professional chefs.

Her husband, **Andreas Pohl** works as a writer, researcher and educator and has a keen interest in Vietnam's culture and social history. Together they have written two books on Vietnamese food, *KOTO: A Culinary Journey Through Vietnam* (2008) and *Vietnamese Street Food* (2011).

THANK YOU

There were numerous people who helped us put this book together. Many thanks to the team at the Hanoi Cooking Centre for all the logistical support, recipe testing, assistance with photography and translating: Nguyen Manh Hung, Phan Thi Duyen, Nguyen Huu Y, Hoang Viet Linh, Cao Thi Than Thuy and Dinh Phung Linh.

Thank you to Trong Pham Viet for his indispensable help in Dalat. Veteran Hanoi publicist Huu Ngoc for making the time to talk with us and generously sharing his cultural insights. Marilyn Drinkwater for sharing her knowledge of the Mekong Delta, and Sung A Nam from Chapi Aspirant for travel arrangements.

Maria Poulos Conklin and Rebecca Hales for helping us turn first drafts into better, second ones. William Conklin, Juliette Elfick and Lou Wilson for passing on research papers and alerting us to internet links and discussion threads. Cynthia Mann for providing feedback throughout the process of putting together this book.

Katri Hilden in Australia for her detailed editing of the recipes. Helen Withycombe and Paul McNally from Hardie Grant for seeing the project through to its fruition.

We also particularly wish to thank the following local businesses for letting us shoot on their beautiful premises: Manzi, Pots n Pans, Trioh, Hanoi Social Club and Chula.

Published in 2014 by Hardie Grant Books

Hardie Grant Books (Australia)
Ground Floor, Building 1
658 Church Street
Richmond, Victoria 3121
www.hardiegrant.com.au

Hardie Grant Books (UK)
Dudley House, North Suite
34–35 Southampton Street
London WC2E 7HF
www.hardiegrant.co.uk

A Cataloguing-in-Publication entry is available from the catalogue of the
National Library of Australia at www.nla.gov.au

Real Vietnamese Cooking: Homestyle dishes from from Hanoi to Ho Chi Minh
ISBN 978 1 74270 526 2

Publishing Director: Paul McNally
Project Editor: Helen Withycombe
Editor: Katri Hilden
Design concept: Heather Menzies
Cover design: Aileen Lord
Design layout: Susanne Geppert
Photographer: Michael Fountoulakis
Production Manager: Todd Rechner

Colour reproduction by Splitting Image Colour Studio
Printed and bound in Printed in China by 1010 Printing International Limited

Find this book on **Cooked.**
www.cooked.com.au
www.cooked.co.uk